ENGINEERING LIBRARY

Securing the Clicks: Network Security in the Age of Social Media

D1213991

Securing the Clicks: Network Security in the Age of Social Media

Gary Bahadur
Jason Inasi
Alex de Carvalho

New York Chicago San Francisco
Lisbon London Madrid Mexico City
Milan New Delhi San Juan
Seoul Singapore Sydney Toronto

The McGraw·Hill Companies

Cataloging-in-Publication Data is on file with the Library of Congress

McGraw-Hill books are available at special quantity discounts to use as premiums and sales promotions, or for use in corporate training programs. To contact a representative, please e-mail us at bulksales@mcgraw-hill.com.

Securing the Clicks: Network Security in the Age of Social Media

Copyright © 2012 by The McGraw-Hill Companies. All rights reserved. Printed in the United States of America. Except as permitted under the Copyright Act of 1976, no part of this publication may be reproduced or distributed in any form or by any means, or stored in a database or retrieval system, without the prior written permission of publisher, with the exception that the program listings may be entered, stored, and executed in a computer system, but they may not be reproduced for publication.

McGraw-Hill, the McGraw-Hill Publishing logo, and related trade dress are trademarks or registered trademarks of The McGraw-Hill Companies and/or its affiliates in the United States and other countries and may not be used without written permission. All other trademarks are the property of their respective owners. The McGraw-Hill Companies is not associated with any product or vendor mentioned in this book.

All trademarks or copyrights mentioned herein are the possession of their respective owners and McGraw-Hill makes no claim of ownership by the mention of products that contain these marks.

1 2 3 4 5 6 7 8 9 0   DOC DOC   1 0 9 8 7 6 5 4 3 2 1

ISBN   978-0-07-176905-1
MHID   0-07-176905-6

Sponsoring Editor Amy Jollymore
Editorial Supervisor Patty Mon
Project Editor LeeAnn Pickrell
Acquisitions Coordinator Joya Anthony
Developmental Editor LeeAnn Pickrell
Technical Editors Juliette Powell, Connie Valencia
Copy Editor LeeAnn Pickrell

Proofreader Susie Elkind
Indexer Rebecca Plunkett
Production Supervisor Jean Bodeaux
Composition Cenveo Publisher Services
Illustration Cenveo Publisher Services
Art Director, Cover Jeff Weeks

Information has been obtained by McGraw-Hill from sources believed to be reliable. However, because of the possibility of human or mechanical error by our sources, McGraw-Hill, or others, McGraw-Hill does not guarantee the accuracy, adequacy, or completeness of any information and is not responsible for any errors or omissions or the results obtained from the use of such information.

I want to thank my wife Padmini for putting up with me for six months of not being able to do anything outside of writing at nights and on weekends. She has a lot of patience and has been extremely supportive during all my random projects.

—Gary Bahadur

For Mom, Dad, and my brother Arthur.

—Jason Inasi

About the Authors

Gary Bahadur

Gary Bahadur is the founder and CEO of KRAA Security and has more than 15 years of experience in the information security and technology industry. KRAA Security protects organizations from threats through a combination of prevention services in areas such as application security, network security, social media security, operating systems security, and compliance measures. Gary was one of the cofounders and CIO of Foundstone Inc., a $20M security vulnerability risk management firm, conducting business development, corporate strategy development, client management, information systems development, consultant management, public speaking engagements, and security consulting engagements for Fortune 100 companies. Foundstone was sold to McAfee in 2004.

Gary was also Senior Vice President of Bank of America in charge of Global Threat Management and was a catalyst for delivering risk mitigation strategies. In addition, he was the president and cofounder of Ether2 Corporation, a manager at Ernst & Young where he developed security practices, and a senior consultant at Price Waterhouse. Gary is a frequent speaker at information security conferences. You can reach Gary at baha@kraasecurity.com.

Jason Inasi

Jason Inasi is CEO & Creative Director of The Factory Interactive, The Digital Design & Marketing Agency. In 1998, he founded The Factory Interactive, a full-service digital design and marketing agency with a focus on convergent media. The Agency leverages the best of design and technology to create engaging and effective media campaigns. In September 2007, Jason launched Veridoo.com™ a rewards-driven, social network platform that has been white-labeled by corporate clients to create branded networks of their own. In January 2009, The Factory Interactive launched SEOtrack™, a comprehensive search engine optimization (SEO) and marketing (SEM) program designed specifically to leverage the power of online search and social media opportunities.

The Factory Interactive has won numerous awards, was recently honored as one of the Top 100 Minority Owned Businesses in South Florida, and is ranked in the Top 10 of Interactive Agencies by the *South Florida Business Journal*. The Factory Interactive's corporate clients have included AOL Latin America, American Airlines Arena, Estefan Enterprises, Cable & Wireless, Coverall, Carnival Cruise Lines, and the Miami HEAT Group. Jason is an active board member of the Greater Miami Advertising Federation, an avid Twitterer, distance runner, and overall adrenalin junky.

Alex de Carvalho

Alex de Carvalho is Vice President of Business Development and Community at VoxMed, cofounder of The Startup Forum, Director of Social Media at Medimix International, and adjunct professor of social media at the University of Miami. During the past four years, he has founded and continues to organize regular South Florida web and technology meetups, including RefreshMiami (2,500 members), BarCampMiami (over 1,200 participants), MobileMondayMiami (500 members), and Social Media Club South Florida (1,500 members). Previously, Alex directed business development efforts at online media and mobile content companies and also cofounded a leading European application services provider specialized in permission-based direct marketing.

About the Technical Editors

Connie Valencia

Connie Valencia is Principal of Elevate Consult. She developed the evolutionary "next step" to approaching and implementing enterprise risk management (ERM). Her client case study for her new risk management approach was with the United Nations (UN) in New York. She has been asked by the outgoing chair of the North American Board of the Institute of Internal Auditors (IIA) to participate on both the ERM Certification Committee and the Governance Committee and is currently negotiating with a large national publisher to design a risk management training platform.

   Prior to joining Elevate, Connie served in leadership roles as Director of Internal Audit for a $2 billion real estate/assessment management firm as well as Practice Leader overseeing advisory services for the South Florida offices of Grant Thornton. Connie began her career with Arthur Andersen serving the Audit and Assurance Services practice. She is also a board member and former (two term) president of the Miami Chapter for the Institute of Internal Auditors (IIA) and is currently overseeing the Caribbean for ten country islands. She is a Certified Internal Auditor (CIA) and has her Certification in Controls Self Assessment (CCSA). Connie has a bachelor's degree in accounting from the University of Wisconsin.

Juliette Powell

Juliette Powell is a media entrepreneur, a community catalyst, and the author of *33 Million People in the Room: How to Create, Influence and Run a Successful Business with Social Networking* (January 2009, Financial Times Press). Drawing on first-hand experience as a social media expert and cofounder of The Gathering Think Tank, an innovation forum that connects technology, media, entertainment, and business communities, Powell writes about the patterns and practices of successful business leaders who bank on social networking to win. With her deep knowledge of the people and technologies at the forefront of social media, Powell has gained a solid reputation for discovering the latest developments and distilling their social and business implications. Her consulting services have been employed by corporate, government, and new media organizations, including UBS, the United Nations, the Department of Justice, the Department of Finance, Microsoft, The Knight Foundation, Research in Motion, and Cirque du Soleil. Juliette is currently working with the E-G8, a new addition to the G8 summit created to inform G8 leaders on the future of the Internet and connected society.

Contents at a Glance

Contents

Foreword

Just when you thought it was safe to use the Internet again, those ADD technorati types cook up a whole new interface between the physical and virtual worlds. Whether you call it social media, social networking, or some yet-to-be-popularized term like groupthink (oh, wait…is that taken?), the phenomenon is real and it has deep implications for our day-to-day lives.

Unfortunately, like many prior adaptive radiations (think dot com), the technology and appetite for more page impressions is way out in front of the desire or ability to control things. As the authors of *Securing the Clicks* cite in their opening chapter, "A New York court recently referred to the users' reasonable expectation of privacy on social media websites like Facebook and MySpace as merely "wishful thinking." As a long-time (and still actively practicing) security professional, I can attest that this may be the biggest understatement of this still-young century.

One of the first questions I always ask clients who seek my advice on information security is "What are you trying to protect?" This question starkly defines the level and type of investment one will make in securing the asset. Social media is intently and expressly designed to leverage our most valuable asset—the essence of ourselves, where we are ("presence"), who we associate with, our daily activities and habits, our reputation/brand, even our most impromptu thoughts expressed 140 characters at a time via Twitter. What would you spend to protect everything that makes you, you?

On the more practical side of the coin, people are social animals. We've historically shared lots of things about ourselves well before Facebook. (Remember browsing the local telephone book? Names, numbers, addresses…) Perhaps naïvely, perhaps not, we all perceive a balance in the risk-reward equation when it comes to information commerce: we get more than we give, right? Not surprisingly, the Internet is based heavily on exactly this risk-reward proposition: immense value is given freely (Wikipedia, YouTube, Farmville…), all in exchange for the ability to know about you and introduce you to commercial suitors. We are complicit in this scheme, like it or not.

So, if you're looking for a safer social media experience, you are fighting an uphill battle, perhaps against the tide of human evolution itself. Fortunately, you have made an excellent choice, and that is to seek the counsel of the authors of this book (some of whom I have worked with in the field of information security for a very long time). They have collected in these pages an invaluable compendium of insider tips, tricks, strategies, and tactics that have steered the world's most recognized corporations steadily across the tumultuous seas of the social media phenomenon. From policies to staffing, budgets to strategic planning, technical investigations to PR response, *Securing the Clicks* covers the fundamentals as well as the advanced issues that confront anyone attempting to do business in today's technological climate. So, start reading, and be confident as you stride out into this brave new social world!

Joel Scambray

CEO, Consciere
Author of *Hacking Exposed: Network Security Secrets & Solutions,*
Hacking Exposed: Web Applications, and *Hacking Exposed: Windows*

Introduction

Why This Book?

The Internet is the fastest-growing medium in the history of civilization. It has far surpassed television and radio in terms of adoption and reach over time. The decade just prior to the millennium heralded in the dawning of a new age in human communication and, in a large sense, reshaped our view of the world. This new world has also opened a Pandora's box of privacy and corporate security issues. The potential for damage from the disclosure of sensitive data, internal communications, or employee codes of conduct are real threats to all business in today's world.

As Internet use becomes ubiquitous and familiar to everyone, increasing numbers of people and employees are publishing their own unfiltered opinions and experiences through easy-to-use and massively distributed social media technologies. These technologies make it simple for virtually anyone with access to a connected computer or device, and for countless amateurs and aficionados everywhere, to publish unedited text and media. They can create all types of media using freely available software tools and can post such content anonymously. The wired and wireless masses, connected through social media platforms, now have the ability to make or break a brand in as little as 140 characters.

This book serves as a practical guidebook for corporations wishing to protect their interests, assets, and brands from social media risks and to defend their digital assets and reputation from attackers using social media platforms, while simultaneously engaging with internal and external communities through the secure use of social media tools and platforms. There are many books on how to utilize social media, mostly from a corporate marketing or customer service perspective as well as for personal branding. We want to educate people on how to properly "secure" their use of social media and the information and corporate resources being freely shared or given away.

Social media has made it into just about every aspect of our lives. Twitter alone grew 1,382 percent year-over-year since February 2009. Facebook has over 750 million members, including 100 million mobile users, and continues to grow. Skype has topped 600 million users. The local community you once lived in can now be reached globally, and you can hold a conversation with someone in India just as easily as you would with your next-door neighbor. What we are willing to share about ourselves, our jobs, our families, and our activities has expanded our network, but it has also made privacy violations, identity theft, misuse of information, leaks, copyright infringements, and trademark violations easier and led to the general devaluing of corporate assets and professional reputations.

By defining boundaries around corporate interests, safe and productive conversations may flourish, even when these reflect negative customer experiences. Risks can be minimized and business processes put in place to deal with the eventualities of open communications. As the world learns about the use of social media, corporations, employees, individuals, and the social media platforms themselves will evolve to become more sophisticated. This book will help companies undertake their voyage of discovery safely.

Who Should Read This Book?

Our primary focus is the corporation and challenges to corporate assets. The book focuses on corporate staff—directors of Information Technology, Human Resources (HR), Marketing, Sales and other executives, and on the employees themselves. The HR director may need guidance in writing corporate policy. The IT director may need guidance on which tools to use to secure the changing social media environment. The Marketing director needs to set up campaigns but, at the same time, do so securely and in a way that protects brand reputation. Executives may have personal social media outlets that show the company in a bad light.

Employees can gain a lot of insight into what is appropriate in how they utilize and leverage social media in the workplace and for business as well as how social media can hurt them if they use it inappropriately, negatively affecting their company. Employees have to understand how not to damage their company's corporate reputation when using social media and how to avoid legal trouble, for example, by not infringing on the corporate brand.

The secondary reader of this book is the small business owner and employees. The same lessons that apply to a corporation can be utilized in the small and medium-sized business (SMB) market. In an SMB, employees are less easily controlled than in a corporation; therefore, there is more leeway for inappropriate social media usage. SMBs can use this book as a roadmap for developing a very cost-effective, secure social media strategy—without needing to hire external consultants to implement a costly strategy.

How to Use This Book

Corporations and professionals face challenges in monitoring online conversations for mentions of their products, brands, services, and key employees, for understanding customer sentiment, for identifying trademark infringements and copyright violations, and for understanding trends in their industry and the competitive landscape. Companies face additional challenges in determining the influence of certain people, as well as the impact of what those people are saying. Moving down the chain, further challenges associated with social media include:

▶ Creating appropriate strategies to deal with numerous inherent risks

▶ Allocating the right amount of resources for planning, maintenance, and corrective action

▶ Developing enterprise-wide social media policies

▶ Hiring, training, and developing Community Managers from within the company and from the community

▶ Determining metrics and performance measurements related to various objectives for social media, including risk mitigation objectives

▶ Implementing security controls over data movement and tracking, and monitoring potential data loss over social media channels

Most chapters begin with a case study—a practical, real-world example of companies facing social media challenges. We provide practical solutions in each chapter; steps that you can follow to implement your own strategy; and checklists, tools, and resources that can you can use to manage your social media security strategy. Our website—www.securesocialmedia.com—is the place to go for policy templates and important updates on the ever-changing social media landscape.

What's the H.U.M.O.R. Matrix?

The impact of social media can be felt throughout the organization and often challenges conventionally accepted operating procedures. To prepare your organization to participate securely on social media platforms, you need a framework to assess and address the areas in need of improvement. In this book, we present a flexible methodology for deploying, managing, and securing your social media strategy. The H.U.M.O.R. Matrix provides the foundation for assessing, addressing, controlling, and monitoring social media in terms of your organization's **H**uman resources,

Utilization of resources, **M**onetary spending, **O**perations management, and **R**eputation management. This framework will help you understand the social media challenges and it provides a structured approach to reducing your risk.

How Is This Book Organized?

We have developed a security framework so you can follow an assessment process to develop a real plan that addresses the risks of social media and methods for controlling and monitoring usage. The book is divided into five parts that mirror the process for implementing a social media security framework.

Part I: Assessing Social Media Security In Part I, you determine what is going on in your environment regarding social media usage. In this part, we outline the strategy for how you will assess your current environment. Chapter 1 defines a process for assessing your global social media presence. First, you have to understand how you conduct business, what your industry is doing, and what your competitors are doing. Chapter 2 defines the H.U.MO.R. Matrix process in detail. Each section of the matrix is explained and provides you with steps to fit your organization's current challenges into a specific framework. In Chapter 3, we finalize the assessment of your environment based on what your customers, competitors, and employees are saying about your company. Your understanding of all mentions about your company lays the groundwork for understanding the threats you face and the controls necessary to manage your social media landscape.

Part II: Assessing Social Media Threats In Part II, you determine how threats are impacting your organization. In Chapter 4, we outline the process for identifying social media threats. You have to assess threats from employees, customers, and competitors and understand the changing threat landscape. Chapter 5 walks you through the process of how threats are utilized, launched, and correlated by nefarious individuals. Threats can be targeted at individuals or against companies, and you should understand the different threat vectors that can lead to attacks.

Part III: Operations, Policies, & Processes In Part III, you learn how to apply controls on how social media is used in your organization. Chapter 6 describes the social media security policy that has to be put into place to address the threats to your social media usage. We define the best strategies for using social media securely so you can determine how to develop an effective security policy and procedures for social media.

The following chapters—7, 8, 9, 10, and 11—develop the necessary operational policies and procedures for each section of the H.U.M.O.R. Matrix. They provide you with the implementation guidelines necessary to address threats, both current and future, to your social media strategy.

Part IV: Monitoring & Reporting   In Part IV, you learn how to implement tools and techniques to monitor and report on your company's social media activities—both internal and external. Each chapter corresponds to a portion of the H.U.M.O.R. Matrix and defines the specific actions you need to take to maintain your security infrastructure over time. As social media platforms change, your processes will be able to accommodate any new technologies and services.

Part V: Social Media 3.0   In Chapter 17, we analyze what you have learned and how you can implement the processes outlined in this book to develop a security strategy to assess how your organization utilizes social media. And finally, in Chapter 18, we start to plan for what we foresee as the future of social media and the resulting social media security challenges ahead.

The Appendix is a compilation of all the tools and social media resources we cover in the book.

> **NOTE**
>
> We also provide supporting information and links to relevant tools we have discussed on the book's website at www.securingsocialmedia.com. Check this site frequently for new updates and new tools, which we'll review as they become available to help increase your social media security.

Once you've finished reading this book, you will walk away with a practical next-steps approach to changing your company's use of social media to a more secure and comprehensive process. Using the tools we discuss, the policy documents we provide, and the step-by-step H.U.M.O.R. Matrix framework, you will not be overwhelmed by the risks posed by social media ever again.

Thanks,
Gary, Jason, and Alex

PART

Assessing Social Media Security

The Social Media
Security Process

S ocial media security starts with understanding your environment and the global scope of the challenges every company faces as a result of this new communications medium. The use of social media has exposed companies to a new category of challenges. Information technology (IT) departments are required to evolve to work more closely with Marketing, Human Resources, Legal, Finance, and Operations to implement tactics to reduce social media risks.

This chapter sets the stage for taking that first step in assessing the risks inherent in using social media across your organization, by your customers, and by your competitors. You will learn how to

▶ Determine how you analyze your industry for good and bad practices.

▶ Assess your existing social media security processes and determine your current gaps in how you utilize different tools, websites, and business processes.

▶ Measure the impact of social media on your organization from employee usage, customer interaction, and competitive landscape and industry practices in an effort to reduce overall risk posed to the organization.

Case Study: Reputation Damage from an Unprepared Social Media Strategy

A company that has not implemented a strategy for managing social media risks is vulnerable to attacks to its brand and its financial bottom line. In the summer of 2010, the petroleum giant British Petroleum (BP) faced a crisis of extraordinary proportions as oil continued to gush into the Gulf of Mexico after the explosion of the Deepwater Horizon oil rig. During the 107 days the company struggled to stem the flow of oil into the sea, BP mounted a public relations campaign to address concerns over the crisis. Company spokespeople touted the company's cleanup efforts and the $20 billion recovery fund for the region. However, BP could hardly do anything to contain negative mentions online as countless numbers of people posted their concerns on Twitter and on blogs and organized themselves into protest groups on Facebook. In addition to their worries about the effect of the oil slick on the environment and on local fishing and tourism jobs, people were turned off by BP's apparent lack of transparency. The company's CEO, Tony Hayward, came under increasing fire online for remarks that were widely perceived as perfunctory, careless, and sometimes callous.

The company closely controlled media access to the oil spill areas and prohibited cleanup crews from wearing protective gear. Whereas BP's own social media outlets had less than 18,000 followers, irate citizens created a Twitter account (BPglobalPR) that had more than 150,000 followers within weeks. The Twitter account, named @BPglobalPR, raised over $10,000 for the Gulf through the sale of t-shirts and other merchandise.

What Went Wrong?

BP's usage and response to the social media community illustrates a number of areas in which the company did not have a process in place for addressing threats to the company and brand. Arguably, the explosion of BP's oil rig in the Gulf of Mexico was an unforeseen event that no one could have predicted. The company's own operational procedures should have prevented the blowout, but that is outside the scope or purpose of this book.

The social media reaction to a blowout or any large oil incident could have been anticipated by the organization well in advance, however. Clearly, people will react publicly to any such incident by posting their concerns and their outrage online. BP could have planned for the eventuality of such incidents by safeguarding the organization against social media fallout and specific attacks to the company's reputation and assets.

In terms of *human resources,* the company could have employed online community managers to oversee their social media presence. Instead, the company barely had a presence and responded through messages prepared by the PR department. As a result, the company's official Twitter account, @BP_America, has only 18,000 followers as of the writing of this book, whereas the fake account that spoofed BP's efforts, @BPGlobalPR, grew quickly to have many times more followers, about 179,000 at last count.

In terms of *utilization* of the company's assets, BP's green logo was "remixed" by people online to reflect the oil's impact on the environment. The @BPGlobalPR account, for example, uses an all-black logo with a drop of oil dripping from it. Numerous other remixes were posted to Flickr and Facebook, and some of them were sold as t-shirts. The company had no plan for safeguarding its trademarks and logos or understanding of how these may be misused in the case of an industrial accident.

In terms of *monetary considerations,* the very large number of negative mentions about BP resulted in a lot of bad press that ultimately impacted the company's valuation. As the oil flowed into the Gulf, public outrage grew and investor confidence waned. BP's valuation decreased so much as to make it a possible target for acquisition by a competing oil giant.

In terms of *operations,* some of BP's actions were highly criticized in social media and the press. There were reports of BP allegedly preventing reporters and photographers from coming too close to the oil spill or from flying overhead. Other reports told of cleanup workers without adequate protection or masks, so photographs of them would not look too negative. Some of BP's critical business decisions, which the company failed to adequately explain, were also highly criticized. These included the use of dispersants, which also pose an environmental hazard, not implementing blowout preventers, and not having a relief well ready. Even if the blowout itself was not foreseeable, the reaction to the news about what the company could have done before or after was entirely foreseeable.

In terms of *reputation,* the vast majority of online mentions about the company were negative. This spilled over to the press, which reported on the reaction of people online. People get upset about industrial accidents; knowing this, the company could have done more to build rapport with frank acknowledgments and more open lines of communication with concerned consumers online.

In these five key operational areas—human resources, utilization of assets, monetary spending, operations, and reputation—BP could have implemented a number of strategies that we will clearly define throughout the book.

How Security Has Changed in the Recent Past

In the past, companies concerned themselves with the nefarious actions of hackers and corporate espionage activity. A relatively small but highly skilled group could represent a major threat to the operation of any size business. Today, anyone with a connection to the Internet and a proverbial "axe to grind" can cause irreparable damage to even the most beloved of brands. The types of attacks a company faces has evolved from purely technical hacking attacks to include attacks on brand image and corporate reputation. The casualties have been many and include The Gap (public derision over the new logo), Southwest Airlines (negative outcry resulting from kicking Kevin Smith, the actor/director, off a plane for being too fat), and Nestle (online attack coordinated by Greenpeace over environmental damage from deforestation when harvesting palm oil). Seemingly, no company today is immune to the many threats posed by a single individual, let alone a socially engaged and networked population.

As the influence of social media grows, security issues will continue to be a major concern for both companies and their active online customers and communities. The most popular social media security concerns have been in the areas of violated privacy rights and identity theft. A New York court recently referred to the users' reasonable expectation of privacy on social media websites like Facebook and MySpace as merely "wishful thinking."

NOTE

You can read more about the courts, privacy, and the admissibility of material posted on social networking sites at the Traverse Legal website. Go to http://tcattorney.typepad.com/digital_millennium_copyri/2010/10/breach-of-privacy-across-social-media-sites-addressed-by-two-court-rulings-in-new-york-and-californi.html.

If someone were to steal your employee's identity over social media channels, that person could use the stolen credentials to break in to your company. If an attacker can capture the password that an employee uses on Facebook via an application like Firesheep (more to come on this), then the odds are high that employee uses that same password across multiple sites, including your corporate network. Finding a person's name and key things, such as birth date, school name, or children's name, about them is easy—and how many people use these as the basis of their passwords. As more companies become present and active on social networks, the explosion of attacks on individuals has now escalated to corporate-level attacks. As we'll discuss in Chapter 4, threats emanating through social media channels are getting more complex, and a company without a good social media security strategy will be as vulnerable as a company without an IT security strategy.

The Assessment Process

The first step toward implementing a strategic social media security practice includes mapping out the current environment to understand the immediate, medium, and long-term implications of engaging communities online. Once initiated, the organization's involvement with the communities they develop online changes through time, with varying risks and challenges along the way. To prepare for the journey, the organization must conduct an audit of sorts, or rather, what we call a *social media assessment process*.

The process we have defined will seem familiar to anyone who has conducted a security audit or performed a security assessment. The book will progress through the following steps:

1. **Strategy analysis**   Define what social media strategies and tools are currently in place and how they are being used, and determine what social media security measures are in place. Assess the whole environment and determine where the gaps are.

2. **Threat analysis**   Define and summarize the threat landscape and determine entry points. The *threat landscape* refers to the different methods by which a company can be attacked, whether it's a technology attack using spyware or a Trojan horse application in a Facebook application or a customer bashing your brand on Twitter.

3. **Operations, policies, and controls**   Define and implement operational tactics to address threats. Implement new policies and controls to reduce the risk.

4. **Monitoring and reporting**   Implement a lifecycle process for continuous monitoring and reporting on the social media tools, projects, and strategies that you implement and the security implications of each. Perform consistent reporting to ensure that new security strategies remain in effect and effective over time.

Why Follow the Assessment Process?

The assessment process allows you to identify the organization's current social media activity, the tools and platforms being used, the personnel responsible for community engagement, and the gaps in security and social media policies across existing accounts, social media profiles, and personnel policies. An assessment process is an ongoing and iterative process and, as such, has to track what is being said online about the brand, the company's products and services, as well as the way communities are communicating about the company and brand, outside of any corporate social media initiatives.

This "ear to the ground" approach enables a constant research and response process that informs the organization about changing community preferences around tools, tone, and user interface so the company can remain flexible enough to react quickly to threats and real attacks against the company's technologies and reputation. Short- and long-term communication objectives must be created, along with proposed deployment methodologies for each platform. In the chapters that follow, we describe how to assess the internal and external environment and will present a flexible methodology for deploying, managing, and securing your social media strategy.

Category	Description
Human Resources	Human Resources provide companywide policies, procedures, and guidance on acceptable employee use of authorized social media tools. These guidelines and policies provide the correct processes for utilization of social media in all areas of the company, including Marketing and Information Technology.
Utilization (of Resources and Assets)	Utilization defines the capabilities of secure social media tactics and how these tactics are implemented across technologies and policies to protect a company's resources and assets.
Monetary (Considerations)	The monetary resources dedicated to creating a social media strategy and tactics as well as a security strategy have to be aligned to best serve the company.
Operations (Management)	Operations management is the day-to-day processes that must be followed to implement a security framework, from a technology perspective, as well as from an ongoing maintenance perspective. The objective is to ensure that social media is handled securely as technologies and social media platforms change.
Reputation (Management)	When all interaction scenarios with social media are calculated, the company's reputation ultimately benefits. Reputation management is the result of good or bad implementations of social media strategies as well as tactical decisions and provides a monitoring and reporting function that helps to maintain an acceptable level of security and policies over time.

Table 1-1 *Definition of the H.U.M.O.R. Matrix*

We call this methodology the *H.U.M.O.R. Matrix* (**H**uman Resources, **U**tilization of resources and assets, **M**onetary considerations, **O**perations management, and **R**eputation management). You'll learn more about the H.U.M.O.R. Matrix in Chapter 2; however, Table 1-1 gives you a brief overview of the matrix's components.

Organizational Analysis: Your Industry Online, the Good and the Bad

Social media permeates the Internet and affects most departments within the organization. Social media strategies are often implemented piecemeal and independently by each department within an organization, which becomes complicated when each department has its own priorities and agenda. Depending on your role within the company, you will be faced with answering these questions related to the impact and use of social media by your current organization and by prospective employees:

▶ **IT Security**   If you are in charge of security, you will be asked: What tools are available to secure usage? How can you monitor, block, and report on activity? What are other companies in your industry doing for their social media practices? How many resources have they dedicated to social media and what risk strategies have they implemented?

▶ **Human Resources**   If you are in charge of Human Resources, you will be asked: How will social media platforms impact the organization? What can or can't employees say or do on social platforms? What types of policies need to be in place? What type of training should be provided? How does this affect the decision-making process for hiring new employees? What are the legal ramifications?

▶ **Marketing**   If you are the Marketing manager, you will be asked: How are competitors leveraging these platforms? What are the best practices for realizing the full potential of social media, even while protecting the company from anticipated challenges and unanticipated problems? How can we best leverage social media for internal collaboration within the enterprise?

Analyzing Your Social Media Initiatives

Determining which platforms are relevant to your objectives, what metrics to use, and how to put systems in place to monitor, measure, and report on various social media activities can be challenging. For example, let's say you are the Marketing Director of a Fortune 100 company tasked with developing your company's marketing efforts through social media. The factors you use to determine success may vary widely from those used by the Sales department or Customer Support. Should you develop a social media presence through creating a Facebook page, focus on growing your Twitter followers, or both? Are you looking to generate direct sales through dedicated channels like @DellOutlet or @JetBlueDeals on Twitter? But your responsibility doesn't end here. In the new world of social media security, you then have to interface with the IT department to understand how the technologies you select for your campaign might introduce a weakness into the environment or subject the company to attack. Each approach has its pros and cons, and each industry has its share of case studies highlighting great successes and epic failures.

Analyzing Your Existing Internal Processes

One of the first questions to ask is Who is responsible for the creation and dissemination of the corporation's social media policy? And the social media security policy? No one department can create these documents. Your existing IT security policy was most likely a collaboration among IT, Human Resources, and Legal. The analysis requires the following steps:

▶ Inventory your IT assets and associate them with marketing activities and social media tools.

▶ Facilitate brainstorming sessions with key stakeholders together in one room for each new project.

▶ Set goals for your social media campaigns and allocate the right IT resources to execute those goals.

▶ Identify the risk and failure potentials for each project.

A key new collaborator is the end-user employee. IT typically does not work with employees when creating policies. This has to change when developing social media policies and security controls that actually work over social media technologies that are not actually owned by the IT department. Employees who are more digitally literate will want to respond and become involved in the co-creation process around social media policy. Because of the participatory nature of the process, employees will feel more engaged, stimulated, and a sense of ownership of the result, thus motivating them to follow and enforce the rules they helped create. IT cannot wholly own this process.

The tone, frequency, timeliness, and authenticity of your process and response to the end user can make the difference in successfully addressing and extinguishing potential social media wildfires. Conversely, an ineffective process can quickly destroy any hard-earned gains that your organization may have built over time.

Securing Customer Data

As BP illustrated, social media technologies make it simple for virtually anyone with access to a connected computer or device to publish unedited text and media. Clearly, corporate interests are at stake, as a brand image that took decades to build can be greatly tarnished or destroyed online in a few hours through word of mouth activity that spreads virally online. The list of case studies grows longer each year, and notable examples include the likes of Dell, Kryptonite, Comcast, United Airlines,

Target, Nestle, Motrin, Amazon, BP, Domino's Pizza, Google, and many others. To start off most chapters in the book, we use a case study to show the relevance of that chapter using a real-world example.

In this new era of engagement, companies must set the ground rules for handling customer data in the social world. The release of private medical files by a doctor's office or the legal ramifications of financial advice from a wealth manager are but two examples of the critical need for companies to establish a social media policy framework.

Securing Channels of Communication

This book serves as a practical guideline for corporations wishing to safeguard their interests, assets, and rights while simultaneously increasing their level of engagement with internal and external communities through the secure use of social media tools and platforms.

By defining boundaries around corporate interests, safe and productive conversations may flourish, even when these may reflect negative customer experiences. The guidelines we discuss will cover all the areas of risk associated with open communications through social media tools and platforms. The chapters ahead contain implementable information, case studies, quick tips, and best practice advice.

Individuals involved in social media should secure their channels of communication and pick the right medium for the company to engage with clients and the general public. In this book, we give examples of what can be said in a public forum and what should be encrypted via offline communications. Understanding the difference between these plays a part in the multilevel defense of a company's online reputation while, at the same time, allowing for real end-user engagement.

To remain competitive, companies must constantly monitor the sentiment of online mentions in order to evaluate the strength of their brand equity and identify potential threats. Online reputation management is a key component in your social media strategy's success. The whole world is talking, and it's up to you to monitor (and at times respond to) what people are saying about you and your organization.

Identifying the Current Gaps in How Your Company Utilizes Social Media Securely

Many corporations involved in the social media space have been ineffective in dealing with issues of security or consumer privacy. In many cases, the people involved are woefully unaware of the rapidly changing legal landscape or the frequently modified privacy policies of many social networks. The responsibility for securing social media is completely undefined in most companies today. Social media is constantly evolving, and one of the goals of this book is to define the strategies, tactics, and best steps needed to navigate the social media sphere securely. But companies are not solely to blame. Facebook, the current de facto leader in the American and worldwide social media space (over 700 million users at the writing of this book), has been historically notorious for continuing to test the limits of the end-user's need for privacy and for poorly communicating changes in its privacy policy. If the social networks themselves expect users to protect themselves through ongoing vigilance, then how should companies provide protection for their customers, their employees, and their assets?

Does your corporate responsibility extend to protecting your employees at home when they use social media? If employees are using social networks to communicate about your organization on their own time (whether sanctioned or not), how can you protect your brand? If it's your responsibility to protect the laptop the employee takes home with firewalls and antivirus and to protect the applications the employee uses on that laptop, by extension do you have a responsibility to protect the social media messages posted by that employee as well?

Clearly, IT's operating guidelines need to include a new section for social media operations or a completely new policy has to be created. These new guidelines should address existing gaps in your organization's secure use of social media by responding to questions such as these:

▶ Who is responsible for social media technologies and policies?

▶ What activities are being conducted using social media technologies?

▶ What is the impact of those activities?

▶ When do social media activities occur and are appropriate notification, tracking, and monitoring systems in place?

▶ How is each social media project managed and reported, and how are problems escalated?

Competitive Analysis

How can you find out what your competitors are saying about you? The comprehensive audit process developed throughout this book will address the accounts, platforms, and resources allocated companywide to your social media initiatives. Before joining the conversation online, however, monitoring what consumers, competitors, regulators, and potential leads are saying is vitally important. Your organization already has technologies in place (hopefully!) to track attacks and log activities of the bad guys. Now, you need similar capabilities and tools for monitoring and measuring the social media space.

By tracking your reputation and online sentiment, you are in a better position to shape your brand equity actively in the social media space, identify potential "disgruntled" consumers and groups, evaluate their potential for challenging your online initiatives, and proactively counter those challenges quickly and effectively. A number of online utilities are available for this purpose, including Google Alerts, Social Mention, Radian6, and Reputation.com, to name but a very few. At the most basic level, you can use Google Alerts, as shown in Figure 1-1, to see when your company name or an executive of your company is mentioned (we used Gary's name here as an example). You can also use the same process to assess what is being said about your competitors. You should probably also know what customers are saying about your competition to help inform your decisions and to help you react more quickly to changes the competition may be implementing.

We will guide you through using several relevant tools as practical sources for monitoring and securing the constantly changing social space around your organization. (One important caveat is that these companies are relatively new, so we don't know whether they'll be here a year from now.) The players may change, but the demand for monitoring your online reputation is here to stay. As such, we are constantly monitoring and reviewing new solutions as they arrive on the market and have developed the resource section of our website (www.securingsocialmedia.com/resources) as a guide to these and many other invaluable tools that you will need to develop a successful social media security strategy.

Figure 1-1   *Using Google Alerts to track any mentions of a name*

Wrap Up

When building your social media security framework, what worked for another company or brand may not necessarily work for you. Each department and every employee should be expected to follow the corporation's social media security policy, which should be built around the company's stated communication initiatives, short-term goals, and long-term objectives. These policies will change over time as the company's involvement online increases as new platforms are developed and through a dynamic and evolving relationship with their communities.

A new process has to be followed to implement a security policy that works for all departments and meets the operational requirements of social media usage. A clear and transparent operational framework that provides insightful guidelines on **H**uman Resources, **U**tilization of resources, **M**onetary considerations, **O**perations management, and **R**eputation management is an essential element of your social media success.

Improvement Checklist

- ☐ Use an assessment process such as the H.U.M.O.R Matrix as the basic foundation of your security framework.

- ☐ Analyze your existing processes and identity gaps in the tools you use to secure social media communications going forward.

- ☐ Identify new threats to the organization via social media platforms.

- ☐ Implement practical procedures for monitoring, reporting, and analysis.

- ☐ Implement coordinated efforts across all departments for a comprehensive companywide strategy.

Security Strategy Analysis: Foundation of Your Security Policy

Every corporation has a process to accomplish every goal. The process could be good or bad. Companies that do not follow a set process tend to make mistakes, achieve unexpected results, have teams going in different directions, and miss their targets. As the motivational speaker and author Zig Ziglar pointed out, "People don't plan to fail; they fail to plan!"

In this chapter, we define the first steps toward developing a secure social media framework so you can track, measure, and monitor your social media usage over time. More specifically, you will learn about the different aspects of the H.U.M.O.R. Matrix and how you can use it to assess your current environment. A framework for security must anticipate future social media developments and how they will impact security.

Case Study: Hacking Is an Equal Opportunity Sport

Not having a strict process for managing security, whether in the social media sphere or general IT infrastructure, can have unwanted consequences. With social media, the constant pace of changes makes managing security tactics more difficult. A recent example of not following a strict process for managing controls is the hack of the Facebook Fanpage of Facebook's own CEO Mark Zuckerberg. In January 2011, his Fanpage was hacked, as shown in Figure 2-1. Although this incident had limited impact on the company's reputation, it shows how even the largest companies are subject to attack.

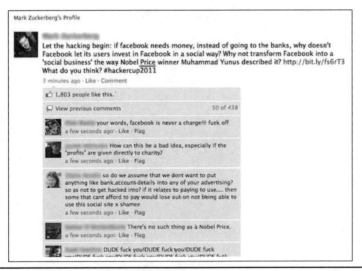

Figure 2-1   *Hacked Fanpage of Mark Zuckerberg*

It is not clear how the hack occurred. Facebook did not provide many details about how the account was compromised. There are a number of ways that it could have occurred—anything from a weak password being guessed to the password being captured over an unencrypted connection to infrastrucre problems. For a large company such as Facebook, whose market valuation is estimated at $50B, its security budget should address these potential weaknesses. Security measures have to take into account people, processes, and technology controls to provide for a secure environment.

Oddly enough, the same week that Mark Zuckerberg's page got hacked, Facebook announced that it would be forcing encrypted login over HTTPS, even making the feature available to developers to secure their secure connections to Facebook. This seems more like a reaction to the hack versus a controled change in the way Facebook handles the insecure login process. But this technology control will be of no use if a process is not in place to ensure users follow good security guidelines or if policies are not developed to provide security training.

The H.U.M.O.R. Matrix

What framework should a corporation use to secure social media? Organizations first need a methodology to analyze the security environment. The content within the methodology should address the organization's overall security strategy, including departments such as Information Technology, Human Resources, Marketing, and Legal. To outline the key components of our framework for the implementation of a complete strategy, we've developed the *H.U.M.O.R Matrix,* which we introduced briefly in Chapter 1.

We utilize this framework throughout the rest of the book to provide a structured approach to developing and implementing a secure social media strategy. Each section of the H.U.M.O.R. Matrix outlines all the requirements, tactics, policies, and implementation processes necessary to move your organization to a new secure process over time, no matter which social media applications are currently in vogue.

The goal of this book is to allow you to implement practical and secure strategies that last for years. Table 2-1 illustrates a way to gather metrics on social media activities. In the left-hand column, we list the areas of control. We use the three right columns to track activity and progress in implementing secure strategies. Throughout the book, we'll also reference a fictional company, JAG Consumer Electronics, to illustrate how your company can implement these strategies. JAG, a manufacturer of a variety of custom electronics, operates in several countries. They have their own Research and Development team. The Marketing department manages social media; however, like many companies, JAG hasn't really developed a robust marketing plan for using all social media outlets appropriately. There is no dedicated position for managing social media; for the most part, the Marketing team shares the responsibility. They do not, however, work hand in hand with IT and Human Resources whenever launching new campaign or social media initiatives.

To start out, JAG evaluated how they generally felt social media was managed in the organization across the five areas of the H.U.M.O.R. Matrix. Through this assessment, JAG discovered that Human Resources was not providing enough training and policies for using social media. The IT team was not integrated with Marketing in utilizing all the different social media tools necessary. There was neither a specific budget for securing social media, nor operational guidelines for IT, Marketing, HR, and Legal to consult for daily operations. The company also lacked robust tools to track the results of social media outlets. JAG completed their self-assessment, indicating their current ratings and where they would like to be in the H.U.M.O.R Matrix over the coming year. By following our framework, JAG can achieve this desired security posture within 12 months. The rest of this chapter defines each section of the matrix.

In the JAG matrix in Table 2-1, we see JAG thinks all five areas currently rate "Poor." Once you have read this book, you can conduct an assessment of your "Current State" and determine what your numbers are today. Normal security practices would define "Poor" as a weak implementation of security practices, or no implementation, lack of standards, and inconsistent management. "Average" security practices are defined as basic practices being in place, meeting the average standards of what is implemented in your industry, but with room for improvement. "Best Practices" usually mean very strict controls, detailed policies and procedures, best of breed implementations, and consistent practices that are kept up to date over time.

Process	Current State 1 - Poor 2– Average 3– Best practices	Maturity Level Desired Within 6 Months	Maturity Level Desired Within 12 Months
Human Resources	1	3	3
Utilization	1	2	3
Monetary	1	2	3
Operations	1	2	3
Reputation	1	2	3

Table 2-1   *Matrix for Measuring H.U.M.O.R. Metrics*

Human Resources

Human Resources (HR) is the main driving force of the security framework. HR makes all other policies or approves all other policies such as IT security policies, so it should be no different for social media policies. Whether your company is large or small, a department or person handles the HR function. The Information Technology (IT) staffing company Robert Half Technology (http://www.roberthalftechnology .com/Small-Business-Resource-Center) found that in 2010 54 percent of U.S. companies had banned workers from using social networking sites at the office and 19 percent restricted use to business use only. In light of this restrictive HR trend, how does your company handle this issue?

Whether an employee posts communications that might impact his company from home or from work is a gray area that the company needs to clarify. If an employee tries to post information to social networks at work, you can easily forbid this with a policy document or even block it with technology such as a data loss prevention tool like Symantec's Vontu program. If that same employee posts to social networks at home, you cannot block it. Still, the employee may effectively be limited or restricted from posting confidential or derogatory information about the company by company policy and contracts between the employee and company. However, case law isn't clear on employees' full rights vis-à-vis their employers when posting to social networks. In a recent case ("NLRB Backs Worker Fired After Facebook Posts Ripping Boss"[1]), the National Labor Relations Board is defending an employee fired for a Facebook post as a freedom of speech case. American Medical Response of Connecticut fired a medical technician for criticizing a supervisor online. By no means are these cases clear cut on what companies can legally do.

Assessing the Current Environment

Human Resources and Information Technology department management must first understand what policies and processes are in place. IANS, a Boston-based research company, found that in 2008 under 10 percent of survey respondent enterprises had an implemented social media policy; this figure jumped to 34 percent in 2009. This is definitely a step in the right direction. Analysis of current HR practices in regards to social media security can be broken down into the categories shown in Table 2-2.

---

[1] Susanna Kim, "NLRB Backs Worker Fired After Facebook Posts Ripping Boss," ABC News, November 10, 2010, http://abcnews.go.com/Business/facebook-firing-labor-board-takes-stand/story?id=12099395.

Category	Description	Best Practices
Current HR Policies	1. What are the current policies that impact employee use of social media at work?	1. Social media policies for all departments should be clearly defined.
	2. What are HR's responsibilities?	2. HR defines all the requirements for business usage that can then be supported by other departments such as IT, Marketing, and Legal.
	3. How do you determine what makes a good policy?	3. HR has to research the legal ramifications and IT must research the technical capabilities of resources to enforce security.
	4. How do you compare your policy to industry regulations?	4. Each organization has to assess the regulatory requirements and the applicability on social media usage.
	5. Should you publish your social media policy externally to the world?	5. Publication of the social media policy is a business decision.
	6. How would HR build a case (chain of custody) for termination for inappropriate use of social media?	6. A very clearly defined procedure for incident response and chain of custody events has to be defined between HR and IT.
	7. What policies are in place for what social media can be used at work?	7. HR must specify what is allowed and work with IT to enforce usage.
	8. When does Legal get involved?	8. Legal departments must be aware of what technologies are in use and how HR plans to restrict and monitor users with the help of IT.
Current IT Security Policies	1. Who is responsible for developing the security policies related to social media?	1. The responsibility is a business decision that must come from HR and Marketing.
	2. How would IT develop these policies, in conjunction with whom?	2. IT must work with HR and Marketing and Legal to develop the appropriate security policies. Even more effective is to also consult with employees who contribute to social media from other departments.

Table 2-2   *HR Practices*

Category	Description	Best Practices
	3. Who is responsible for managing social media security and response to social media breaches?	3. IT is responsible for incident response, but Marketing is responsible for reputation damage and follow-up.
	4. What security policies must be in place to implement HR policies?	4. A technology plan must be implemented by IT to manage HR requirements for social media usage, monitoring, and reporting requirements.
Training Regimen	1. What tactics are currently being used by HR to educate employees in social media usage?	1. Training on the appropriate usage of social media must be defined and managed by HR.
	2. How is security training conducted, specifically in regards to social media tactics?	2. IT is responsible for developing (based on HR requirements) and disseminating the appropriate training modules.

Table 2-2   *HR Practices (continued)*

If we look back at the hack of the Mark Zuckerberg Fanpage, could more stringent policies on how pages are accessed, limits on who accesses the page, and restrictions on sharing of passwords or other procedures have prevented the hack?

Your initial assessment of current practices has to identify the company's business goals. What is allowed runs to different extremes, and policies have to map to how a company intends to address social media usage by employees and how it intends to respond to customers over social media. Strategies and tactics must not only include responding to customer groups, but also any and all influential communities (whether they are customers or not) that are talking about the brand and the company's products and services. Most companies have no middle ground when it comes to their social media policies. Extreme restrictive practices often block all sites, completing record all activity, register all profiles, and limit authorization. A very relaxed environment allows companywide usage without restrictions on sites or times of usage and no monitoring and reporting.

Information Gathering

After you have completed your current assessment steps, you then review all policies regarding social media use. Each department—Human Resources, Information Technology, Marketing, Legal, and any other department involved in social media—must first assess what policies are in place. Table 2-3 identifies the steps that each department goes through during the information gathering phase. The review JAG performed is detailed in the third column.

Steps	Description	Example
1. Policy owner	For each current policy, identify that policy.	Jag has identified that there is an "Information Technology Security Policy" owned by the Information Technology Department.
2. Policy characterization	Describe the policy.	This policy defines JAG's security practices.
3. Policy scope	Describe the applications and responsibilities defined in the policy.	This policy covers all security technologies and operations for the organization. The current policy does not have a specific social media section for security.
4. Target audience	Define whom the policy applies to.	This policy applies to all departments in the organization.
5. Dissemination	Describe how the policy is disseminated in the organization.	The IT department posts the policy on the internal Intranet website.
6. Impact analysis	Identify the key risks addressed by this policy.	The IT department addresses computer security risks in this policy. Control measures to address possible attacks are covered in this policy. Social media is not currently a risk addressed by the policy.
7. Technology mapping	Define what technologies, if any, are necessary for this policy's implementation.	The policy defines all technologies to secure the internal servers and workstation, perimeter devices. and remote users. There is no technology defined to secure social media usage.
8. Security implications	Describe the policy's security impact.	This policy is specific to security for the organization. It details specific security steps that must be taken to secure the systems and users and data. It does not impact secure social media tactics.

Table 2-3   *Information Gathering Steps*

Document and Process Review

After you have gathered all policies from all the departments, you must analyze each policy in detail and identify and evaluate the processes that impact social media security. After reviewing each policy, you can determine the impact on social media. Table 2-4 lists examples of how this part of the process can be applied to our fictional company, JAG Consumer Electronics.

Policy	Social Media Security Impact	Owner
IT Security Policy	No specific sections address the use of social media. Instant messaging is specifically denied within the company, but no technology is in place to block IM to the outside world.	IT
Human Resources Policy	Social media technologies are defined with this policy, and employees are not supposed to use social media sites, specifically Facebook and MySpace, in the office.	HR
Acceptable Use Policy	The Acceptable Use Policy covers any form of communication from the company computers. Although no specific mention of social media is made, all communications must adhere to acceptable standards such as no inappropriate language or disparaging remarks and company assets should only be used for work purposes.	IT
Termination Policy	The Termination Policy does not specifically state how social media usage can lead to reprimand or termination. An organization cannot truly restrict the use of social media on personal time, even within the military, regardless of what the policy states. The ability to use avatars and false information as well as alternate e-mail addresses when registering on social networks makes reinforcing the restriction practically impossible. A Termination Policy will be hard to enforce without adequate proof.	HR
Marketing Social Media Policy	The Marketing Social Media Policy lists the different social media technologies that are used by JAG. Specifically, the Marketing department lists Facebook, MySpace, LinkedIn, and Twitter as communication mediums. The Marketing team has designated a specific manager who authorizes usage of these platforms for communication but does not specifically state if other employees may use these mediums for purposes other than marketing.	Marketing

Table 2-4   *Impact of Each Policy on Secure Social Media*

Measuring the Current State: H.U.M.O.R. Matrix

The analysis of how all the policies and processes associated with the security impact social media usage prepares you to identify your organization's ability from a policy perspective to use social media securely. Our final analysis of the Human Resources metric is to identify all the tactics that make up a robust security environment. Table 2-5 shows the metrics that Human Resources needs to measure

HUMAN RESOURCES	Current State 1 - Poor 2 – Average 3 – Best Practices	Maturity Level Desired Within 6 Months	Maturity Level Desired Within 12 Months
Human Resource Policy			
Specific social media security policy	1	3	3
Social media conduct defined by HR	1	3	3
Capabilities of HR to manage social media	1	2	3
HR's dissemination capabilities	2	3	3
Capability to engage employees through policies and processes	2	3	3
Capability of HR to manage training	1	2	3
Capability of HR to communicate policies	1	2	3
Capability of HR to respond to social media breach	1	2	3
IT Security Policy			
Applicability of social media policies	2	3	3
Social media security technology defined in IT policies	2	3	3
Capability to respond to social media breach	2	2	3
Training Regimen			
Training for employees on social media usage	1	2	3
Training for employees on social media security issues	1	2	3

Table 2-5   *Human Resources Matrix*

their security capabilities, with IT providing the right tools. Let's use JAG again as our test company. After reviewing its current HR tactics and policies, JAG has filled in the matrix in Table 2-5, first by determining where they are and where they would like to be in the next 12 months. JAG currently scores a 1 on the policy items because no social media policies are really in place. JAG does have IT security policies, which is why it garnered a 2 in those components; however, JAG hasn't updated these to address social media. JAG rates a 2 in dissemination and communication because the capabilities exist, if only the right policy content was available to disseminate it. Finally, no training is provided for IT staff or employees, so that rates a 1.

Utilization of Resources and Assets

So we have completed our "H" in the H.U.M.O.R. Matrix. Next, we move on to Utilization. Determining how to track social media usage requires a concerted effort. Utilization analysis aims to identify all the tactical and strategic steps a company takes to create a secure social media framework. Social media places assets at risk in the organization. Assets include hard assets such as technology equipment and soft assets such as a Microsoft SQL customer database or intellectual property information. A process has to be in place to protect assets and determine how security resources are used in the environment, specifically in regards to the changing social media landscape. We divide the Utilization metric into three categories: technology, intellectual property, and copyright. Table 2-6 describes the categories.

Category	Description
Technology	What technologies are used to distribute social media content and to monitor social media activity, both to and from employees and from customers?
Intellectual policy	How does a company track its intellectual property in the social media universe,where restricted information is easily shared?
Copyright	Using social media can easily compromise corporate copyrighted information as well as compromise copyrighted materials from other organizations and individuals. How does the company track possible infringement of copyrighted information?

Table 2-6 *Utilization Categories*

Assessing the Current Environment

As you did for Human Resources, you first conduct an assessment of the current environment. For each Utilization category—technology, intellectual property, and copyright—you must take steps to determine your current security posture. Your company has to first assess how social media affects your assets and what is currently being done to protect those assets.

Technology Assessment

After developing a social media security policy (as performed under the Human Resources portion of the matrix), technology is your next line of defense in protecting against social media attacks or inappropriate dissemination of information. The responsibility of the IT or Information Security department is to implement technologies to manage how assets are controlled. Companies that tie their social media usage and interaction to their corporate resources, such as accessing customer information or using payment gateways over social media, must put very robust tools in place to manage social media usage. Online social gaming company Zynga, which makes the popular Facebook games Farmville, Citiville, and Mafia Wars, got hacked by a British IT professional in 2011. He broke into the company's system and stole 400 billion in virtual poker chips (potentially $12 million dollars in value). Although this didn't lead to a material loss for the company, it did impact the company's reputation with customers.

Follow these steps to assess the technology needed to secure social media:

1. **Inventory** List all technologies currently in place to secure social media and the mediums used. Focus only on what impacts your social media usage or could impact your social media usage or connectivity to your other assets.

2. **Capability** Assess the capabilities of the security technologies utilized in managing assets to manage your social media activities. If a particular piece of technology can't protect you in the social media world, you are not concerned about assessing it here. For example, if you use McAfee's Data Loss Prevention solution (www.mcafee.com), you have the ability to block files and confidential data leaving the organization. You can apply this same product to social media channels, such as posting files on a website like Facebook or sending out IM messages with confidential files or information using Skype.

3. **Policy mapping** Map the security technology that impacts social media usage to the corresponding requirements in your IT security policies and HR policies. You are reviewing the current environment at this point, so if nothing maps back to policy requirements, don't try to make it fit. You are focusing only on what works today. You should also map your social media strategy at this point to your social media usage policy. Then, within your IT security policy, you have to build hooks into social media usage and apply the appropriate security tools.

Technology utilization crosses all boundaries in terms of how social media is used in your company and how assets can be put at risk. Social media uses different types of communication channels—from web and mobile social utilities like Facebook (www.facebook.com) to location-based applications like foursquare (www.foursquare.com). Shared cloud services such as Basecamp (www.basecamphq.com) provide collaborative sites for information sharing but open the company to data loss through third-party hosted software services.

Social media applications may be categorized as open source, cloud, or both. *Open source* applications are based on code made available for public use with certain restrictions. WordPress is an open source application you can download and install, but it can also be accessed as a cloud application. *Cloud* applications can be open source and are available in a publicly hosted environment. Most social media sites are cloud-based applications such as Facebook and Google Buzz. The key risks that need to be assessed when using these technologies include:

▶ Inadvertently violating the open source license model

▶ Using open source material in products that are then sold as proprietary

▶ Not assessing the security controls properly in open source code, making the assumption the code is stable

▶ Loosing future development if the open source project fails

▶ Violation of third-party intellectual property because a contributor used proprietary code

WordPress(www.wordpress.org) places almost no restrictions on usage, as they state on their website:

> WordPress is an Open Source project, which means there are hundreds of people all over the world working on it. (More than most commercial platforms.) It also means you are free to use it for anything from your cat's home page to a Fortune 500 web site without paying anyone a license fee and a number of other important freedoms.

But contributors could still expose your company to risks other than licensing issues through code infringement or inherent security weaknesses in the code you download.

As just mentioned, most social media platforms are considered cloud computing. Consider that all the data handled by Facebook, Twitter, Blogger.com, Google Buzz, MySpace, YouTube, Flickr, Reddit, StumbleUpon, and so on, is hosted and stored on their servers. You have access to your accounts and data, but you do not know what will happen to the companies running those sites—especially when they do not have a business model for revenue in place as of yet. Twitter may be extremely popular, but it still does not make enough money to cover its operating costs. What happens to all the information Twitter has gathered if the funding runs out and the company shutters its doors or gets acquired?

Intellectual Property

Once you have understood how technology is utilized in the current environment, you need to look at what your company is doing regarding the next critical asset—intellectual property (IP). Remember, you are still in the information-gathering phase. First ask yourself: What IP do we need to protect and how can it be lost through our employees' utilization of social media?

In the "Human Resources" section, you determined what your current policies are and where the appropriate policy might be lacking. One specific area to consider is intellectual property. Also information about intellectual property can damage a company. If you determine you need a policy specific to IP, then you must now assess how to utilize that policy. Such a policy can be for your own information, but it can also be for your customers. If your employees have access to customer IP or your own IP, you have to determine how IP management is affected by social media usage.

Follow these steps to assess risks to IP over social media:

1. Determine if IP is currently being sent out via social media sites using technology controls.

2. Determine if you have the capabilities to manage, track, and block IP assets over social media platforms.

3. Determine types of communications used to disseminate IP information, for instance, a Twitter message about your customer's latest product development or a Flickr photo showing restricted customer information.

4. Determine if your company might be impinging on a customer's or another company's IP, for example, taking data from crowd sourcing sites or social media sites and using it internally to your company. The Nielsen rating company did just this when they captured information from Patientslikeme.com's forum pages for Nielsen marketing purposes (more on this in Chapter 4).

Finally, as you assess your utilization of technology, list all the tools necessary for protecting IP. Key tools used today for normal IP protection are Data Loss Prevention technologies such as Symantec's Vontu (www.vontu.com) or Trustwave's Vericept (www.vericept.com). When you are using social media sites, tools necessary to track IP going out the door should be focused more on URL filtering technologies such as Websense (www.websense.com).

Copyright

Copyright protection is very similar to IP protection. An employee can easily compromise her own company's copyrights and trademarks or infringe upon those of other organizations and individuals. What steps are you are taking to assess copyright protection? For example, take a blog post by your Marketing department that references some company or topic. Let's say they need a good picture to go with the post. They can easily search Google for images and then copy the image and use it in the post. This could lead to copyright infringement associated with your company. Or, what if your Marketing department sends out an e-mail newsletter with copies of stories about a pertinent topic from a magazine or news website. This is exactly what happened in February 2011 to Webcopyplus. The company had to pay US$4,000 to settle a lawsuit based on the fact that a copywriter used an image in a commercial piece of work. The image was available on the Internet, but Webcopyplus neglected to pay for it.[2]

The other side of the equation is the actual desire to protect certain copyrighted property. This is a business decision and goes beyond the realm of IT or Marketing. Take, for example, Nestlé's problems in 2010. The environmental group Greenpeace been targeting Nestlé's use of palm oil, which Greenpeace says is a source of deforestation, greenhouse gas emissions, and threatens endangered species, particularly orangutans. Greenpeace's video was posted on YouTube and Nestlé tried to have the video removed from YouTube, citing copyright. Greenpeace retaliated by having followers change their Facebook profiles and send Twitter messages using Nestlé logos and copyrighted data. Nestlé received a very negative response, as sited by CNET: "Hey PR moron. Thanks, you are doing a far better job than we could ever achieve in destroying your brand," to "It's not OK for people to use altered versions of your logos,

---

[2] PR Web, "Copywriter Pays $4,000 for a $10 Photo Due to Copyright Infringement," February 15, 2011, http://www.sfgate.com/cgi-bin/article.cgi?f=/g/a/2011/02/15/prweb5061854.DTL.

but it's OK for you to alter the face of Indonesian rainforests? Wow!"[3] The brand's ability to navigate the social media landscape backfired.

Outside of traditional law enforcement tactics to respond to negative campaigns, the company had no strategy in place. This is another reason why companies need digital literacy training and community management best practices, in addition to the general security training already given. Companies must have protection mechanisms in place to track the use of copyrighted assets on social media. Your company has to assess which tools can be used in this arena and the capability of the IT staff to manage those tools and work with Marketing, Legal, and Human Resources to protect those assets. In assessing the need to protect copyrights, utilize the same steps as you do when assessing intellectual property.

Regulations regarding social media are still very vague. Some industries have best practices they would like to apply to social media usage. Industries such as the legal and healthcare professions are already very heavily regulated. Those regulations in theory apply to social media usage as well. There are numerous regulations on the books regarding intellectual property, so these can easily be applied to social media usage. How a company tracks adherence to those regulations in social media poses a new challenge.

Measuring the Current State: H.U.M.O.R. Matrix

Once you have determined the assets that need to be protected and the technologies you need to have in place to protect them, you can complete the next section of the H.U.M.O.R. matrix, measuring your current Utilization capabilities. Table 2-7 shows the key aspects of the Utilization metric you need to track. Let's go back to our test company JAG to see how it's doing in this area. JAG rated a Poor due to several key factors, which include:

▶   Lack of technology controls in place to monitor what is happening in the environment, from users posting information to tracking customer mentions on social media platforms.

▶   JAG has no tools to monitor the social media sphere for risk to IP.

▶   JAG does not know if its own employees might be infringing on other copyrights when posting blog information because it does not strictly control blogging content.

---

[3] Caroline, McCarthy, "Nestle Mess Shows Sticky Side of Facebook Pages," CNET News (March 19, 2010), http://news.cnet.com/8301-13577_3-20000805-36.html.

UTILIZATION OF RESOURCES	Current State 1 - Poor 2 – Average 3 – Best practices	Maturity Level Desired Within 6 Months	Maturity Level Desired Within 12 Months
Technology			
Appropriate technology in place to track user access to social media	1	2	3
Appropriate technology in place to track regulations in social media utilization	1	2	3
Appropriate technology in place to track data storage in social media utilization	1	2	3
Appropriate technology in place to track access to data to social media utilization	1	2	3
Appropriate technology in place to track shared services for resources in social media utilization	1	2	3
Appropriate technology in place to track business continuity to social media utilization	1	2	3
Appropriate technology in place to provide support services for social media utilization	1	2	3
Intellectual property			
Ability to track inappropriate use of intellectual property	2	2	3
Ability to track inappropriate use of third-party intellectual property by company	1	2	3
Copyright			
Ability to track copyright data of the company	1	2	3
Ability to track inappropriate use of third-party copyrights by the company	1	2	3

Table 2-7 *Utilization Matrix*

Monetary Considerations

Medium to large-sized businesses usually have a budget dedicated to both marketing and information security practices. Although this may not necessarily be the case for the small company, most likely some money is dedicated, however unstructured, to these two areas. Here you need to access the budget for securing social media and determine if it comes from the IT or Marketing budget?

Assessing the Current Environment

Putting all of the tools, policies, and procedures in place to attain your security goals requires a budget. Where does the money for the security budget come from? Social media budgets are being developed, but not many companies have yet set aside a budget specific to social media security. Knowing what's needed is difficult as social media changes so frequently, so budgets have to be focused on building processes and operations irrespective of the actual social media platform being used. It shouldn't matter if your company is using Google Buzz or Facebook, a budget needs to be in place for the tools and processes needed to secure the medium being used, which is a cloud service.

Information Gathering

Assessing current security controls is a difficult process. The value of a control compared to the value of a deliverable is extremely difficult to determine in social media. There are no accepted formulas for calculating the value of social media and metrics for properly measuring results. Security is such a new part of social media you have to determine what value you want to place on security. How do you measure the cost and value of a control?

To measure your social media security spending, you have to identify what tools are necessary, how many resources are required, and what part of your IT Security budget or Marketing budget will be required to meet those security goals. If no budget is dedicated to social media, who is to blame when you do not have the controls for social media security in place and a problem occurs? A security budget also has to include the cost of data loss through social media channels.

Social media monetary spending can be tracked and categorized to more easily organize your budget in regards to security requirements. This cost model is a good place to start if you do not already have a dedicated model for creating social media security budgets. Table 2-8 shows the breakdown of the Monetary spending portion of the H.U.M.O.R. Matrix.

Budget Item	Department	Implementation Costs
Technology	Information Technology	Identify cost of software purchases.
Personnel	Human Resources	Identify cost of resources needed to manage social media.
Policy Development	Information Technology Human Resources Marketing Legal	Determine cost of effort needed to develop and maintain social media policies.
Enforcement	Human Resources Information Technology	Determine cost of technology and people needed to monitor and maintain security over social media.
Monitoring	Marketing Human Resources	Determine cost of technology and activities needed to monitor usage.
Reporting	Human Resources Information Technology	Determine cost of resources needed to report on activity and follow up on inappropriate activity.

Table 2-8   *Monetary Spending Requirements*

Monetary spending has to work in conjunction with how employees conduct business. The more you positively reinforce valuable social media activity by employees, the more likely they are to

▶   Report on inappropriate social media activity from within the company environment.

▶   Actively champion the brand through social media (whether this is in their job description or not).

In other words, positive reinforcement helps you train your employees to do a big chunk of the monitoring for you, which lowers resource budgets over time, regardless of technology.

Measuring the Current State: H.U.M.O.R. Matrix

Table 2-9 shows how you would track your monetary spending. Here is how our test company JAG Electronics rated. JAG's key problem is that the company does not have a budget dedicated to social media security. Nothing has been set aside from the IT security budget. No tools or services have been purchased to monitor the brand, report on threats to the company, or secure employee usage of social media.

MONETARY SPENDING	Current State 1 - Poor 2 – Average 3 – Best practices	Maturity Level Desired Within 6 Months	Maturity Level Desired Within 12 Months
Track budgetary spending for social media	2	2	3
Cost of tools needed to track participation	1	2	3
Cost of tools needed to track social buzz, on a real-time basis	1	2	3
Cost of tools needed to measure brand awareness	1	2	3
Cost of tools to track positive, negative, or neutral mentions	1	2	3
Cost of tools acquired for measuring monetary spending for social media security tactics, software, and person-hours	1	2	3
Value of brand equity determined	1	2	3

Table 2-9   *Monetary Considerations Matrix*

Operations Management

Operations management is about managing the day-to-day activities related to using social media. A company has to have structured processes for these activities and clearly defined roles for operations. Operational weaknesses can lead to downtime of the social media tools being used, lost opportunities or increased risk resulting from incoherent or incomplete business processes, or the loss of data through weak restrictions on social media.

The role of IT in providing security for a dispersed medium such as social media has to be clearly defined and articulated both to the IT department and to the end user. In the "Human Resources" section, you defined the IT security policies that must be applied to social media. Operations are the implementation of those policies. How involved should security be and where is the line between IT and the business unit owners such as Marketing and Legal? The roles of defining the security issues may fall on the IT department, but working and educating employees and the business unit owners may fall to different groups.

Assessing the Current Environment

The key responsibility for Operations lies with the Information Technology department. To a lesser extent, Operations will also be handled by other departments such as Marketing, Human Resources, and Legal for certain aspects of social media management.

Assessment Steps for Understanding Operational Risks

To understand how operations impact the ability to utilize social media tools properly, your staff and employees have to know the appropriate steps to follow. Different tactics and job functions will determine what tools are necessary on a day-to-day basis. Key areas that will drive your operational capabilities include access to information, the impact of regulations, data management requirements, shared service models, business continuity, and necessary support services.

▶ **Access**   Your employees may be storing sensitive data on social media sites such as work documents they might e-mail to themselves for later use or key information about themselves that can be used to guess their passwords such as a birth date or children's names. Determine who is accessing that information internally by logging visits within your company to social media sites with web filtering technologies such as FireEye(www.fireeye.com). Determine how employees are accessing that information. Can you tell if they surf the Web or go online using smart phones provided by the company?

▶ **Regulations**   Do you know if the social media site meets any regulatory requirements? Are you under a regulatory requirement that might bar you from using third parties that have not been audited or met certain standards? Do your employees know whether the data they may be submitting to social media sites is breaking a regulation? Determine a fast and effective process for removing information from each of the social media platforms, as well as any third-party applications used in conjunction with them, to comply with regulations. When it comes to social media and the ability to share content across mediums at the click of a button, rapid response is critical.

▶ **Data storage**   Do you know where the servers you are using for your social media activity actually store your data and interactions? What if it's in another country? Or, in the case of Blackberry, which runs all enterprise traffic through RIM data centers in Britain and Canada, are messages subject to eavesdropping by competent hackers or governments? If it's confidential or sensitive or regulated data, are the encryption levels strong enough or are you at risk of breaking some law? Also, depending on whether you are using Blackberry's own Facebook application or another party's application on a Blackberry to access your Facebook profile, your data may be sitting on multiple servers in several countries without you or your employee's knowledge. Determine where data is stored—depending on the location, it might impact the ability of your organization to use social media platforms for business.

▶ **Data access**   After spending dozens of hours submitting content and media to a website and establishing relationships and creating a community, can you export that data? How often is the data backed up? Determine your backup and recovery strategy for social media content.

▶ **Shared services**   The concept of cloud computing is about shared services. What if you have access to a server with thousands of others and data gets comingled? Determine if there is a risk of your data being comingled.

▶ **Business continuity**   If you have spent vast sums on a marketing campaign that utilizes a social media site or process, your business could be dependent on that site or process. If that site goes away, you could be out of luck, losing data and customers and wasting time and resources. You do not control social media sites. Determine if there is a business continuity plan in place for the particular social media platforms you are using.

▶ **Support services**   Social media sites are notorious for not having support. You are usually on your own. How do your employees use these sites and do they need assistance, which could be a drain on your own resources? First understand how employees use the social networks and what applications are truly needed. What functionality do employees need? You can then determine the level of support necessary to meet a specific business goal.

Assessment Steps for Cloud Resources

When using cloud or open source technologies, assessing the risk of using both types of technologies is important:

1. Identify how information is stored.
2. Identify how information is controlled.
3. Identify the channels for creating and accessing information.
4. Identify any information access mechanism by users.
5. Identify their identity theft response capabilities.
6. Identify their third-party credential storage management routines.
7. Identify their capabilities to protect against spam, viruses, and malware.

8. Identify hacker attacks on stored data or applications.

9. Identify data loss prevention techniques.

The IT department's final responsibility lies in determining and implementing the necessary toolset to protect social media usage. Until recently, all the IT security tools were focused on the network layer, the operating system layer, and the application layer. All the policies and operations guides were geared at securing these environments. Now, social media pushes the control outside of IT and makes the management and usage of data a new responsibility for IT. A list of sites and services and the tools necessary to provide some form of tracking, monitoring, and reporting of those sites and services should be created and updated as social media changes. With the many options you have, a tracking mechanism to manage all your technologies is definitely a requirement.

The desired outcome of the use of tools and security processes should be defined in the "Human Resources" section through the policies and procedures created. For each technology used, define the effects of a specific attack and how the appropriate response from a technology perspective and a policy perspective will address the attack. We will go into more details later in Chapter 4 on defining threats and how to respond. This section should only assess what the current environment is and set the stage for implementing IT audit controls.

Information Gathering

Operations management procedures are part of the standard processes IT follows for day-to-day security management. The difference is that social media has to be specifically addressed as a landscape that changes on an almost daily basis.

To assess the current environment, the various departments, with IT leading, should address the following questions:

▶ Do you have a secure social media operations guide or a subset of guidelines within normal operating procedures?

▶ What practices are currently being followed?

▶ Is there a specific correlation between Human Resources and IT security policies and social media tactics?

▶ Have responsibilities been designated to specific departments?

▶ Does your company follow any industry best practices for operations?

▶ How do you find industry best practices for social media security operations?

▶ How does IT track new social media sites and technologies to anticipate security concerns or different data usage paths?

▶ Who is allowed to conduct social media practices?

▶ Is there a process to inform operators of social media platforms and new usage by other departments?

▶ Where do the operators learn about new social media security problems and solutions?

Measuring the Current State: H.U.M.O.R. Matrix

After reviewing the operations capabilities of the various departments, you can start measuring your capabilities in the Operations management portion of the H.U.M.O.R. Matrix. As we have done previously, JAG Consumer Electronics has assessed their environment and come up with the following ratings in Table 2-10. JAG is again

OPERATIONS MANAGEMENT	Current State 1 - Poor 2 – Average 3 – Best practices	Maturity Level Desired Within 6 Months	Maturity Level Desired Within 12 Months
Operations identified for social media	1	2	3
Operations responsibilities clearly defined by department	1	2	3
Operations mapped to social media policies	1	2	3
Active monitoring of social media threats	1	3	3
Asset management of social media sites being used in the company	1	3	3
Tracking of employees allowed to use social media	1	2	3
Education of operators that manage social media security tools	1	2	3
Process for determining data usage and storage in social media sites	1	2	3
Recovery process for restoring information from social media sites for business continuity plan	1	2	3

Table 2-10   *Operations Management Matrix*

rated Poor because the company has not clearly identified operational guidelines for social media security. Policies are not being followed, day-to-day activities are not in place, and the IT department has not integrated social media monitoring into its processes. JAG has no ability to track where data is being stored on social media sites and no ability to recover operations if those sites become unavailable or the data becomes unavailable.

Reputation Management

All social media results in both a reputation opportunity and challenge for the company. For a small company, any damaging information spread through social media venues might be disastrous for the company whereas for a larger company, a damaging story can be weathered. But how the reputation and brand of any company gets affected by social media and what the company does to manage, monitor, and report on activity are the key to successful reputation management.

Assessing the Current Environment

Reputation management starts with establishing a baseline for your organization's brand equity. What is your current brand equity and how would you measure it? Unless you can measure the brand value, you do not know how to allocate your security budget and the processes and technologies to secure your brand. Currently, brands worth millions of dollars in value have invested nothing in social media management. A brand and a company's stock price can be damaged by a single viral video on YouTube. A great example is the YouTube song by musician Dave Carroll. His guitar was broken on a United Airlines flight, and the airline did not compensate him and treated him poorly. Dave wrote a song about the incident. The song, which went viral on YouTube, had over 9 million hits. The *Times* newspaper reported that the video caused United Airline stock to drop 10 percent.[4]

Information Gathering

The next step in assessing a brand's reputation is determining the risk of external attacks and the defense tactics needed. Finding this information is a daily 24/7 effort. Your IT security department can implement tools to track reputation attacks. But you

---

[4] Chris Ayers, "Revenge Is Best Served Cold—on YouTube," *The Times* (July 22, 2009, http://www.timesonline.co.uk/tol/comment/columnists/chris_ayres/article6722407.ece.

also need to be aware of third parties that are completely external to your company and determine what kind of response you might need to those attacks on your reputation. One example of a tool to track mentions of your brand or name is IceRocket (www.icerocket.com), as shown in Figure 2-2. Using IceRocket, you can begin tracking what is being said about your company Twitter account or brand name.

Crisis management is a significant aspect of a security response plan. You have to analyze your current capabilities to respond to an attack both from a technology perspective such as stolen profile information and from a brand perspective such as the fake BP Twitter account. What policies and practices do you have in place if a crisis were to occur today and how will you address gaps you find in your crisis management plan regarding social media attacks?

In crisis management, there are various roles to play. What is the role of IT versus HR versus Marketing in a crisis? How do you determine when crisis is security-related versus marketing-related? This is a gray area unless you do some scenario analysis prior to actually having a crisis. In some cases, the Marketing department itself may set off a crisis. A bad campaign can launch a chain of events that leads to an attack on the company's brand and reputation. For example, the hugely successful online

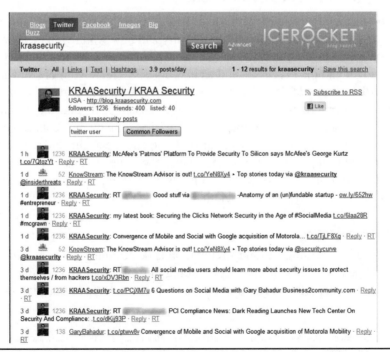

Figure 2-2   *IceRocket tracking of key Twitter terms*

couponing website Groupon ran controversial Super Bowl ads in 2011 making light of some serious social causes. Their efforts to raise funds for those same causes were completely lost on the public, who expressed their disapproval across social media platforms. How do you analyze whether your marketing campaigns affect your security model? Does your marketing team actually notify your security team when a major social media campaign is about to be launched? Are there team meetings between the groups? What is Marketing's responsibility in terms of monitoring activity versus IT's responsibility when a new campaign is launched? IT and Marketing should work together to select the right reputation management tools. One example of a tool is Social Mention (www.socialmention.com). Figure 2-3 shows an example of the data that can be tracked using Social Mention. Key functions of these types of tools include measurements of "sentiment," activity, keywords, along with what is being posted and tracking important mentions.

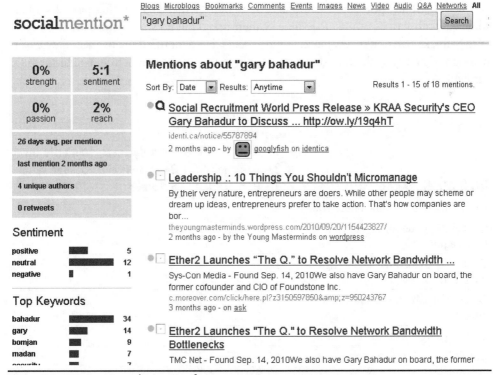

Figure 2-3   *Using Social Mention for reputation managment*

Prior to social media campaigns, if a marketing campaign were to be launched, there might be some IT support involved. Perhaps IT would set up e-mail lists or a new website. Now Marketing teams can create social media profiles on Facebook and launch a whole campaign without involving IT and determining beforehand if there are any security implications. A marketing campaign can instigate a cyber attack against the brand without IT being involved. Without the proper tools in place, measuring reputation attacks is hard. What tools should IT use to support Marketing functions and understand the impact on reputation management? Whose responsibility is it to defend the brand? There are a number of challenges that IT needs to address along with other departments to address reputation risk.

Measuring the Current State: H.U.M.O.R. Matrix

Table 2-11 shows how these risks can be assessed in our fictional company JAG Consumer Electronics. JAG is, of course, weak in this area as well because no real tools have been implemented to track what the public is saying about JAG. There is no tracking of any potential mentions of JAG in a Twitter post or blog post. JAG has some capability to determine the value of their brand but no way to measure the effect of the attacks that could devalue the brand. As IT is not notified in advance, they can't work consistently with other departments when it comes to launching social media campaigns.

REPUTATION MANAGEMENT	Current State 1 - Poor 2 – Average 3 – Best practices	Maturity Level Desired Within 6 Months	Maturity Level Desired Within 12 Months
Capability to determine brand equity	2	3	3
Capability to identify risk against brand equity	1	2	3
Capability to identify attacks against the brand	1	2	3
Defense capabilities against brand attacks	1	2	3
Crisis management capabilities	2	3	3
Capability of Marketing and IT to coordinate	1	2	3
Tools to manage reputation	1	2	3

Table 2-11   *Reputation Management Matrix*

Wrap Up

This chapter outlined the primary steps toward understanding your social media security framework. First you must assess your environment before you can move onto defining the relevant threats and the required controls to implement security. The H.U.M.O.R Matrix allows you to put together a complete social media security analysis. The next chapter will outline how to monitor the social media landscape to complete your picture of what is currently happening in your social media practices.

Improvement Checklist

- ☐ Do you have HR policies that cover social media?
- ☐ Have you conducted an analysis of all the tools used by your company in social media?
- ☐ Have you defined a budget for social media security technologies?
- ☐ Have you written operational guidelines for how all departments use social media?
- ☐ Do you know what kind of monitoring you need to have for reputation management?

Monitoring in the
Social Media Landscape

Monitoring is an integral part of your social media security practices. If you can't monitor activity, you cannot control activity. Monitoring has to target three audiences: your customers, the public, and your employees. Threats and attacks are both internal and external, and so your monitoring activities have to manage both sides of the attack scenario.

In this chapter, we discuss what you need to monitor. We also explore different tools and processes you need to follow to determine where the threats are on the Internet and how people use social media platforms to compromise your company and brand. Finally, we look at the importance of creating a "what if" scenario to protect against leaks of confidential information and examine some of the relevant court rulings about privacy and monitoring.

Case Study: A Dangerous Public

In December 2010, a group of hackers took aim at Mastercard.com's website and launched a denial of service (Dos) attack that took the website offline. The activists launched their denial of service attack to show support for WikiLeaks and WikiLeak's founder Julian Assange. WikiLeaks had posted confidential documents about a number of governments and corporations, and, as a result, MasterCard decided to stop processing donations to WikiLeaks. The attack was called "Operation Payback."[1] One credit card payment service reported that it could not process payments because of the attack. Although this attack did not ultimately impact MasterCard's ability to process credit card transactions, consumers saw how vulnerable MasterCard was to attackers. Facebook and Twitter were then used to promote the attacks against the MasterCard brand. On Twitter, the attackers tweeted:

> *The MasterCard action was confirmed on Twitter at 9.39am by user @Anon_Operation, who later tweeted: "We are glad to tell you that http://www.mastercard.com/ is down and it's confirmed! #ddos #WikiLeaks Operation: Payback (is a bitch!) #PAYBACK."*

---

[1] Esther Addley and Josh Halliday, "Operation Payback Cripples MasterCard Site in Revenge for WikiLeaks Ban," *The Guardian* (December 8, 2010), http://www.guardian.co.uk/media/2010/dec/08/operation-payback-mastercard-website-wikileaks.

What Could Have Been Done?

By monitoring these networks, MasterCard could have responded faster to the attacks, even as they were being discussed online. MasterCard's communications with the public could have been swifter to reassure customers that charges were still being processed. The whole episode might have even been avoided if MasterCard had done more research into the ramifications of pulling the plug on WikiLeaks payment processing.

This type of activity can shift consumer sentiment about a company's security capabilities, and MasterCard may have lost brand value (though this is hard to measure). MasterCard did not have a proactive response to communicate with consumers about the attack; it did not utilize other social media outlets to ensure people that a proper response was in place. If MasterCard had had social media influencers in place, those influencers could have released information quickly to different channels about the attacks. Social media was not the cause of the actual problem, but MasterCard could have used it as a countermeasure to inform consumers about what was happening.

How's JAG Doing?

A company does not have to be as large as MasterCard to face the same challenges and need to understand the environment. Our fictional company, JAG Consumer Electronics, has the same problems. JAG needs to know what customers are saying about its service, the friendliness of employees, and even what competitors might be saying about prices. JAG currently does not have a process in place to capture what's being said online about the company. JAG isn't tracking mentions of brand names, key employees, leading products sold, or competing firms, and the company is not aware of check-ins to retail locations on foursquare, Gowalla, and other location-based services. Furthermore, JAG is not scanning its own products using mobile barcode scanning services, which would show competing retailers' prices and locations.

What Are Your Customers and the General Public Saying?

Are you listening to the compliments, complaints, and sentiments expressed by your customers online? Do you know what information exists online—both from your own efforts and those external to the company? Have you produced podcasts and webinars and, if so, how are these being monitored and syndicated? What impact have whitepapers, articles, or company presentations had on your brand? Companies today must constantly measure their brand reputation online to determine the sentiments being expressed and assess any possible threat levels.

A simple, fast, and free basic solution begins with a Google search. To start, do a quick Google search for your company and/or any of its products or services. This internal (also known as an "ego search") will quickly reveal any indexed websites, news mentions, or blog posts related to your brand. In many instances, these searches will return the company's official website and any recent press or news mentions. And, at times, they will provide your first glimpse into your brand's online reputation.

A recent search on Wal-Mart returned the company's website (www.walmart.com) and listing of store locations. However, as illustrated in Figure 3-1, there are negative sites about Wal-Mart as well: Wake-Up Wal-Mart (wakeupwalmart.com), an anti-Wal-Mart website; and Wal-Mart Watch (walmartwatch.com), a "nationwide campaign to reveal the harmful impact of Wal-Mart on American families and demand reform of their business." You will also find links to an anti-Wal-Mart movie and the humor website peopleofwalmart.com. This simple search shows a significant amount of negative sentiment expressed toward Wal-Mart, Inc.

In early April 2010, one of Wal-Mart's official website's (www.walmartcommunity .com for their Community Action Network, or CAN) was hacked and spam links with the title "die mommy die" were injected across the site, as shown in Figure 3-2. This social network, CAN, is a good marketing tool, but when it gets hacked, it becomes a brand management nightmare.

Upon further investigation, Wal-Mart discovered that the spam code was injected into the footer template of the website. Although these attacks may seem frivolous, and possibly humorous at first glance, they are early warning signals of potentially more serious security attacks. This combination of attacks against the web application with the attacks on the social community website can result in serious damage against a brand image.

Figure 3-1   *Negative sentiment sites about Wal-Mart*

What to Monitor

To protect your company from online social media attacks, you need to employ a series of monitoring solutions. Certain monitoring solutions, which we'll discuss shortly, observe the chatter and monitor key terms and sentiments, both from a customer perspective and an attacker perspective.

Walmart's Support for Military Families & Veterans - Walmart ... ☆
Download Full Movie Online Sky High download movie **Die, Mommie, Die!**
download movie Lethal Weapon 2 download movie Black Rain download movie
The World Is ...
www.walmartcommunity.com/military-support/ - Cached

Hats off to Walmart - Walmart Community Action Network ☆
5 Mar 2010 ... cell phone free bollywood ringtonesSky High download movie **Die,
Mommie, Die! download movie Lethal Weapon 2 download** movie Black
Rain download movie The ...
www.walmartcommunity.com/2010/03/hats-off-to-walmart/ - Cached

⊞ Show more results from www.walmartcommunity.com

Figure 3-2   *Hacker message on Wal-Mart's Community website*

The most prevalent problems that you need to monitor include:

► Copied sites

► Negative posts

► Misleading information

► Fake profiles

► Trademark/copyright infringement

► Bad news coverage

► Confidential documents disclosure

► Complaint sites

► Competitor attacks

► Hate sites

► Employee scandals

► Corporate scandals

► Industry perceptions

A number of services—both free and paid—can assist in this process. Free services, such as Google Alerts, can monitor key terms and track forums, blogs, and negative online posts, whereas commercial online reputation monitoring services, such as

Radian 6 and Reputation.com, can be set up to monitor and track online sentiment and potential privacy breaches. These services can

- ▶ Monitor posts and make requests to remove information that may not be appropriate (such as names, addresses, ages, phone numbers, past addresses, and other personally identifiable information)
- ▶ Block trash or unwanted paper mail
- ▶ Prevent online ad tracking so your activities are not monitored by the ad networks

As mentioned previously, negative online sentiments can serve as an early warning sign of possible security threats. They can help you identify sources of discourse and the impact of your online reputation control efforts. By monitoring key terms and online mentions for positive, negative, and neutral sentiment around your company's products or services, you can determine what's being said. In addition to this monitoring solution, you should also assign company resources (company staff) to monitor, analyze, and react quickly to online social media mentions in an effort to protect the company from potential threats.

When to Dedicate Resources to Combating Negative Mentions

Negative threats can originate from any source: blog post, video commentary, disgruntled Tweet, or online forum. Prior to deploying resources, you need to assess the nature of the threat to determine the source, influence, and potential fallout.

If the threat is singular in nature (for example, a customer complaint), then the best possible response is to reach out to the individual or individuals with an olive branch in hopes of remedying the situation personally. This dedication to customer service can many times repair the relationship and turn negative commentary into positive sentiment about your company's responsiveness.

In the event that the negative threat is more widespread, then you need to implement a systematic policy of engagement, long-term PR efforts, and security strategies. In Chapter 6, we review more details of what your actual policy should cover. These can involve activating online influencers who may be integral to repairing your company's image and online brand equity. These social media influencers can take the form of bloggers, Twitter personalities, or freelance industry reporters, to name a few. Combine this with any security technologies necessary to report on any corporate assets that may be threatened, and you have a complete monitoring solution. If you do not have these monitoring solutions in place, you might face attacks that lead to brand damage or even loss of operations if you experience a technology-related attack on your brand.

Establishing a relationship with advocates and tracking their online movements prior to an attack can be your first line of defense, proving invaluable to securing your company's brand reputation and online security. In addition, these wired influencers can readily persuade those who are easily won over. This can significantly impact public opinion in the event of a negative attack and have, at times, even rallied cybersecurity experts to aid in the defense of organizations under continued online attack.

TIP
Train and empower your employees to use social media as well; they are far more credible and have authentic voices in advocating your brand.

One recent example is the lawsuit brought by an Alabama law firm against Taco Bell in early 2011. The suit claims Taco Bell's beef is not real beef, the key ingredient in its product and company identity. This claim could do more damage to the company than any other type of cyberattack. Taco Bell came out on the offensive, launching a marketing campaign and using social media platforms to promote its side of the story. Its Facebook page now has over 5,860,000 followers! And people are saying great things about the company on the company's Fanpage, as shown in Figure 3-3. These "brand ambassadors" are "Liking" the brand and promoting it to their friends.

Figure 3-3   *Taco Bell Fanpage*

Processes to Track the Conversations Leading Up to an Attack

The problem of technology and staff resources has been a recurring theme for many companies. How many people do you actually have who can do all this work, and do you have the proper budget to buy the right tools? Finding the right resource and having the right resource are two separate challenges. Knowing how to monitor potentially harmful discussions, prior to a threat occurring, is critical in defending and securing your social media strategy. As mentioned earlier, reputation management and monitoring services can provide daily digests and real-time alerts that you can use to gain insight on current online sentiment. With a simple Google Alert, as shown in Figure 3-4, you can select keywords to track, source type (blogs, news, video, discussions), how often to track, types of results you want to see, and how the results should be delivered to you.

Once the source of the threat, or even just an informational post, has been identified, you'll want to search for any additional outlets. Where else might that threat be disseminated that could impact your company? It could spread to other media channels. If there is a history of threats from a particular source, such as a blogger who does not like your company, you should put that "threat" source on your list of sites to monitor for future activity.

Another free tool you can use to see what's being said is Yahoo! Pipes (pipes.yahoo .com). Using Pipes, you can create your own, very comprehensive search program. Figure 3-5 shows a created "Pipe" that searches different social media applications

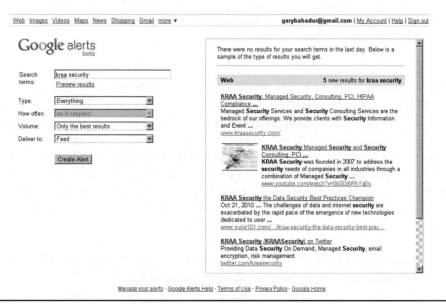

Figure 3-4   *Setting up Google Alerts*

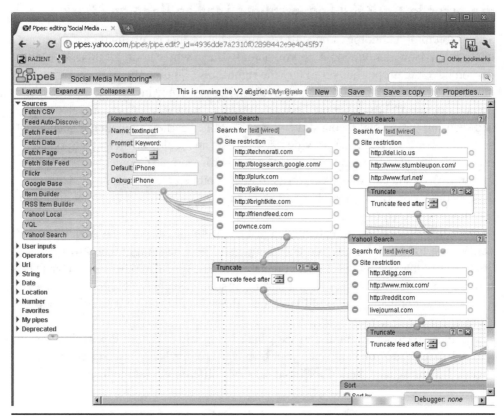

Figure 3-5   *Building a Yahoo! Pipe search*

and news outlets and delivers any results written by Charles Heflin. Figure 3-6 shows a search on the company name "KRAA Security." Look at the results in Figure 3-6; notice a LinkedIn Profile for a "Mugambi Daniel" listed as an accountant at KRAA Security? There is no such person as Daniel living in Kenya working at KRAA Security. A coauthor of this book, Gary Bahadur, is the CEO of KRAA Security, and he certainly would know who is on the payroll! Obviously, this profile is a fake. Someone is probably trying to run a scam using the KRAA Security name! If you get a result like this and have an incident response policy in place, as we discuss in Chapter 6, at this point you would take several steps:

1. Contact LinkedIn and get this person removed as an employee of KRAA and notify LinkedIn that it has a scammer in the network.

You're logged in as gbaha (logout)

My Pipes   Browse   Discuss   Documentation   [Create a pipe]   [Search for Pipes...   🔎]

Social Media Monitoring Tool

Monitor what people are saying across multiple social platforms. To use this tool enter a keyword to query the social media sites for that keyword. Hint: use quotes around keyword phrases. Follow Charles Heflin on Twitter at http://www.twitter.com/charlesheflin

Pipe Web Address: http://pipes.yahoo.com/socialmedia/monitoring

[☆ | View Source | Clone]

Configure this Pipe

Keyword: [kraa security]   [Run Pipe]

Use this Pipe

[📇 Get as a Badge] [➕ MY YAHOO!] [➕ Google™] [📶 Get as RSS] [📶 Get as JSON]   More option▶

List	45 items

Maria Nowak profiles | LinkedIn
View the profiles of professionals named Maria Nowak on LinkedIn. ... student at Kraa Security. Demographic info. Bydgoszcz Area, Poland | Information Technology and Services ...

Kraa Security - Company Profile | LinkedIn
KRAA Security was founded in 2007 to address the security needs of companies in all industries through a combination of Managed Security Services and...

YouTube - managed network security austin
(512) 407-8324 | http://www.allcitytech.com | AllCity Technology has been providing quality computer service and support since 1999. From our flagship TECHME...

Mugambi Daniel profiles | LinkedIn
View the profiles of professionals named Mugambi Daniel on LinkedIn. ... Kraa Security. Demographic info. Kenya | Information Technology and Services. Current: ACCOUNTANT at Kraa ...

Figure 3-6   *Results of the Yahoo! Pipe social media search using the keywords "KRAA Security"*

2. Determine if you can turn on any restrictions in LinkedIn to stop this from happening in the future.

3. Implement a routine monitoring practice to identify future activity for anything related to the company name.

Another way for the public to find you is with location-based services (such as Gowalla, Facebook Places, foursquare, and Scvngr). A simple "check in" from an employee at a customer office or visit from a potential employee can inadvertently cause a leak of sensitive information about the company to the public. Location-based services give the public a way to track your company and may lead to some form of attack based on where your employees check in. As location-based services become more integrated, this form of communication will be subverted. Persons involved in social media activities for your company have the responsibility to monitor, enforce, and adapt your social media security policy as new threats emerge and additional departments participate in new and emerging social media networks.

What Are Your Employees Saying?

Social media threats can also originate internally. Disgruntled employees can post sensitive information to blogs, Twitter, or wikis, and cause irreparable damage. Does your corporate policy extend to employees accessing Facebook, Twitter, or other social media networks? (We discuss your full social media security policy in Chapter 6.) Can employees openly engage in transparent conversations with customers? If so, who monitors these interactions? Are you reviewing daily Facebook activity or Twitter digests and are these monitored manually or through an automated solution?

What to Monitor

Key points to monitor in employee conversations include:

► Potential leaks of confidential information or proprietary information or intellectual property

► Breaking acceptable use policies by posting inappropriate material

► Any employee social connections that may cause an HR violation such as discussing company secrets in a public forum

► Employee sentiment about the company

► Employee conversations with customers and competitors

► Potential regulatory violations

► Inappropriate dissemination of customer information

► How employees discuss company products and services

► Dissemination of company security programs or processes that could allow attackers access to network resources

▶ Productivity loss

▶ Job search requests

Facebook is of particular concern when it comes to social media security. With over 600,000,000 users, many of whom check in daily, Facebook traffic is 500 percent greater than any other social network (according to a report by Palo Alto Networks, The Application Usage and Risk Report, October 2010). Although most Facebook usage is passive (checking messages, status updates, and so on), accounts and credentials can still be hijacked through URLs with embedded malware. These types of attacks "can help uncover corporate roles or answers to security questions," according to the Application Usage and Risk Report (http://www.paloaltonetworks.com/researchcenter/2010/03/ new-application-usage-and-risk-report-now-available/). This type of URL attack has been so prevalent that products like Bit.ly have changed how they shorten URLs. Twitter made the use of shortening URLs popular because of the limited number of characters per post. Bit.ly can turn a long URL into a much shorter one. Until recently, however, it hid the original URL so you didn't actually know the real link behind the shortened URL. Now when you click a Bit.ly short URL, a pop-up shows you the actual link before you go to the page, as shown in Figure 3-7 in TweetDeck (purchased by Twitter in May 2011). This is definitely a requirement for safe surfing.

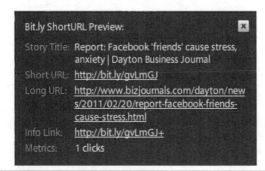

Figure 3-7   *Bit.ly now shows you the actual URL.*

The behavior of your employees in the social space can also affect threat levels and increase security risks. Without a clear social media policy, a simple response can launch a tidal wave of attacks. This was what happened as a result of Nestlé's response to users repurposing its logo online as a sign of protest. The company's aggressive response to its Facebook fan users and its accusations of intellectual property theft left many shocked and activated the wrath of hundreds more. The result: Nestlé was bombarded with thousands of logo variations and made global news over a relatively minor issue. Had the response been handled by a trained community manager, the issue could have been addressed more judiciously. The result would have been more in line with the company's original intentions. Instead, the result brought awareness to the protesters cause—propelling their issues onto the global stage, resulting in a tremendous negative impact on the Nestlé brand. If you look at the stock price chart during the period when the attack took place (shown in Figure 3-8), you see a drop in price. We can't say for certain what this drop is attributable to, but all the negative reputation attacks may have contributed to the drop.

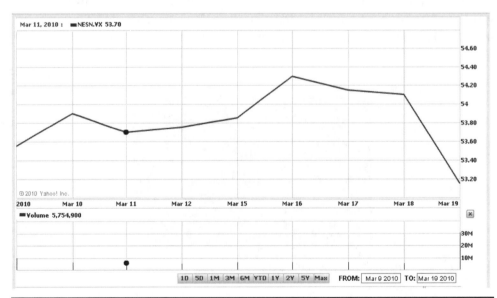

Figure 3-8   *Nestlé Stock price drops during brand attack.*

Public relations nightmare aside, this incident undoubtedly created additional online security threats to the company's social media profile as news spread beyond the realm of Facebook and into the wider online (hacker) populace. In addition, the incident gave Nestlé's competitors an opportunity to capitalize on the issue and position themselves strategically against the company's policies and operational practices.

Corporate social media missteps are made every day. However, under the global microscope of social media, these minor hiccups can quickly become major issues. The resulting damage can be measured in the disruption of productivity due to a change of focus, potential disruptions in the supply chain, loss of revenue, and a concurrent negative impact on the overall company image and bottom line.

The "What If" Scenario

Your social media security policy needs to address the "what if" scenario surrounding possible leaks of confidential information. Apple Computer found out firsthand what a leak of confidential information combined with a wired population can do to a brand's global image and competitive advantage.

The short version goes like this: A guy walks into a bar with a coveted, yet-to-be-realized Apple iPhone 4 prototype. The guy has one too many drinks. He loses his phone in the bar. His phone ends up in the hands of one of the most widely read Internet gadget websites, Gizmodo.com. The website writes a detailed blog post on every aspect of the phone generating over 13,049,935 visits to the article (see http://gizmodo.com/5520164/this-is-apples-next-iphone).

The story quickly spreads around the globe and generates a PR and potential product launch nightmare for Apple, as the article reveals problems with the iPhone's antenna. Apple, famous for secrecy surrounding its products, immediately unleashes a barrage of legal counter strikes, including filing charges of theft against Gizmodo founder Jason Chen based on a California law dating back to 1872. The criminal investigation includes the issuing of search warrants and the seizure of laptops, flash drives, and credit card statements from Chen's California home. The loss of proprietary data and subsequent detailed broadcasting of this information was a major embarrassment to the carefully polished image Apple tries to maintain.

Although Apple may have a legal case regarding the physical property, Gizmodo, as an online news organization, is wholly and legally in its right to broadcast this sensitive data, which it did, leaking the confidential information all across the social connected Web. In 2001, the U.S. Supreme Court ruled that confidential information leaked to a news organization could be legally broadcast (http://www.techeye.net/business/apple-calls-coppers-on-gizmodo).

This ruling may come as a surprise to many organizations. With over 133 million blogs online and novel forms of news sources appearing on the horizon, the definition of a "news organization" is radically changing. Websites like WikiLeaks, Consumerist, Angie's List, and countless others generating millions of visitors every day create a legal gray area for many organizations mentioned negatively on these sites. In October 2010, WikiLeaks released over 400,000 documents called the Iraq War Logs, documenting sensitive information on the wars in Iraq and Afghanistan. An enlisted serviceman allegedly copied the data from secure internal servers and sent them to WikiLeaks. What was proprietary to the U.S. government has been made public via this website.

These issues illustrate the difficulty of protecting and monitoring your company's intellectual property and online reputation. Securing your intellectual property and assessing potential threat levels is getting increasingly more difficult as social networking tools become more accessible. Add to this the global nature of the Web, international policing issues, and conflicting judicial rulings and the issues multiply exponentially. In June 2009, the U.S. Supreme Court ruled in a 9-0 vote that an employee's privacy becomes void while using company-issued equipment.

However, a U.S. district court ruled in *Buckley H. Crispin v. Christian Audigier, Inc. et al.* that items posted on social media sites such as Facebook and MySpace that were not available to the public could not be subpoenaed. Google Alerts will not track keywords on social media sites when they are included in comments that are posted in a way in which the content isn't posted publicly. If you have 4999 friends on Facebook and publish a post to your friends, that monitoring technology will only pick up those 5000 potential leaks when they go public, by which time, it might be too late to stop the viral surge.

Wrap Up

With conflicting views of corporate privacy versus the right of the individual, you may be wondering what you can actually do to protect your company from potential social media threats. As with all potential threats, the first line of defense is monitoring potential hot spots of activity. Key websites, such as digg, Twitter Trends, Technorati, and industry forums, along with Google Alerts can function as simple, but effective, early warning systems. All company employees engaged in social media activity (especially those with access to sensitive information) should report on their activity on a daily basis, and their interactions should be monitored for possible breaches in protocol. Additionally, employees should be made aware that accessing individual social network profiles during company hours or via company-provided equipment subjects them to investigation in the event of a security breach. This strategy does break down when employees are on their own time and using devices or cellular networks that cannot be tracked by the company. We will discuss more monitoring solutions that can look for all information like this in Part IV of the book.

A system of response and enforcement should be an integral part of your social media security policy and developed in tangent with your Legal department. Clear analysis of the threat level is necessary to gauge the appropriate response and determine the correct channels for engagement and/or legal action, which you can do with a clearly defined policy and careful implementation of the H.U.M.O.R. Matrix outlined in this book. We show you the steps to take to develop a successful social media security strategy that not only keeps you secure but also engages your community in a constructive manner that does not alienate them.

To know what is being said about your company requires consistent processes for monitoring sentiment. Specific steps need to be in place for what to monitor and how to monitor those mentions that impact your company.

Improvement Checklist

☐ Are you monitoring what is being said about your company across the Internet?

☐ Do you have a process in place to respond proactively to any potential threats?

☐ Do you receive consistent daily reports on what is being said online about the company?

☐ Are you monitoring employees' activities with the company name being mentioned?

☐ Do you have scenarios designed to test for potential damage to the company over social media?

Assessing Social Media Threats

Threat Assessment

Threats constantly evolve, and those in the social media sphere are no exception. We are all familiar with spyware, and most of us have probably installed spyware scanners and antivirus products from companies such as McAfee and Symantec. But is the current crop of antispyware/antimalware software capable of stopping malicious apps in Facebook or ones that are downloaded via shortened URLs in a Twitter post? One of the original spyware hacks for Facebook was "Secret Crush." This application would purportedly tell you if someone secretly liked you. (Having to rely on Facebook for this is a whole different problem for some.) When you installed the application, however, it actually installed Zango Spyware. That software then delivered ads to your computer. *Clickjacking,* of which this is an example, is the latest buzzword for malicious applications and links in social networks.

The challenge for antispyware products is that the user, who is usually logged in as administrator on his own machine, is consciously authorizing the installation. Spyware blockers are going to have a harder time as people integrate business functions with Facebook and interact with more Facebook applications. A company has to have stricter control of the end-user system, restrict the end users' ability to install applications on their machines, and monitor for new malicious social networking hacks. The home user, who does not have an IT support team on her side, is more prone to being tricked into installing these malicious applications. And as people become more educated about the potential danger of installing applications through social media, the threats will evolve.

This chapter identifies the threats that your company faces from attacks from people, processes, and technology. There are malicious users, competitors, and customers who can impact your company, right along with the typical cyberattacks we are so used to seeing. Threats have to be identified, managed, and stopped to reduce the risk you face in the social media landscape. In this chapter, we walk you through the various threat scenarios that may be new to you because the use of social media is relatively new, and we identify current threats that have made their way onto social media sites. We then categorize these threats using the H.U.M.O.R. Matrix, and finally we delve into the process of assessing the damage and developing a response.

Case Study: Political Hacking

The reasons for hacking are pretty varied. Real monetary rewards for hacking have been escalating in the past few years. Social and political hacktivism has also been on the upswing. In a recent case of political hacktivism, the Twitter account of Fox News Politics (foxnewspolitics) was hacked by the group named Script Kiddies.

On July 4, 2011, a tweet went out: "Breaking News: President @BarakObama assassinated, 2 gunshot wounds have proved too much. It's a sad 4th for #america #obamadead RIP" (See the news article from the *Guardian* at http://www.guardian .co.uk/technology/2011/jul/04/hacking-twitter-feed-fix-news.)

Considering that Fox News leans right and to the conservative Republican Party in the United States, this tweet was a direct attack on their political positions. The attack was directed toward Fox News' brand and reputation.

What Went Wrong?

Although no money was actually lost, this form of attack is prevalent. Hacktivists have more opportunities to spread their message by hacking into social networks that do not have a history of implementing good security protocols.

However, the Script Kiddies did not hack into Twitter or another web application in this case. They left no smoking gun as to how the hacktivists got into the Twitter account. Fox News says they are working with the Secret Service and Twitter to find out what happened. It could have been an easy-to-guess password. A user of that account may have shared it with someone or posted the password in a file that was stolen by the hacker group. When companies do not share information on these attacks, it makes it harder for others to learn how to better protect themselves.

How's JAG Doing?

How is our company JAG Consumer Electronics doing when it comes to threat management? As we reviewed in Chapter 2, JAG really hasn't put together too many business processes and tools for social media. From a threat management perspective, JAG does have your typical IT security tools in place. JAG runs an IDS solution; they have a disaster recovery plan with some business continuity scenarios mapped out; and they read the typical security news portals such as Securityfocus.com. JAG does a decent job in terms of IT infrastructure security threats, but the company does not have social media tools in place to identify brand threats. JAG has antimalware and antispyware in place but does not monitor user interaction with sites such as Facebook, so it knows what users are doing and what applications they may be installing. Like many companies, JAG has not implemented a process for the evolving threat that social media networks pose to corporate environments. Can JAG address the changing landscape and be proactive in identifying social media threats?

The Changing Threat Landscape

A threat in the social media landscape works differently than in traditional IT security. If you are an IT security manager today, you are accustomed to a variety of threats to corporate data and networks, including hackers trying to break through your firewall, viruses and malware in e-mails or on suspicious websites, insiders trying to steal company information, and your company's exposure to corporate espionage activities. While these threats continue to exist as before, social media has opened new avenues and possibilities for these threats and for new types of risks to occur.

The threat landscape has changed pretty quickly as compared to most IT concerns. The new technologies and processes employed in social media have exposed companies to new risks. For example, ten years ago identity theft was about someone gaining access to your credit by physically stealing a credit card or stealing a credit application when you tried to get financing to buy a car. Even then, it was difficult to obtain all your information successfully. But today, identity theft has become easier because people give away their information more freely on social networks like Facebook and LinkedIn. The threat is now based on how social platforms collect information and on what motivates people to give away their sensitive data. For example, some password recovery systems require people to answer a personal question, such as their mother's maiden name, their birth date, or the name of their favorite teacher. And yet this type of information is often the same banks request from customers when they call in to check on their accounts. Over time, social networks gather increasing amounts of information about users as the users themselves interact more through status updates, social games, and by simply filling out their own profiles more completely. This means that not only is the sanctity of their identity dependent on the social network's security environment, but also their identity is increasingly unveiled in more detail to their contacts and acquaintances on their social networks.

Identifying the Threats

You have to determine the vectors of threats being launched against your company. Social media includes blogs, microblogs, instant messaging, mobile applications, and community pages on Facebook, real-world community networking groups organized through Meetups and Tweetups, YouTube, Flickr, and much more. New avenues of online social interaction develop every few months; these channels have to be assessed for potential threats, for damage they can cause, and for the company's capability to respond immediately. In the summer of 2010, security firm ProofPoint commissioned a study[1] on data loss prevention for U.S. companies and found the following:

- ▶ 36 percent of respondents said their organization was impacted by the exposure of sensitive or embarrassing information during the past 12 months.

- ▶ 7 percent of companies terminated an employee for social networking policy violations.

- ▶ 11 percent of companies terminated an employee for blog or message board posting policy violations.

- ▶ 13 percent of U.S. companies investigated an exposure event involving mobile or web-based short message services during the past 12 months.

- ▶ 25 percent of companies investigated the exposure of confidential, sensitive, or private information via a blog or message board posting.

- ▶ 18 percent of companies investigated a data loss event via a blog or message board during the past 12 months.

- ▶ 17 percent disciplined an employee for violating blog or message board policies.

A focused attack from social media channels will come from the following sources:

- ▶ **Blogs**   An attacker can disseminate incorrect information about your organization, which is picked up by other bloggers who further perpetuate the myth.

- ▶ **Video**   A disparaging video can easily spread. Videos tend to have more weight than blogs with viewers/customers because they can see the issue, rather than just read about it. On March 27, 2010, U.S. Department of Agriculture official Shirley Sherrod addressed the NAACP's 20th Annual Freedom Fund Banquet. Months later, a small excerpt from Sherrod's speech was posted by Tea Partier Andrew Breitbart on YouTube. The excerpt went viral, stirring up controversy over Sherrod's racially biased statements. As a result, Secretary of Agriculture Tom Vilsack had to force Sherrod to resign. Later, however, further footage of the speech showed Sherrod's comments to be taken out of context, prompting the USDA to offer Sherrod a new position (see http://www.thenewamerican.com/index.php/usnews/politics/4133-shirley-sherrod-fiasco).

---

[1] Outbound Email and Data Loss Prevention in Today's Enterprise, Proofpoint (2010), http://www.proofpoint.com/id/outbound/index.php.

▶ **Microblogging** Quick hits can occur through sites like Twitter that can quickly impact your image and spread lies about your company. Without a preplanned counterstrategy in place, the misinformation could spread faster than you can address it and share fresh information with your community.

▶ **Mobile** Mobile applications for social media make sharing information much easier and can target specific types of users based on mobile usage or even geolocation of the customer.

▶ **Social Meetups or Tweetups** The offline world of "meetups" to promote social media activities are frequent, very well informed, and attended by active online sharers, so an attack here has the potential to greatly impact your brand, both online and offline in tandem.

The Attackers

The attackers in the social media space are often different from typical IT attackers. The attacker profile can be categorized into the following types:

▶ **Hackers** The pure thrill of breaking into a secure resource just to prove you can is still there. Hacker can do it for profit by stealing your sensitive information such as customer lists, can compromise your social profiles to launch botnet attacks, or do it on behalf of some competitor, agency, or activist group.

▶ **Disgruntled employees** This category of attacker is probably the largest. Never before has a single person had the capability to attack a brand so quickly, spread lies and misinformation, and become an online resource without being vetted. Negative mentions that had been reserved for friends and family are now publicly shared online.

▶ **Employees** Employees may inadvertently compromise the brand by saying negative things about the company, posting sensitive or confidential information, or allowing information to be leaked through social media.

▶ **Competitors** A competitive attack can focus on your brand image or your customers, and competitors can even steal data from your company resources. These attackers can easily hide behind fake profiles and sources to seem legitimate or make determining who is launching the attack very difficult. Moral hazard alone is never a sufficient deterrent for unethical activity by competitors.

Threat Vectors

A number of different threat vectors, both internal and external, can impact your business. As we discussed in Chapter 3, once you have your monitoring solutions in place, you need to make sure you are looking at the right threat potential. Threats come from people, processes, and technology, and you have to understand the different groups in social media.

Users

The main threat to corporate social media usage is the user. The user is uneducated in security and most are untrained in social media security. Users go to inappropriate websites, click phishing links, and give away information about themselves and your company. The user is already authenticated to your network, which is another challenge for security: you already trust them to access and use your resources.

Customers

Although you undoubtedly need customers, they also pose a big challenge when it comes to social media. In traditional IT, you could restrict customer access by giving them very limited privileges to your ecommerce website and other customer-related IT systems. Nowadays, dissatisfied customers generate negative content, affecting sentiment about your company through communication channels you have no control over—just because they can. It used to be a quick rule of thumb that, on average, an unhappy customer would tell nine of their friends about their experience. If those nine shared with just two more each, you can see how bad it can get pretty quickly.

$\rightarrow 9 \rightarrow 18 \rightarrow 36 \rightarrow 72 \rightarrow 144 \rightarrow 288 \rightarrow 576 \rightarrow 1152 \rightarrow 2304 \rightarrow 4608 \rightarrow$ 9216 bad mentions!

Human Resources

The Corporation itself can even create a threat vector due to a lack of knowledge, training, and common sense. As of this writing, only a small percentage of companies has implemented HR policies, guidelines, and training that cover social media use by employees.

Social Networking Worms

According to Internet security vendor Kaspersky Lab, "malicious code distributed via social networking sites is ten times more effective, in terms of successful infection, than malware spread via e-mail."[2] Worms targeting social networks have an easy

---

[2] "Kaspersky Offers Online Guide in the Wake of the Latest Facebook Phishing Attack," *PC World,* http://pcworld.com.ph/kaspersky-offers-online-guide-in-the-wake-of-the-latest-facebook-phishing-attack/.

time taking over accounts, spreading across different users, and propagating. One reason is that users are now accustomed to having antivirus check their e-mails, but they are not used to getting attacked through web applications such as Facebook or Twitter. Statistics also show that people are spending more time on social networks than with e-mail. ComScore found that e-mail usage was down 18 percent in their 2010 US Digital Year in Review (http://www.comscore.com/Press_Events/ Presentations_Whitepapers/2011/2010_US_Digital_Year_in_Review). People are more trusting of websites they frequently use, like Facebook, which leads to more easy attacks. For example, *Koobface*, a popular worm in 2010, was used to steal sensitive data on Facebook, MySpace, Twitter, LinkedIn, and Bebo. Koobface tricked users into downloading a Trojan that, once installed, opened access to important information from the user. These types of worms are spread virally through videos or links shared by unsuspecting users.

Botnets

A rogue botnet, in this context, is a controlled collection of malicious software and automatic agents on compromised computers that seeks to attack and steal information. Social media has enabled the spread of botnets, which have evolved to use social networks to obfuscate the malicious link. For example, most long URLs shared on Twitter are shortened through link-shortening services such as tinyurl.com or kiss.ly. With shortened URLs, people cannot easily make out what the original URL was and thus click a link that takes them to a site controlled by a botnet without thinking. Once on the botnet site, new links are generated that serve to compromise users' computers.

Web Scraping

Web scraping has evolved into sophisticated automated programs that log into websites and automatically collect information. For example, a program can log into a discussion forum about healthcare and capture peoples' comments about the problems they face and the drugs they take. Because social media is all about sharing, technologies can be used to collect and mine all that information for nefarious purposes, whether it's to hack into your accounts or to send you targeted advertising for drugs the "scraper" has found out you use. A recent example is Nielsen's scraping of the PatientsLikeme.com website for data about forum posters. Patientslikeme.com administrators saw that a new user was using software that was "scraping," or copying, every single message off PatientsLikeMe's private online forums. Nielsen was logging and gathering the data, capturing users health information, presumably to sell this data to marketing companies.[3]

---

[3] Julia Angwin and Steve Stecklow, "'Scrapers' Dig Deep for Data on Web," Wall Street Journal (October 10, 2010), http://online.wsj.com/article/SB10001424052748703358504575544381288117888.html.

Data Devaluation

Sharing may have been highly encouraged and praised in kindergarten, but it's less laudable when putting your personal information online. Embarrassment is the least of your worries now. Think about all the questions your bank asks you for authenticating your account, such as your first school, your birthday, your dog's name, your mother's maiden name, the street you grew up on, or the best man at your wedding. All these bits of information are now available on social media sites as well, either through their own authentication questions or through the data and photos users share about their lives. It is far too easy to collect this information through web scraping. Once scarce and privileged information, which was used to identify and authenticate individuals, is now freely available online.

Phishing

Phishing allows attackers to simulate a legitimate site and attempts to entice users to give up their information, thinking they're logging onto the real site. The forged e-mails you got from PayPal or Citibank asking you to reset your password information were phishing attacks. Now you get the same e-mails asking you to sign into fake Facebook or LinkedIn websites that look like the real thing. Applications in Facebook that look legitimate may, in fact, be phishing for your information. The evolution of phishing has further evolved into *spear-phishing,* or targeted phishing. The threat involves spam e-mails sent out to users, attempting to gain financial and banking information, confidential information, or intellectual property. Attacks usually are disguised as sources the victim trusts and, when clicked, will usually download malware onto the victim's computer. Another regular occurrence is a 419 Operation (this refers to the relevant section in the Criminal Code of Nigeria). The target receives an unsolicited e-mail or letter asking for money, often needed for nefarious money-laundering purposes. After gaining access to someone's account, the scam tries to entice the victim's contacts to send them more money through Western Union, for example. An offshoot of the scam is to tell the victim that a person they trust is stranded abroad without their credit card and needs cash wired to them. Often, access to someone's profile is gained in Internet cafés using keyloggers or when users forget to log out of their session. These scams prey on both the victim's good faith that they are communicating with friends (a trusted source) and on the gullibility and good faith of the victim's contacts.

Impersonation

How do you know who is really behind that social media profile? Is your employee or even your competitor saying things in another person's voice or using another person's account or profile? Has someone created an account specifically to attack you? Fake user profiles are a dime a dozen online.

Threat Assessment and the Threat Management Lifecycle

The threat assessment process, which is illustrated in Figure 4-1, should provide you with a methodology for identifying threats, determining their potential impact, and identifying which steps you need to take to mitigate the risk. It's important to note that social media threats are still evolving, so determining their real impact on corporations is hard. With more data in another year or two, we can probably better quantify the effects. These next sections cover the basic structure of the threat assessment process and introduce the Threat Management Lifecycle.

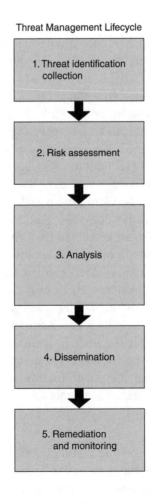

Threat Management Lifecycle

1. Threat identification collection

2. Risk assessment

3. Analysis

4. Dissemination

5. Remediation and monitoring

Identify and Assess

Identify and assess potential threats to the organization through social media sources:

▶ Where can the threat attack and compromise the corporation?

▶ What methods can the threat use to attack the company?

▶ What risk does the company face?

▶ What options exist to monitor against such threats?

Analyze

Based on information you have collected about the threats your organization faces, what can you determine about the organization's ability to respond to a threat?

▶ What are the organization's weaknesses in collecting attack information from social media sources?

▶ What are the actual causes of the threats?

▶ How can the company actually identify a threat is taking place?

▶ What resources are available to handle the threat?

▶ Do you have a method in place for prioritizing social media threats? What is that method?

▶ Which controls and tools are available once you have identified a threat?

▶ Is there any current known method of remediating potential or existing threats?

▶ Can threats be correlated to remediation processes?

Execute

The company must then respond to the threats it has identified:

1. Create an action plan approach based on how you will monitor and identify the threats.

2. Dedicate specific systems to and train specific resources in threat resolution.

3. Plan for future threats and for how the company will respond.

The basic threat management process is similar to, or even the same as, what you would use to handle typical hacking activity against IT resources. Our definition of the *Threat Management Lifecycle* is detailed in Table 4-1.

Threat Lifecycle Steps	Detailed Results
1. *Threat identification/collection*	Review internal and external threat sources for company relevance, using available threat information. Identify historical threats that may have already impacted the company for underlying systemic causes. Identify historical threats to competitors in the same industry and to similar companies in other industries. Analyze Business as Usual (BAU) processes to identify potential future threats from a social media perspective and environment. Conduct project analysis for ongoing and future activities that may be vulnerable to the current threat.
2. *Risk assessment*	Assess if the social media attack paths impact company assets/brands. Review inventory of social media activity that might be at risk based on the threat. Compile identified list of assets and social media activities that are vulnerable; see Table 4-2 for some examples. Determine level and priority of risk factors. Assess the total risk of the threat (people, processes, and technology) and its potential impact and provide a risk rating for each identified threat. For example, hacking the Twitter feed might be considered a high risk for Dell because the company can track real revenue to twitter posts.
3. *Analysis*	Develop a threat resolution, including impact on current corporate social media activities and impact on marketing. Assess wider business impact of threat and resolution implementation costs.
4. *Dissemination*	Determine who needs to be notified, including campaign owners, process owners, subject matter experts (SMEs), monitoring teams, remediation teams, business unit owners, public relations, human resource managers, and finance and auditing teams. Send notification of potential impact of the social media threats and resource requirements to owners/end users as required. Meet with the impacted business activity owners (marketing, HR, IT) to discuss your response to the threats, scheduling of resources, and remediation activities. Determine escalation procedure based on risk of threats and, in certain cases, on the type of information that may be being spread online about the threat.

Table 4-1 *Threat Management Lifecycle*

Threat Lifecycle Steps	Detailed Results
5. *Remediation and monitoring*	Implement solution to respond to threat (such as education and training, implementation of tools and data loss prevention solutions, which we cover more in Part IV).
	Monitor for potential and actual threat activities.
	Monitor external sources for threat activity and morphing of the threat.
	Review processes for results of remediation activities.
	Develop reporting metrics.
	Communicate results to stakeholders, be transparent, and share results and lessons learned with employees.
	Involve employees in security processes.
	Document lessons learned and consider need to update policies, business processes, and employee training.

Table 4-1   *Threat Management Lifecycle (continued)*

Threat Management in Action

Following the Threat Management Lifecycle for social media is not as simple as tracking down a technology threat such as an unpatched Microsoft server. Describing a social media threat is still a challenge in terms of how the terrain is shifting through rapidly evolving technologies, behaviors, and ground rules.

For example, early in 2010, a hospital employee was "encouraged to resign" for sending a tweet identifying Governor Barbour of Mississippi as a patient, even though no confidential information was sent out.[4] When the Governor tweeted, "Glad the Legislature recognizes our dire fiscal situation. Look forward to hearing their ideas on how to trim expenses," the administrator of University Medical Center (UMC) responded with "Schedule regular medical exams like everyone else instead of paying UMC employees overtime to do it when clinics are usually closed."

Since the employee's tweet referenced an incident that had occurred three years prior, when the Governor had a checkup conducted at the hospital, it was deemed a violation of the Health Insurance Portability and Accountability Act, or HIPAA. Even though vague, the employee had revealed patient information. In fact, HIPAA covers a wide range of employees, not just doctors and nurses. This type of threat might simply be a result of not properly educating employees on applicable laws; however, it still poses a threat to the organization.

Step 1, "Threat Identification/Collection," was easy to determine: it was the tweet itself. Step 2, "Risk Assessment," was based on HIPAA violations and potential fines

---

[4] Julie Straw, "Woman Out of a Job After Sending Tweet to Governor Barbour" WLBT (December 21/22, 2010), http://www.wlbt.com/global/story.asp?s=11713360.

to the organization. Step 3, "Analysis" of the mitigating resolution was the resignation. Step 4, "Dissemination," was the hospital notifying the proper authorities about a possible HIPAA violation; and Step 5, "Remediation and Monitoring," was encouraging the employee to resign. But remediation could also include ongoing training for all employees.

H.U.M.O.R. Threat Assessment

Within the H.U.M.O.R. Matrix, we can continue to break down the threat assessment process and identify what the problem may be within each category. Let's take an example of a threat against a well-known brand. In October 2010, Porsche AG announced it was banning employees from using social media sites.[5] They were not specific regarding whether the ban applied only to work hours or to home hours as well. Obviously telling someone what they can do during nonwork hours is difficult and probably illegal, but Porsche's identification of a significant threat had driven them to this decision. Porsche was worried that employees might post company confidential information to social media sites. "The social media websites may expose the automaker to unwanted observation and these services imply a certain threat potential," Porsche spokesman Dirk Erat was quoted as saying. If we map this back to our H.U.M.O.R. matrix, this threat could be associated with Human Resources policy violations and Utilization copyright and intellectual property violations.

Using the H.U.M.O.R. Matrix, we can identify threat vectors that can be launched either from "hackers," customers, employees, or any other sort of potential attacker.

Human Resources Threats

These threats target processes that are either inappropriate or not in place:

▶ **Policy violations**   Employees can violate the social media policy or social media security policy. But this is predicated on the company actually having a policy that outlines the restrictions in place. Policy violations are an internal threat.

▶ **Termination**   Human Resources must have developed and communicated a termination policy that addresses potential threats posed by disgruntled ex-employees, with a specific response by the company as a consequence of any such policy violation.

---

[5] "Facebook Access Blocked to Porsche's Employees on Espionage Threat," *International Business Times* (October 12, 2010), http://www.ibtimes.com/articles/70846/20101012/facebook-porsche.htm.

▶ **Personal usage**   Employees' personal usage of social media can affect the corporation's reputation when they post things such as inappropriate pictures or the like or confidential information about the company.

Utilization Threats

Resource Utilization threats are focused on how assets can be put at risk through social media mediums:

▶ **Technology**   Technology threats are easy to identify. Threats encompass everything from malware to Trojans to phishing sites and scams. These are known methods of attack against corporate use of social media.

▶ **Intellectual property**   Threats to intellectual property (IP) may come from the employee, a supplier, or a competitor. The employee can try to specifically disseminate IP or may just inadvertently give away IP over social media channels. The supplier may have access to sensitive IP through enterprise-collaborative applications. The competitor might scrap social media channels for IP that should not have been made available or might use social media channels to disseminate IP about your company or even plant false IP to damage your reputation.

▶ **Copyright**   Copyright threats are more widespread, and most attacks are generally inadvertent and minimally damaging. People may use your logos and other publicly available information without your express permission, and they may "remix" or change it for their own activist purposes. In many cases, these illegitimate uses are hard to detect, although sometimes they become viral and widely shared. The majority of copyright attacks will be external to your company.

Monetary Threats

These threats result in financial loss by malicious theft, resource costs due to security remediation measures, loss through inefficient use of assets, or opportunity loss due to threats distracting the company from its focus:

▶ **Financial loss**   Social media can be used by an attacker for immediate financial gain through impersonation and by accessing employee accounts. The financial loss may all be inadvertent if an employee were to cause damage. One example occurred in November 2010, when an underwriter for the General Motors IPO was dropped because the underwriter's employee leaked information via e-mail.[6] Although e-mail is not a true social media platform, it can easily be used as such and connect to other platforms such as LinkedIn or Facebook. Now you can actually claim your Facebook e-mail account, which is something like gary.bahadur@facebook.com.

▶ **Resource costs**   Responding to social media attacks may require purchasing new systems, monitoring tools, and other dashboards and utilities. Tools are a requirement; however, training employees will prove extremely useful and reduce the need for technology controls.

▶ **Time to recovery**   The amount of time spent recovering from a data breach can be extremely expensive.

▶ **Opportunity loss**   Responding to social media threats can easily distract company IT or HR personnel from more productive activities.

Operational Threats

Operational threats will usually have a direct impact on the functioning of the IT, marketing communications, and/or HR departments. Day-to-day activities will likely be disrupted.

▶ **Downtime**   Downtime can occur for many reasons. If the company relies on many social media outlets, any threat that can take a marketing campaign offline can affect the functions of the company. On October 6, 2010, Facebook went down for some hours. If your company had dedicated staff to working on a Facebook campaign that day, what would the impact have been on your marketing budget and expected results from your campaign? You could not recover any costs from Facebook. What if a hacker was launching a denial of service (DOS) attack against a particular social media site you are using; this could greatly impact your revenue model. Downtime costs have neither been calculated for external social media sites for most companies, nor is there a model for calculating these costs because results greatly depend on community and consumer sharing and engagement. How do you calculate the lost opportunity from engagement that never occurred because the social platform was not available?

▶ **Data loss**   Compromising accounts on social networks is very easy. A corporate Facebook account that is taken over by an attacker might contain confidential data about customers along with marketing lists.

---

[6] Tom Krisher, "UBS Employee Leaked Information on GM IPO" (November 10, 2010), http://abcnews.go.com/Business/wireStory?id=12108775.

Reputation Threats

A Reputation threat is more dispersed but no less dangerous. It might take a while for something like a Twitter attack to become known, but it can definitely impact the company's brand value:

▶ **Competitive disadvantage**   An attacker can launch an anonymous attack against your brand very easily. They can hide behind new profiles, spread disparaging remarks, and send out fake information about your company. Although your competitors can launch these attacks without your knowing where they are coming from, it is unlikely they would do so because someone will always find out where the attacks come from and your competitors' reputation would eventually take a hit.

▶ **Disgruntled customers and employees**   A disgruntled customer or employee can start posting to their blog and social networks about disappointing product and service experiences. For example, an aggrieved musician created a music video about how United Airlines broke his guitar; the video quickly went viral and currently has amassed over 9 million views. According to a Forrest Research report, "Do Your Employees Advocate for Your Company?", employees surveyed put detractors at 49 percent, those who were neutral at 24 percent, and promoters at only 27 percent.

▶ **Activist attacks**   A consumer group or activist organization can mount an attack against your social media properties. When Nestlé started a Facebook page for KitKat, Greenpeace quickly built a grassroots digital campaign denouncing Nestlé for harming native species when harvesting key ingredients for their chocolate. It was a marketing fiasco for Nestlé.

▶ **False information**   Customers and consumer advocacy groups may simply be posting erroneous information about the product, its origins, and its utilization. Such misrepresentations lead to misperceptions that can significantly impact the competitiveness of the product in the marketplace.

▶ **Management crisis**   Without a structured approach, a social media crisis can easily spin out of control. Recall BP's lack of social media response to the fake BP Twitter account that was set up to disparage the company after the Gulf of Mexico oil spill. The response quickly spun out of BP's control and became a PR nightmare. Reputation is a key driver of purchasing, and if a company's reputation is damaged, word of mouth can affect trust, which, in turn, affects sales. Nielsen reported in their 2009 Global Online Consumer Survey that some form of trust was very important in advertising and brand awareness, as shown in Figure 4-1. Once trust is lost online, rebuilding it is very difficult.

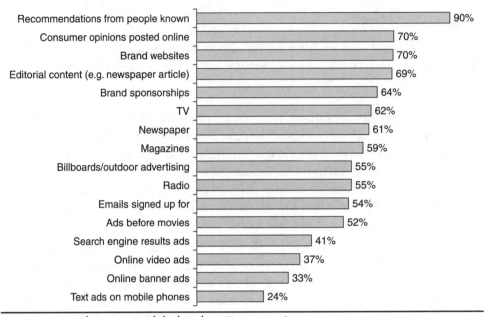

Figure 4-1 *Nielsen 2009 Global Online Consumer Survey*

Reputation threats challenge corporations on many levels:

▶ **Transparency and authenticity** Does the initial attack and/or the company's response (or lack thereof) confuse the customer?

▶ **Reaction time and behavior** Does the company address the threat quickly and appropriately before it negatively impacts reputation value?

▶ **Trusted relationships** Has the company built a strong and trusted reputation online that can withstand some period of attack?

▶ **Companywide response capabilities** Are the company's responses across departments, channels, and geographic regions coordinated and consistent?

▶ **Compromise of the influencers** Do the brand's online influencers understand how the attack is affecting the brand? Otherwise, this misunderstanding can impact customers.

▶ **Customer service** Are customer services issues responded to appropriately? Otherwise, customers will quickly become disaffected and negatively influenced.

▶ **Multiple communications channels**   Negative mentions can occur through many different social platforms at once. Are all of the possible social platforms and distribution mechanisms being used effectively and simultaneously to deal with the problem?

Assessing Damage

If, having accessed the attack vectors, you recognize a social media threat that may impact your company, you need to determine what damage may occur. Damage is measured in three ways: operations, brand impact, and monetary loss.

Measuring damage has never been easy when it comes to determining the security impact of an attack. The return on security investment for technologies such as implementing a firewall, web URL filtering, or even antivirus systems is very difficult. In the previous section, we discussed the threats. Once you have determined those, you can manage your reactions to those threats. Build a damage assessment matrix, as shown in Table 4-2. The column labeled "How to Prioritize the Damage?" serves as your next-steps guideline.

What Is the Potential Damage from the Attack?	How to Determine the Damage?	How to Prioritize the Damage?
Operations		
Downtime	Did the attack cause downtime and for how long?	How did the attack impact the delivery of customer service?
Data loss	Was data stolen?	What is the value of the data or cost of compliance fines?
Brand Impact		
Competitive disadvantage	Are customers enforcing the attacks and saying negative things about your brand?	What method of attack is getting the most response?
Crisis management	What does it cost you to recover from the crisis? Both in hard costs and brand valuation?	What is the costliest response scenario?

Table 4-2   *Damage from Social Media Threats*

What Is the Potential Damage from the Attack?	How to Determine the Damage?	How to Prioritize the Damage?
Monetary Loss		
Financial loss	Can you measure real dollar losses?	Measure hard dollar costs.
Time to recovery	How much is the cost to recover full operations?	Measure time to recovery and convert to dollar costs.
Opportunity loss	What other projects/practices were impacted by the attack?	Determine potential value of lost sales, customer service backlog, or incomplete projects.

Table 4-2   *Damage from Social Media Threats (continued)*

Developing a Response

Identifying threats is a complicated task in itself. But once you have identified what those threats are and you've assessed the damage, what do you do next? A response team can encompass multiple departments. As we have been discussing, a combination of staff from HR, IT, and Marketing will usually need to be called upon for most large-scale threats.

If you are in charge of defending the company website and an attack is launched from an IP address in Russia and you only do business in the United States, you could easily block that IP address from even being able to see your website. If you see a new virus launching attacks, you could easily update your virus scanner with new attack signatures. But with social media attacks, you can't really shut off access to your blogs, and you definitely cannot stop people from using Twitter. You have no real way to stop an attacker from disparaging your brand: users have freedom of speech, and cease and desist defenses tend to backfire. So what is your response to this type of threat? We will get into actual controls in later chapters, but for now, having identified the threats, categorized them, and accessed the damage, you have to decide which responses or countermeasures to launch.

Threat identification is the first step, as discussed previously. But who identifies these threats? The most important groups for identifying threats are IT, Marketing/Communications, and Customer Service (they are usually the first to be notified by a customer about problems with the company, its service, or its products, and are a great first response team). If the IT team has the right monitoring software and resources in place, they can see when a brand attack is being launched. With the right tools, such as a reputation management service, IT can monitor what's being said, or they can see if company pages are being taken over by attackers if the company's social media resources are compromised. The Marketing team can identify an attack by paying attention to social media monitoring dashboards, feeds, and alerts, and seeing what is being posted. Budget limitations are no excuse. Free and simple methods for finding content posted on the Internet are available. Google Alert (http://www.google.com/alerts) can alert you instantly, by e-mail if you'd like, when key words you're tracking pop up. Another free resource is Addict-o-matic (www.addictomatic.com). You can track information about a company, person, or topic for free, as shown in Figure 4-2. (Alex is very popular, although there is another Alex De Carvalho who is a dancer, as you can see in the YouTube listing.)

And once the threat has been identified, who is responsible for analyzing and defending against the threat? Clear roles and responsibilities have to be proactively implemented. As with any technology threat, certain people or groups are responsible, depending on the type of threat. If the threat is a false story about how bad the company product is, then it might be up to Marketing, Sales, Customer Service, and/or Legal to respond, depending on the context. If an attacker compromises the corporate blog or Facebook page, IT should be involved with recovering the site,

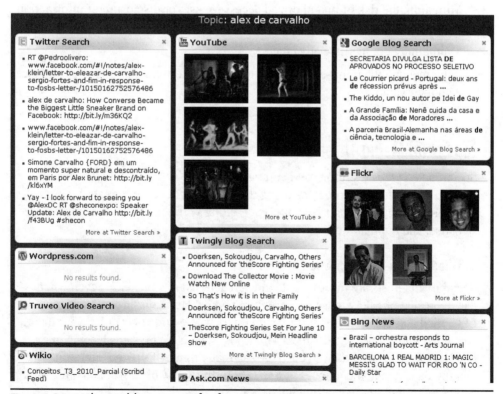

Figure 4-2   *Utilize Addict-o-matic for free monitoring.*

changing passwords, cleaning up any malicious software that may have been installed, protecting against further compromises of the account, and helping to identify the perpetrator should legal action be considered.

All threat response should be based on a defined policy. As with an IT security policy, the social media security policy must include an incident response component. This component contains the threat management steps that everyone who has a social media responsibility should know and can use as a guideline for resolving future threats. The main advantages of implementing an enterprise-wide threat management process include:

▶   Addressing regulatory compliance issues that affect operations when social media is used to communicate information or manage customer data

▶   Complying with regulations such as HIPAA Security Rules, RedFlag, or PCI DSS. We will touch on various legal issues throughout the book.

▶   Improving privacy for, security of, and information about customer information assets

▶   Mitigating the risk of unauthorized access to, use, or disclosure of information on social media channels

▶   Maintaining competitive advantage

▶   Implementing the right security tools to protect information assets in accordance with their value

Top Social Media Threats

Social media websites, tools, and companies change so frequently it's hard to point to a specific technology as being the top threat. The top threats against social media can be categorized, however, along with the affected technologies, websites, and applications.

1. Libel/Slander/Defamation

Social media posts are discoverable in legal actions, in some cases even when they're posted privately to a select group of people. Horizons Group Management, LLC, filed a libel lawsuit against a Twitter user who claimed his or her apartment contained mold. Specifically, the Twitter post stated, "Who said sleeping in a moldy apartment was bad for you? Horizon realty thinks it's okay." Horizons is seeking damages in the amount of $50,000 (http://www.blackweb20.com/2009/08/06/libel-and-social-media/).

2. Copyright/Trademark

It's extremely simple to copy and share protected information and very hard to track copyrighted information and very easy to infringe on a trademark. In November 2010, GAP, Inc. launched a lawsuit against a small startup, Gapnote.com, stating that the goods and services marketed under GAP, Inc. and Gapnote.com were similar, which infringed on GAP trademarks. Because Gap has such a wide social media footprint, they filed a serious infringement lawsuit against Gapnote.com (http://www.siliconrepublic.com/business/item/18766-retail-giant-gap-inc-in/).

3. Changing Technology

Social media sites and tools are constantly changing. By the time this book comes out there will probably be a whole new set of sites we haven't covered.

4. False Information

Since everyone and anyone can create content, you don't know if the content in a profile is true. The fake BP Twitter account (@BPGlobalPR) initially looked like a real corporate account (until they started posting some really funny tweets!).

5. Location-based Activity

With just about every new service having a location component, stalking someone with a publicly open account, cross-referencing information, and potentially finding where competitors are meeting clients, or infringing on an employee's privacy can be easy.

6. Corporate Espionage

As employees and employers put information online, it's actually become much easier to conduct corporate espionage over social media than ever before. By following your rival on Twitter, you might garner confidential information employees disclose unknowingly. If your competitor's sales staff uses foursquare, perhaps they'll check in at a client site. If you want to break into their e-mail account, finding a Facebook and LinkedIn profile with lots of personal information such as a pet's name, street address, and kid's name—all of which many people use as passwords—is easy. Just start guessing their password.

7. Identity Theft and Impersonation

If a social media profile is compromised, impersonating someone is simple. The amount of information available makes re-creating an identity easy. Identity theft can happen through spoofing or phishing. A hacker can send phony posts from "friends"— posts you might believe— and once you click a link, you may be rerouted to malicious sites or remote code may be executed to compromise your computer.

Wrap Up

Threat assessment is the first step in defending the company from attacks. If you do not know what form an attack is taking, you won't be able to defend yourself. Having a logical process in place to identify the threat, the danger it poses to the company, how it can be exploited, and how the company will respond is critical to providing a secure environment, whether defending against traditional hacker attackers or social media attacks.

Improvement Checklist

- ☐ Can you identify the methods by which threats can be launched against your company?
- ☐ Can you identify who is launching an attack?
- ☐ Can you determine what damage may occur from a social media attack?
- ☐ Have you developed and tested threat response scenarios?
- ☐ Have you detailed a response plan that all key employees who use social media can follow?

CHAPTER 5

What Can Go Wrong

Traditional attacks have taken the form of identity theft, corporate espionage, supply chain disruption, phishing, and hardware/software attacks such as SSL and DoS. However, as discussed in Chapter 4, social media threats can originate from almost anywhere and quickly challenge a company's traditional IT security policy. Unethical hackers now have much more nefarious designs when launching their attacks. This chapter builds on the previous chapter by looking specifically at

▶   The dangers of social media and the importance of encryption

▶   Cyberstalking and corporate cyberstalking

▶   Validating the end user

▶   Data scraping

Case Study: Firesheep, A Real-World Example of Social Media Hacking

Firesheep, a Firefox extension created by software developer Eric Butler, allows anyone to access anyone else's social media accounts so long as both parties are connected to an unsecured wireless network, such as a coffee shop's free Wi-Fi. According to Butler, the attack is relatively simple and works by exploiting "cookies" on the user's browser. As stated on the Firesheep site (http://codebutler.com/firesheep): "When logging into a website you usually start by submitting your username and password; if an account matching this information exists, you receive an automatic reply with a 'cookie,' which is used by your browser for all subsequent requests."

If you log in to your bank's web portal, the whole time you are checking your account you should see an "HTTPS" in the address bar. But this is not the case with all sites that allow a login. What many sites do is encrypt the login but then stop encrypting the rest of your browsing session, which means the user authentication can become vulnerable. An attacker can get a hold of the user "cookie" and basically have access to the user's session. This problem is a real threat when you log in to accounts that do not properly handle the complete session over encrypted tunnels, like when you're between client meetings and using the free wireless at Starbucks.

So anyone logging into Facebook or another social network from an open wireless network may be subject to attack and compromise. In the case of Firesheep—see Figure 5-1—this exploit was developed to expose the continued vulnerability of

Figure 5-1   *Firesheep in action*

many of the leading social networks, generate awareness, and effect a change. This example is capturing traffic of other users on the open wireless network. Here you see a capture of Gary's Facebook login.

Social media hacking can happen to anyone, just ask actor Ashton Kutcher. His Twitter account was compromised. The tweet read:

> Ashton, you've been Punk'd. This account is not secure. Dude, where's my SSL?

And with that, Ashton Kutcher learned about the dangers of Firesheep. The event occurred at 17:30 Pacific time, during the 2011 TED Conference. Presumably Kutcher was using an unsecured web session. A few minutes later, his Twitter name, @aplusk, was used to tweet out to 6.3 million followers who saw the message posted to his Twitter account:

> P.S. This is for those young protesters around the world who deserve not to have their Facebook & Twitter accounts hacked like this. #SSL

To date there have been over 1.3 million downloads of the Firesheep plugin.

The backend of Firesheep uses WinPcap; it's essentially sniffing network traffic, a technology that has been around for a long time. Putting Firesheep into a nice packaged installation is what made it so popular. As with any unencrypted traffic, an attacker can engage in various activities such as ARP poisoning and session hijacking. Encryption adds a lot of overhead, which is why some sites usually don't encrypt the whole session over SSL. Forcing encryption would be expensive, but it's the best defense against this type of attack, and in the end, the overhead is worth the security.

But, as with any arms race, there are technology countermeasures and procedural countermeasures. The company ZScaler released BlackSheep by Julien Sobrier. BlackSheep tricks Firesheep with a fake login cookie. It notifies the user when Firesheep has been detected, displaying the IP address of the attacker so you know a bad guy is in the room. In Figure 5-2, you can see the message displaying the IP that is running Firesheep.

Figure 5-2   *BlackSheep notification of Firesheep*

The result of some of these hacking stories is that social networks are making changes and addressing some security issues. Facebook has made encrypted login available. The whole session is not encrypted, however. Hopefully, all social networks will encrypt user access eventually—by default. Twitter, however, still does not force encryption.

Dangers Specific to Social Networks

The IT security team has a number of responsibilities in enabling social media security. As you'll see in Chapters 8 and 10, where we talk about processes and policies for utilizing resources and operations management, IT has to expand its toolset to include new technologies to help manage the risk posed by social media. Many of these tools and processes have to be managed by the IT team in conjunction with other groups in the company (such as Marketing and Legal).

With the rapid growth of social media, the stealing of e-mail contacts, passwords, and other personal information is yesterday's news. According to a recent paper by a group of Israeli cybersecurity experts, a new threat called "stealing reality" has emerged from the social media world (http://arxiv.org/abs/1010.1028). Stealing reality is a process whereby the perpetrator preys on your entire social network, slowly pilfering information about your behavior and life. This type of attack is extremely disruptive, as the user is not likely to change his or her entire pattern of behavior, which makes defending against future attacks exceedingly difficult. The ability to clone behavioral patterns and discern information about an individual or network through these nonaggressive methods illustrates the serious nature of these types of attacks. The tried and true methods of defense no longer apply. New radical approaches to security need to be devised.

The typical company response to a cyberattack is to identify the source of the attack and systematically update security procedures, shut down access to the compromised point of entry, and monitor for future attacks. The question today is how do you protect your networks from an intruder who *looks* like and *acts* like you? How do you even know the intruder is there or has created a fake you? How much data is available, unbeknownst to you, that could effectively compromise your security over time? The social media monitoring tools we discuss in Chapters 13 and 15 can help you find some of these social network intruders. A study, led by researchers at Northwestern University, collected a dataset of around 11 million Facebook profiles by exploiting a now-discontinued default Facebook feature. According to the report, messages tempted users with offers such as ringtones or used a social trap like announcing that someone had a "crush" on them. Of the messages, 70 percent were phishing attacks, but the others were attempts to gain Facebook account details—a strategy that could lead to more spam, or worse.

The H.U.M.O.R. Matrix outlined in this book stresses the importance of monitoring the conversation in an effort to identity threats to security. In Chapter 4, we identified the various threats to the different components of the matrix. At times, however, no amount of monitoring can protect your data from prying eyes. In April 2010, 15 percent of all Internet traffic was hijacked and redirected to Chinese servers. A report by the US-China Economic and Security review commission (http://www.uscc.gov/) stated that Internet traffic was rerouted for 18 minutes, and among the websites involved in this hijacking were the U.S. Senate, Office of the Secretary of Defense, NASA, and the Commerce Department. China, however, has "denied any hijack of Internet traffic."

This begs the question: *Who are you really conversing with?* How much information was compromised during those 18 minutes, and what were the potential short- and long-term effects? If the person having the conversation appears to be legitimate, how can you truly authenticate the source? A fake source attack is basically TCP session hijacking. TCP session hijacking has been around for a long time. A hacker takes over a TCP session between two machines, and since the session authentication occurs at the beginning of the session, the attacker can take over the machine and reroute traffic to another site, capturing data and then rerouting traffic back to the legitimate site.

IT Security Restrictions to Protect Your Networks

You are already aware of some of the basic controls IT has in place or can easily put in place. With social media, fake sources and man-in-the-middle attacks are more prevalent. When an employee is at home checking into a social media site or on the road at a conference or hotel checking sites, protecting them from these types of attacks is difficult. With some products that are installed to protect against malware, viruses, and Trojans, you do get some protection from malicious or fake sites, but only to a limited degree. In Chapters 8 and 10, where we discuss tools, you'll get a more in-depth look at software that can further manage the social networks that can impact your network security. But with networks that are under a company's control or for web applications the company develops, some technologies are easy to put in place:

▶ An open source solution is Arp handler inspection, or ArpON, which can block man-in-the-middle attacks through ARP poisoning and spoofing. It is agent based, however, so it may pose a problem because you have to manage the agents.

▶ You can use a long random number or string for a session key, which makes it harder to guess session keys.

▶ After a session has started, you can regenerate a session id.

▶ You can encrypt the whole session, and although more costly in overhead, it is probably the easiest method. Whenever your employees log in to any application, whether internal or external, encrypting the login and session will protect against an insider attacker and prevent an external attacker from capturing your data as it crosses networks.

▶ You can change the cookie with each request.

This countermeasure won't work when your employees are outside of your controlled environment, like when they're sitting in Starbucks using the free Wi-Fi. Then you have to rely on educating them not to log in to their social networks from unsecured networks. In Chapter 7, we review education in more detail.

Cyberstalking

> *Make no mistake: this kind of harassment can be as frightening and real as being followed and watched in your neighborhood or in your home.*

> —former Vice President Al Gore[1]

Cyberstalking is using the Internet (or other electronic media) to harass individuals, groups, or organizations. Cyberstalking can manifest itself as threats, accusations, identify impersonation, and sexual solicitation. Social media allows for these types of attacks to be mounted anonymously and to spread quickly across multiple networks.

---

[1] 1999 Report on Cyberstalking: A New Challenge to Law Enforcement and Industry, Department of Justice, August 1999, http://www.justice.gov/criminal/cybercrime/cyberstalking.htm.

Many of these attacks cause extreme personal distress to the individuals being targeted, in some cases even resulting in suicide (as in the case of Megan Taylor Meir, October 2006, the thirteen-year-old girl who was cyber-bullied on MySpace). In 2010, two teenagers in Pamlico County, North Carolina, were charged with a class 2 misdemeanor for cyberstalking their principal through a fake Facebook profile they created. The ensuing negative press, national coverage, and legal fees caused significant disruption that could be measured in the tens of thousands of dollars.

By tracking search results, forums, discussion boards, chat rooms, e-mail communications, instant messages, and the many social networks, identifying the source of the threat is possible. Many states have implemented cyberstalking laws: California, which was the first state, was followed by Alabama, Arizona, Connecticut, Florida, Hawaii, Illinois, New Hampshire, and New York. Unfortunately, prosecution at this time has been extremely lax and many perpetrators go unpunished.

Commonsense rules play an important role in protecting against cyberstalking. Since the Internet makes being anonymous so easy, knowing who the stalker is and where he or she is coming from is very difficult. An expert might be able to track down an IP address, but even that can be easily hidden with anonymous proxies. The ease with which attackers can create fake profiles, send fake requests, and take over other people's identities has made it much easier to gain information about victims without too much fear of being found out.

NOTE

A complete list of government resources and filtering technologies can be found in the resources section of our website, www.securingsocialmedia.com/resources. To find state laws, check the site for the National Conference of State Legislatures at http://www.ncsl.org/IssuesResearch/ TelecommunicationsInformationTechnology/CyberstalkingLaws/tabid/13495/Default.aspx. Other sites include QuitStalkingMe.com and WiredSafety.org.

Corporate Cyberstalking

Attackers can use completely legal means to gather information about their victims because that information is freely given on social media sites. Cyberstalking doesn't have to be personal; it can also be used against corporations. If your competitor wants to know what clients are taking sales meetings with you, they might track down your sales teams on LinkedIn and see if they've "checked in" at or close to a customer's site through Facebook or foursquare, or even track their travel patterns through TripIt, Dopplr, and other social travel services. Stalkers can find a lot of information about your sales team's activity. So what are some steps a corporate attacker actually takes to stalk your company?

1. **Company information**   Identify employees at the target. The easiest way to do this is with LinkedIn and Google searches.

2. **Personal information**   Once you know the names of employees working at the target company, find out as much about them as you can on Facebook, Twitter, Flickr Blogs, MySpace, YouTube, etc. You can pull their e-mails, friends' names, pets' names, children's names, schools they went to, and so on. Some folks will even accept a friend request. How many people still use a pet's or child's name as a password? When Gawker Media was hacked in December 2010,[2] the passwords were cracked. As you can see in Figure 5-3, some really simple passwords were being used, including "password."

3. **Locate employees**   Find out where the employees hang out using Facebook Places, SCVNGR, Google Latitude, Loopt, Gowalla, foursquare, and other geolocation services. They might be with a customer and checking into the customer's office!

```
2516 123456
2188 password
1205 12345678
 696 qwerty
 498 abc123
 459 12345
 441 monkey
 413 111111
 385 consumer
 376 letmein
 351 1234
 318 dragon
 307 trustno1
 303 baseball
 302 gizmodo
```

Figure 5-3   *Easy-to-hack passwords*

[2] "Gawker Hack: Hacked Database Compromises User Data," Huffington Post (December 12, 2010), http://www.huffingtonpost.com/2010/12/12/gawker-hack-hacked-databa_n_795613.html.

4. **Correlate information** Use one of the numbers of social media tracking tools to continue to gather information about the competitor or employee of the competitor. Some tools include Seesmic, Social Mention, Addict-o-matic, HootSuite, Lithium, Radian6, IceRocket, CustomScoop, to name just a few.

5. **Cross the line** If you want to cross the line, you will have gathered enough information to get login e-mail addresses and probably enough information to guess passwords to accounts. A real cyberstalker will definitely cross that line.

Validating the End User

While e-mail still presents one of the greatest threats to a company's network via malware, phishing, and so on, social media is quickly becoming a major challenge for most organizations. Internal and external communication standards should be implemented to aid in defense of your networks and user information. Here are a few countermeasures that serve as your first line of defense:

- ▶ Modify and change passwords regularly.

- ▶ Avoid dictionary words for passwords (try a C0mbin@t1on of numbers and uppercase and lowercase letters and symbols, instead of a pronounceable phase).

- ▶ Create individual usernames and passwords for each social media platform (one for Twitter, another for Facebook, etc.).

- ▶ Require DNS authentication on all company e-mail communications.

- ▶ For individuals whose primary role is not social media community management, remove the ability of the end user to install applications on his or her desktop. In the case of community managers and those whose role is to interface with customers online, train them in the proper and secure use of desktop applications and make sure the latest versions are installed.

- ▶ Remove end-user administrator privileges.

- ▶ Implement URL filtering to help block malicious attacks via websites.

One of the first lines of defense is creating easily understandable standards for customer communications via social media channels. These standards should be applied to e-mail, social media, and all other forms of digital communications. By creating these standards, customers will be familiar with communication from your company and instantly suspicious of phishing attacks or malware links.

Here are a few key items that should be implemented to counter customer identity and phishing attacks:

► Standardize your social communications with the customer.

► Do not request personal information.

► Use your customer's full name when possible.

► Implement e-mail authentication.

► Avoid the inclusion of hyperlinks.

Determining Accountability

Your social media policy and IT security policy combine to define the consequences of breaking corporate restrictions. In Chapter 6, we develop the basics of your social media policy. But any company should already have a security policy in place that has been vetted by human resources and tells employees what is permissible and what is not. Employees have to be accountable for either utilizing social media insecurely or utilizing it to break the rules or laws and cross that cyberstalking line.

IT security teams have the capability to monitor activity, or can implement that capability easily enough. With URL filtering and web monitoring tools, you can easily determine what employees are doing on social media sites, if they are doing anything inappropriate, and determine consequences.

Data Scraping

Social media is a platform for sharing. But this information sharing has progressed beyond sharing just with friends and family to sharing with the whole world, which is less social. Corporate sharing has moved beyond just employees interacting with the general public, which can be good or bad. Corporate sharing via social media can attract more customers, followers, and business, but malicious users can turn all that available data against your company. Knowing who is using the information you share, and to what purpose that information will be used, is difficult. This is the erosion of your true social circle.

With a personal profile, an employee can receive random requests to become "friends." These requests do not all come from friends; these "friends" could be spammers or malicious users trying to gather information about the employee. The same problem is occurring with corporate social profiles. Generally, corporate social profiles are meant to be shared with everyone. Fanpages are being created constantly. Your "friends" and "fans" have access to all the information that you post, however.

A targeted information gathering attack might target the marketing person who runs the corporate blog. Becoming friends on the corporate site might lead to the malicious user convincing that marketing person to become friends on her personal social network profile. You can find a person's LinkedIn profile with a generic Google search. Once the malicious user gets access to the marketing person's personal social profile, he has enough information to create a fake profile, or enough data to try and guess the password the marketing person might use to connect to corporate e-mail or the corporate blog. This could lead to a compromise of your internal corporate network.

With the advent of location-based services, we are seeing a rise in physical insecurity based on social media usage. A recently popular site, Please Rob Me (http://pleaserobme.com), takes advantage of the Twitter location feature. Imagine what a stalker following you on Twitter could do or what a deranged ex-boyfriend or ex-girlfriend could do who is able to follow you to corporate networking events you post about attending on Facebook? All this information can be easily scraped up by a malicious user, potentially leading to some disastrous activity for you or your company network.

Information disclosure on social media sites like Facebook, Twitter, LinkedIn, and MySpace can be the downfall of information valuation. With this information completely in the open, how users authenticate may have to change. No longer can a bank authenticate customers by asking the name of street they grew up on or their dog's name; this data is on social media profiles. The ability to share and provide information can completely undo your network security requirements. Social media does not encourage people to be security conscious. Social media encourages

- ▶ Lack of privacy
- ▶ Information sharing
- ▶ Giving away answers to security questions
- ▶ Social engineering

Malicious people are attracted to social networks because gaining trust is easy and because of the amount of data available for social engineering. Relationship building is easier through social media, which can lead to phishing attacks. With these sites, once you trust a new "friend," you may accept a request for an application your "friend" is promoting. Your marketing person may now install that application without knowing he has just downloaded malicious code to a corporate computer. There are no external third-party audits of these applications before they appear on Facebook. Your computer can be easily infected by a virus or spyware. Without education about the risks of information gathering and theft from social media profiles, employees can unknowingly open backdoors into your company. Here are some of the challenges companies face with users connecting and sharing on these social sites:

► Widespread display of personal information, much of which is used for authentication.

► Almost anyone can view data. Search engines index profiles. And by tricking people into accepting friend requests, access to all the information in those personal profiles is easy to attain.

► Insecure applications being installed. Once a trust relationship is in place, malicious users can get people to click a malware link or install a Trojan application within social sites to gain access to network computers.

► No privacy restrictions. Users are often unaware of all the privacy settings social networks are now implementing and do not restrict access to their data as a result.

► Weak passwords. Users still use children's names or pets' names as passwords, and by allowing people to see your personal data on your profile, you create an opportunity for a malicious user to discover those common passwords.

Wrap Up

Social media makes attacking the end user much simpler. People knowingly and unknowingly give out a lot of information on social media platforms that can be used against them. The social media sites go online and attract thousands and millions of users very quickly, without having a long history of finding and fixing bugs in their applications. If companies are going to allow employees to use social media, they have to educate them on the risks and provide more resources to help reduce the risks to their users.

Improvement Checklist

☐ Has your company provided basic information on social media risks to employees?

☐ Do you restrict logins from particular networks to corporate social media?

☐ Are you following news streams about social media security dangers?

☐ Are you providing information to employees about how to better lock down their personal social media profiles?

PART

III

Operations, Policies, & Processes

6

Social Media Security Policy Best Practices

Best practices for social media are still evolving. In the pure security world, many standards are followed, everything from National Institute of Standards and Technology (NIST) standards to ISO 27001, an Information Security Management System standard. By employing current standards, IT can follow security requirements to secure social media. If you look at social media data as you would any other data stream, you can apply current policy frameworks. For example, to secure communications between the author of your blog posts and the website hosting the blog (assuming you are hosting it), you can enable SSL and require a strong password that gets changed every 90 days. Secure data streams are part of Payment Card Industry (PCI) requirements. If the Marketing department sends data to a vendor, you can secure that communication with e-mail encryption or encrypted file transfer.

But the challenge in the social media environment has to do with the content and destination of outgoing communications, as well as the person who is consuming and responding to the communication. For example, encrypting a blog submitted by an employee will not help your company once it's published publicly. The post may give away company secrets if the employee doesn't know he wasn't supposed to share certain bits of information with the public!

Every company must have policies in place and a framework laid out defining acceptable use of social media. Every organization—from small businesses to governments—need to treat social media policies like IT policies—living documents that guide appropriate use. In this chapter, we discuss social media security policies requirements. Specifically, we cover

- ► The components of an effective policy
- ► How the H.U.M.O.R. matrix fits into your policy
- ► Developing your social media security policy

Toward the end of the chapter, we've also included a sample social media security policy that you can use as a guideline for creating your own policy.

Case Study: Growth of Social Media Policy Usage

In the United Arab Emirates (UAE), 45 percent of the population uses Facebook. The UAE eGovernment has released the Guidelines for Social Media Usage in UAE Government Entities,[1] a progressive move toward implementing a social media security policy. The guidelines provide steps to be taken by the government and addresses issues such as access to social media sites from within government offices, account management, employee conduct, content management, citizen code of conduct, security, privacy, and some other legal issues. The guidelines state: "The main driver behind granting access to employees is to ultimately enhance their work performance and contribute to improving their outputs and deliverables." It recognizes that the lines between personal and professional usage of social media sites are often blurred, making the issue of granting access to one rather than the other difficult. It, therefore, recommends: "Access to social media sites shouldn't be banned. Employees should be held accountable for any improper use of any social media site."

The policy covers a wide array of policy topics, including:

▶ **Policy controls** These outline appropriate behavior and content guidelines when using social media tools.

▶ **Acquisition controls** Examples of these are found in the "Access to Social Media Websites" section of the UAE's policy. The controls allow for greater security and privacy settings and greater control of information (such as setting strict authentication measures or managing cookies) when subscribing to commercial social media sites.

▶ **Training controls** These provide awareness and courses for employees on policy, conduct, and best practices when it comes to using social media tools.

This policy is a great start for the UAE. What the government can do to improve this process is to address policy guidelines for monitoring and reporting. They should also add an incident response policy for when things go wrong. The current policy does not address these key concepts in any detail. As their policy states, however, social media management is an ongoing process, and the UAE will most likely modify the policy as the landscape changes.

---

[1] Ibrahim Elbadawi, "Three Reasons Why the UAE eGovernment Social Media Guidelines of Are Vital," Government in the Lab (Date: March 11 2011), http://govinthelab.com/three-reasons-why-the-uae-egovernment-social-media-guidelines-of-are-vital/?utm_source=feedburner&utm_medium=feed&utm_campaign=Feed%3A+Government20InAction+%28Government+2.0+in+Action%29.

What Is an Effective Social Media Security Policy?

Defining the content of a policy is the first great challenge. Currently, there are no international standards bodies (such as Institute of Electrical and Electronics Engineers or IEEE) to help with this problem. The government is trying to adapt NIST SP 800-53 Rev 3, which is a government standard on information security procedures, to take into account some form of accreditation for services such as Twitter or YouTube as a network system. As these are hosted services, however, you have no control over them; you have to rely on the administrator of Twitter and YouTube to maintain security protocols.

An effective policy has several main components that take into account the type of services used. Social media platforms are both internal and external, and what type you use will necessarily dictate at least some parts of your policy. Here are the key ingredients that policies should have:

► Any regulatory requirements and legal requirements that social media use could impact

► Managing internal and external hosted applications, including monitoring and reporting tools and techniques and testing and auditing

► Enterprise-wide coordination

► Codes of conduct and acceptable use

► Roles and responsibilities for the Community Manager

► Education and training

► Policy management, reporting, and monitoring

How's JAG Doing?

These key ingredients are missing from JAG's policies. They gave themselves a "Poor" rating for most of these categories. To date, JAG's policies have focused on HR and IT: basic Acceptable Use Policies, Employee Code of Conduct, IT Operations Guidelines, IT Security Policy, Internet Use Policy, and hiring policies. Within JAG's HR policies, training and education do not focus on IT issues or social media issues, and within its IT policies, no social media issues are addressed. The Marketing department has not even put out a public version of its social media policy to state the company's position on social media usage. Hopefully, JAG will improve its score in the H.U.M.O.R. Matrix after reading this chapter and implementing new policies.

Regulatory and Legal Requirements

As we've discussed in earlier chapters, the reasons for needing a social media security policy (or a security policy applied to your organization's social media usage) are very similar to any other policy you may have. Employees need guidelines for appropriate usage. The decades-old acronym PEBKAC—Problem Exists Between Keyboard And Chair—certainly applies to today's new social media environment. A number of legal risks also drive the need for documented policies. Several of these include:

▶ **Discrimination claims**   Employees can say anything over social media that might be attributed to the company. For example, you could have a policy basically saying if employees post things on personal sites that impact other employees or the company, they may get terminated. Discrimination claims can lead to an employee claiming a hostile work environment and filing a lawsuit. Or perhaps a supervisor uses social media to disparage an employee during off hours; this could also cause a lawsuit.

▶ **Defamation claims**   Employees may say things over business or personal social media outlets that impact the company or competitors or even customers. Employers may share too much information, including photos, about other employees that can lead to a lawsuit. Case law has not settled on this as yet. A case was pending in which the National Labor Relations Board alleged that American Medical Response of Connecticut Inc. had illegally fired an employee in 2009 after she criticized her supervisor via a personal Facebook post. The firing prompted a lawsuit based on protected speech under Federal labor laws. The case was settled in early 2011. The settlement called for American Medical Response of Connecticut Inc. to change its blogging and Internet policy that barred workers from disparaging the company or its supervisors. The company also has to revise another policy that prohibits employees from depicting the company in any way over the Internet without permission.[2] This is a far-reaching consequence to their overall policy. The modified policy has to very careful in trying to restrict off-hours usage.

---

[2] "Company Accused of Firing Over Facebook Post," *New York Times* (November 8, 2010), http://news.yahoo.com/s/ap/20101109/ap_on_hi_te/us_facebook_firing.

▶ **Confidentiality breach**   This risk is probably the most prevalent. An employee shares too much confidential information, leading to regulatory fines or even competitors finding out too much.

▶ **Regulatory breach**   Many regulations also include educational components for employees, detailing what is appropriate to communicate about regulated products, such as financial investment opportunities or claims about pharmaceutical drugs, or about disseminating confidential customer information. For example, an employee might easily share too much patient information over social media in breach of the HIPAA Security Rule regulations, as illustrated in Chapter 4 in the case involving a Twitter post sent out by a hospital employee.

Your policy should address the consequences of giving out proprietary and confidential company information; making discriminatory statements; and making defamatory statements regarding the company, its employees, customers, competitors, or vendors. It should address how employees can use the company name and what information can be shared. You need to have a well-documented escalation procedure to apply the right enforcement capabilities, create a framework for chain of custody, document all types of legal discovery and proceedings, and provide justification for possible actions against employees, hackers, or other malefactors. Much social media content is beyond the company's direct control so policies and procedures have to suffice where technology tools cannot have an impact.

Managing In-house (Self-hosted) Applications

Your social media security policy should detail security requirements for using social media sites that you do have control over. Companies that build their own policies and apply their own requirements without the benefit of adopting a secure process for developing applications are developing policies based on how technology and privacy of data has been historically treated in typical security infrastructures. Many approaches to securing a social media application or website are similar to securing your company's ecommerce site or proprietary applications. Differences occur when you are compromised by an employee saying something inappropriate, a customer attacking your company brand, or your sales team losing customer data over social media channels. These problems make it into the public sphere much quicker; customer feedback is almost immediate; and your brand can suffer damage within the span of a few hours.

When using social media sites that you *do* have control over, such as your own WordPress-based Blog or wiki site, key security requirements must be baked into the availability of the sites to your employees:

1. Ensure that you have followed a security assessment process to test applications for risk due to traditional attacks, data management problems, and secure coding practices. Your security processes should detail the basic steps you have to follow in testing a web-based social media application:

   a. Information gathering, including application fingerprinting; application discovery; spidering and Googling; analysis of error code; SSL/TLS testing; DB listener testing; file extensions handling; old, backup, and unreferenced files

   ### NOTE

   For detailed technical security analysis of secure software testing, review Hacking Exposed 6: Network Security Secrets & Solutions *by Stuart McClure, Joel Scambray, and George Kurtz (McGraw-Hill Professional 2009).*

   b. Authentication testing, including default or guessable accounts, brute force, bypassing authentication schemas, directory traversal/file include, vulnerable remember password and password reset, logout and browser cache management testing

   c. Session management, including session management schema, session token, manipulation, exposed session variables, HTTP exploits

   d. Data validation testing, including cross-site scripting, HTTP methods and XST, SQL injection, stored procedure injection, XML injection, SSI injection, XPath injection, IMAP/SMTP injection, code injection, buffer overflow

   e. Web services testing, including XML structural testing, XML content-level testing, HTTP GET parameters/REST testing

   f. Denial of service testing, locking customer accounts, user specified-object allocation, user input as a loop counter, writing user-provided data to disk, failure to release resources, storing too much data in session

2. Address post-deployment testing and consistent testing of your application over time.

3. Identify what key company and customer information should be encrypted during each data management step: creation, transportation, usage, storage, and destruction.

4. Review how authentication steps are handled for third-party applications and APIs; weak or plaintext unencrypted authentication can allow inappropriate access to or theft of credentials.

5. Define strong passwords and how they will be enforced and when they should be changed, especially if multiple employees in, for example, Marketing might have access to the company account on sites such as YouTube or Facebook.

6. Address log management issues. Where possible, you want to log which employees access the social media corporate accounts and know who posts information. Log management can be extremely important to incident response plans.

In-house Social Media Site Checklist

Once you have built your self-hosted site, follow the approval process for deployment to production, just as you would for any other IT application being placed into production.

Answer these questions to ensure you are meeting the key requirements for approval:

▶ Are appropriate disclaimers in place?

▶ Is ownership of the site clearly defined and displayed?

▶ Is an operations process in place for site update and content review?

▶ Does content get signed off by appropriate management? Are policies in place for user content moderation?

▶ Are all users and administrators of the application trained in appropriate usage, moderation, and content creation?

▶ Have you developed a community manager process?

▶ Are security testing plans in place to test the application's functions as well as the operating system's and network layer's capabilities to defend against hacker attacks?

▶ Is an incident response process in place for application usage as well as potential damage to the application's functions?

▶ Are operations staff assigned responsibilities for maintaining the site?

Managing Externally Hosted Applications

Third-party cloud applications cannot be handled in the same manner as your own infrastructure applications. You have minimal impact on these third-party companies and their security requirements, and influencing them to modify their security posture will probably not be effective. Alternatively, reliance on your own controls is essential. Examples of internal controls to consider include:

▶ How your employees use these third-party social media sites

▶ What data is allowed

▶ How you will monitor your corporate activity

▶ How you will respond to an external incident

Another key change in how you manage data is that you have to rely on third-party platforms to conduct their own security testing of their applications, and then they may or may not show you the results. You inherently trust these platforms and related applications to keep all the private messages you receive from your Facebook Fans secure from hackers and you rely on third parties not to sell customer lists of your Twitter followers. But has your company asked Twitter or Facebook for a SAS 70 II audit report (which is a third-party analysis of a company's security posture)? As of last year, Twitter agreed to share all public tweets since its inception (2006) and archive them in the Library of Congress—with the exception of deleted tweets. Google already indexes tweets in real time. Yahoo! and Microsoft get copies, too. This could be part of your audit processes. Have you any idea what their security policies are over the data you share with these third-party companies?

The policy framework has to take into account the following major security concepts when dealing with a third-party application:

▶ Social media is generally based on third-party "cloud" applications and, therefore, your company can't control their security.

▶ Social media web applications and downloadable applications have the same security challenges as all other web-based applications and other installed software applications.

▶ The general public is as involved with your company's use of social media as you are, and your policy has to give guidance to your employees on how to handle public interactions.

▶ Your company should have a public version of your social media policy that explains your positions on social media.

▶ Sharing of data is a must in social media, but data sharing is also a key aspect of attacks from both a technological hacking perspective as well as a content perspective.

▶ Malicious code is easier to share via social media portals and downloadable applications that can then connect back to the corporate environment to introduce viruses, Trojans, and other malware.

▶ Reputation management is often more important than secure technology-based controls when addressing the risks due to social media.

▶ Enable encrypted communications to the social media site when possible. This is not easy with most sites, but applications are available that can help with this task. One example is HTTPS Everywhere from the Electronic Frontier Foundation (https://www.eff.org/https-everywhere). As the site says:

> HTTPS Everywhere is a Firefox extension produced as a collaboration between The Tor Project and the Electronic Frontier Foundation. It encrypts your communications with a number of major websites. Many sites on the Web offer some limited support for encryption over HTTPS, but make it difficult to use. For instance, they may default to unencrypted HTTP, or fill encrypted pages with links that go back to the unencrypted site. The HTTPS Everywhere extension fixes these problems by rewriting all requests to these sites to HTTPS.

When you install the HTTPS Everywhere add-on in Firefox, it forces encryption on the sites it covers. In Figure 6-1, you see that going to Facebook without HTTPS Everywhere leaves the website unencrypted. Once you install HTTPS Everywhere, you will see, as shown in Figures 6-2 and 6-3, how the "https" is now forced without any user interaction for social media sites you visit.

Figure 6-1   *Visiting a site without HTTPS Everywhere turned on and no encryption*

Figure 6-2   *"HTTPS" is forced when visiting Facebook with HTTPS Everywhere.*

Figure 6-3   *"HTTPS" is forced when visiting Twitter with HTTPS Everywhere.*

HTTPS Everywhere actually offers protection against Firesheep and the software currently supports other sites such as Google Search, Wikipedia, bit.ly, GMX, and Wordpress.com blogs, and, of course, Facebook and Twitter. (As we mentioned in Chapter 5, BlackSheep can also help identify the Firesheep threat.) As Facebook and Google and other sites make HTTPS connections more readily accessible and a default option, the threat of unencrypted communications will decrease.

Externally Hosted Social Media Site Checklist

Although determining the security measures employed by a third-party site may seem difficult, follow at least a minimal set of baseline standards when allowing your company to utilize any website for marketing campaigns, storing customer data, and communicating with the public. At a minimum, you should attempt to gain a better understanding of the third-party application you are using and ask pointed questions to gain insight into its security protocols. Your policy for gathering information should list, at a minimum, these requirements:

▶ Review the social media site/platform's SAS 70 II audit report. If the site doesn't have one, ask for one to be conducted and get the results sent to you if possible.

▶ Ask for and review a basic financial summary of the company: Are they profitable or on the road to profitability?

▶ Review the site's privacy policy for any steps that may compromise your data or your customer's data.

▶ Ask for the guidelines the site has for its own internal testing procedures for vulnerabilities and review their procedures. What is the schedule for conducting testing?

NOTE

In May 2010, the security company F-Secure discovered a malware attack being run by fake Twitter accounts on Twitter posts with the message "haha this is the funniest video ive ever seen." When users clicked it, a Trojan was installed on their systems! If Twitter had a very proactive security program in place, they would have found this before F-Secure.

► Ask for and review the site's incident response program.

► Review the encryption of the site's data storage, data transmission, and authentication.

► Ask for and review the site's backup strategy.

► What happens to your data if the company goes out of business? This is a question you will probably not get a good answer to, but you may want to ask about a data escrow service.

► Review any documentation the site has regarding industry regulations or types of data stored. Review the site's data breach notifications policy.

► Review the service level agreement with the site. If the site does not have one, ask for one to be developed.

Enterprise-wide Coordination

Like your current human resources policies and IT security policies, your social media policy has to be a companywide program. If only the Marketing team is subject to the policy, other employees will not know what is allowable and will most likely post inappropriate information. If the IT department is the only one following the policy, other departments will not know how to use social media sites in a secure manner or will not receive any training on what can and cannot be posted about the company.

Writing the social media policy is a collaborative effort. Creating more granular social media security policies and educating employees must be a companywide effort. The policy can either be broken down into multiple policies and written as the business functions change, or it can be written in a more generic format to address future changes in related processes, which might be a bit more difficult to do. Most companies currently have a Laptop Policy and a Mobile Device Policy; these are granular policies. The approach you select really boils down to an individual choice. If you do want to write granular policies, you may consider starting out with these:

► Social Media Policy

► Social Media Security Policy

► Employee Code of Conduct for Online Communications

► Employee Social Network Information Disclosure Policy

► Employee Facebook Policy

► Employee Personal Social Media Policy

► Employee Twitter Policy

- ► Employee LinkedIn Policy
- ► Corporate Blog Policy
- ► Corporate YouTube Policy
- ► Social Network Password Policy
- ► Personal Blog Policy

Codes of Conduct and Acceptable Use

For any of the policies you define, there are basic requirements that all employees should adhere to and understand. Any HR professional will know these by heart! Widely used examples of such policy provisions include:

- ► All employees must take responsibility for knowing the policies, just as they do for reading the company handbook. Training is, of course, a requirement to ensure employees can follow the policies properly.
- ► Employees must understand the policy is global for all social networking activities.
- ► Employees are under the same confidential restrictions regarding company information no matter what platform they use.
- ► Any information disclosed publicly should include the appropriate disclaimers, for example, employees should clearly identify themselves as company employees when speaking about the company or about the industry.
- ► The employee cannot infringe on company trademarks or intellectual property whenever communicating outside the company.
- ► Guidelines about sending out certain types of company-related information, from brochures to sales proposals.
- ► Employees can be terminated for inappropriate use of company information or conduct unbecoming an employee that negatively impacts the company.

When different departments collaborate on developing policy and managing technologies, a company can get a better handle on how social media will be used internally and externally and how rules for social media usage can be developed. Here are some basic rules and guidelines that employees must follow:

- ► Employees must read and understand all policies related to social media.
- ► Employees must understand they need to be trained appropriately in social media usage.

- ▶ Employees may use company resources only for approved social media activities during working hours.

- ▶ Employees must not disseminate confidential information.

- ▶ Employees should not use nonsecure social media systems to conduct company-related work activities, unless otherwise specified.

- ▶ Employees are not allowed to circumvent company security procedures and technologies.

- ▶ Employees should not share login information to social media sites in any unapproved manner.

- ▶ Employees will follow company guidelines on using secure passwords.

- ▶ Employees should understand they represent the company when they discuss the company name on social media sites and will respect company policies.

- ▶ Employees should have, at a minimum, yearly training on security processes.

- ▶ Employees are responsible for security along with the IT department.

Roles and Responsibilities: The Community Manager

The Community Manager is a relatively new role as applied to the online environment in Web 2.0 and beyond. Where the role fits into the organizational structure is still up for debate, and largely depends on the company's industry, culture, and objectives for participating in social media. In many companies, the Community Manager role is a Marketing function due to the overwhelmingly communicative nature of social media. Other companies, such as Comcast, use social media primarily for improving customer service. Lego, the toy manufacturer, uses social media for new product idea generation. Dell has successfully used social media for community building and sales promotions. Dell encourages *all* employees, regardless of department, to engage with their communities via social media. Employees spend an average of 20 minutes/day connecting with online communities and customers.

Some companies have recognized the cross-functional nature of social media, setting up a separate reporting line as a cost or a profit center or as a shared support service, based on strategic objectives. Whichever the case, the manager guides strategic, tactical, and operational activities related to social media outlets and implements daily procedures, plans, ad-hoc campaigns, and oversees resources and processes around multiplatform community scalability.

The role must be defined at the outset from the standpoint of secure utilization of social media, however. Part of the Community Manager's responsibility involves interfacing with the IT Security, Legal, and Human Resource departments to ensure a cohesive strategy that reduces risk to the company from the potential social media threats discussed in Chapters 4 and 5.

The current role of the Community Manager usually involves a combination of the following:

- ▶ Welcoming customers to the organization's social community
- ▶ Identification and relationship building with key influencers
- ▶ Real-time monitoring, moderating, responding to, and redirecting conversations
- ▶ Encouraging interaction and community development among members
- ▶ Managing programs and content
- ▶ Managing internal resources allocated for social media
- ▶ Enforcing policies and guidelines
- ▶ Managing tools for social media development programs and communications
- ▶ Reporting on activities and developing new metrics
- ▶ Tracking customer sentiment
- ▶ Developing, implementing, and managing content creation strategy
- ▶ Managing responses to the brand
- ▶ Delegating feedback to internal teams
- ▶ Developing web communications to optimize all customer interactions
- ▶ Managing the company blog for engagement and readership
- ▶ Responding to and managing crises
- ▶ Developing internal communications through thought leadership, employee engagement, and training
- ▶ Online and offline event planning for connecting the company with its community of customers and clients and providing forums for like-minded consumer advocates to meet and interact

Nowhere in this description is there an explicit interface between the Community Manager and the IT, Legal, and Human Resource departments. This integral connection is too often overlooked in policies and by management. The role of the Community

Manager must expand to take on a liaison project management function that goes beyond just managing social media content and communications. To be effective as a real interface for the company, the Community Manager's role must take on these further responsibilities:

▶ Coordinate policy development among all business units.

▶ Work with IT Security to track incidents.

▶ Work with Marketing and IT together to coordinate public response to incidents or customer threats.

▶ Work with Legal to understand application laws to social media usage.

▶ Work with Human Resources to ensure all employees involved in social media understand the restriction on usage and potential dangers.

▶ Work with IT Security to use appropriate tools to track, monitor, and report on employee use of social media tools.

These new tasks take the Community Manager out of his or her current role. A best practice would be to designate someone in IT or IT Security to partner with the Community Manager or even take on some of the Community Manager's responsibilities in the IT realm. In the role of assisting the IT department with helping employees understand the security implications of social media, the Community Manager can share responsibility with IT for reviewing and searching for security information related to the social media tactics being used. This has to be a shared responsibility, as social media site monitoring includes:

▶ Reviewing company profile pages daily to determine if any inappropriate or hacked content has been displayed

▶ Reviewing other sites and profiles referenced or relevant to the company for acceptable use of company information

▶ Creating a routine for checking to see if users and customers connected to the company's social media profiles are conducting their online activities in accordance with company acceptable standards of association

▶ Scanning links to the company to see if any compromised pages have been posted

▶ Working with IT Security to test company sites for weaknesses

▶ Working closely with IT Security to review what new vulnerabilities might impact applications and websites used for social media marketing campaigns

TIP

Sites for tracking vulnerabilities include the National Vulnerability Database (http://nvd.nist.gov/nvd .cfm), Security Focus Database (http://www.securityfocus.com), and Open Source Vulnerability Database (www.osvdb.org). On these sites, you can search for technologies and social media channels you use for any known vulnerabilities that might compromise your security.

The successful implementation of the Community Manager role has to be assessed by multiple departments. IT must be able to communicate technology challenges, threat scenarios from social media, and response capabilities. Human Resources must be able to implement and enforce policies through the assistance of the Community Manager, and together, they must work with employees to enforce compliance with policies. Marketing must be able to coordinate communication projects and business objectives to all other departments through the Community Manager and have access to the right technology resources to accomplish its goals. Legal should be able to coordinate regulatory restrictions on social media usage across all departments through the Community Manager.

With these new responsibilities, the reporting structure will be a challenge, particularly as the role naturally evolves cross-functionally over time. Although an employee should never have two bosses, which is often a recipe for failure, involving other departments in a goal setting process for evaluating the Community Manager's job performance can be effective. The Security Director has a key role to play in working with the Community Manager. A number of security technologies, which many large companies already have in place, can also be applied to secure new media communications. Data loss prevention tools are probably the most comprehensive for monitoring the types of data coming into and leaving the company's environment. By putting a process in place for IT Security to work with the Community Manager, new projects and campaigns, new web applications, and proposed social media tools can be monitored, tracked, and reported on in a more timely manner.

Education and Training

As with any security framework, educating your staff is paramount. A good baseline training program can reduce risk as well make employees less likely to cause inadvertent breaches. Employees can be unaware of how easily social media channels can be used to manipulate users into divulging confidential information or granting computer system access. Using social media, attackers try to use a variety of techniques (just a few a noted here) to gather private information:

- ▶ **Pretexting** Using an invented scenario and a piece of known information to establish legitimacy in the mind of the target. Information is then typically used to try to obtain Social Security numbers, date of birth, or other personal verification measures.

- ▶ **Phishing** An e-mail that appears to come from a legitimate source (like your bank) requesting verification of information and warning of a consequence for noncompliance.

- ▶ **Trojan horse** A destructive program that masquerades as a benign application.

Many employees recognize some of these attack techniques. Unfortunately, not every employee understands the complete attack landscape, which can leave your company and possibly your network vulnerable to attack. Employees need to understand the importance of network security and the key role they can play in helping protect company information. For example, employees may create common passwords to use on social media sites to simplify their interactions and daily status routines, but this ease-of-use scenario can also make it simpler for the attacker to gain access to their social media accounts and possibly leverage further attacks into your network.

The benefits of employee security training include:

- ▶ Employees absorb the importance of "best practices" and then they can, in turn, practice and preach a broader understanding of a company culture of safety and security.

- ▶ Employees are less likely to fall victim to attacks and expose your company to additional attacks.

- ▶ Employees learn a new model of acceptable behavior and culture within the company.

- ▶ Employees learn about their responsibilities to help prevent malicious activity and detect problems.

- ▶ Training helps reduce the risk of intentional or accidental information misuse.

- ▶ Training provides a baseline of compliance for federal and state regulations that may require security awareness training.

Policy Management

Once you have your social media security policies in place, you have to update them continuously. The challenge with social media, as compared to other technologies, is the speed at which the sites, technologies, capabilities, and processes change. New functions are being built so rapidly that a completely new capability, function, or application might be available in six months that is not currently covered by your policies. Securing these new functions and understanding how employees and customers interact with new sites is going to require more diligent updates of your policies than you are used to with normal IT security policies.

Both the IT staff and the Marketing staff must have a process in place for researching new technologies, determining what employees and customers are using, and understanding how these new sites affect the company's assets and resources. For example, geolocation is rapidly rising in popularity with new applications coming out weekly, but most companies have yet to grasp the true capabilities, dangers, and opportunities of geolocation applications. To keep abreast of the latest trends and functions, the Community Manager must work with Marketing and IT to

▶ Select specific sites to read and research such as Mashable.com and TechCrunch.com.

▶ Review employee web surfing to look for what is trending.

▶ Put a process in place to analyze new applications before the company is swamped with something unexpected by employees or customers.

H.U.M.O.R. Guidelines

In Chapter 2, we outlined some basic policy questions that you must address regarding your company's overall social media security strategy. Within the H.U.M.O.R. Matrix, we can also apply policy requirements. In Chapters 7–11, we go into details for each requirement in the H.U.M.O.R. Matrix. Different policy matters have to be addressed for each requirement. Table 6-1 lists the key aspects of social media policy to be captured.

H.U.M.O.R. Requirement	Policy Component
Human Resources	▸ Disseminate policy in an understandable format that is available to all employees throughout the company.
	▸ Disseminate a public version of applicable policy requirements for employees and customers.
	▸ Develop guidelines for using social media for business requirements.
	▸ Assure compliance with all legal and regulatory requirements.
	▸ Develop a clear response plan for incident management and public interaction.
	▸ Create policies for education and training.
	▸ Create policies for restricting access to company private information.
Utilization of Resources	▸ Create policy for clear usage of intellectual property by employees and the public.
	▸ Create guidelines for response to theft of intellectual property.
	▸ Create policy on writing content and plagiarism.
	▸ Develop processes for utilizing the correct technology resources for different social media activities.
	▸ Create policy for updating tools as capabilities change.
Monetary Spending	▸ Create policies for identifying business justifications for spending budget on social media activities.
	▸ Define budgets for education and training.
	▸ Develop process for identifying monetary damage through social media activities.
Operations Management	▸ Develop Operations guidelines for IT, Marketing, Legal, and HR, detailing the responsibilities of each department.
	▸ Define enforcement requirements and activities that will be taken by HR and IT.
	▸ Define the process for understanding what social media resources will be used and what impact the various cloud services will have on the business.
	▸ Create a password policy.
	▸ Develop processes for threat management.
Reputation Management	▸ Develop clear process for incident response management.
	▸ Identify policy for monitoring and reporting on both employees and customer/public social media activities that affect the company.
	▸ Develop processes for controlling reputation monitoring.

Table 6-1   *H.U.M.O.R. Matrix Policy Components*

Developing Your Social Media Security Policy

Once you have determined the key components of your social media security policy according to the H.U.M.O.R. Matrix, you have to actually write it. For each component of the matrix, we go through a number of steps in the following chapters to outline tactical implementation. The first step is to understand the risks your company faces. We discussed threat assessment in Chapter 4 and further in Chapter 5. This section of the book goes through the controls you need to implement with your policies. Your threat assessment should have identified the risks to your tools and the websites you use for social media activities. The intent is to identify risks to your social media activities, understand what could go wrong, and implement mitigating controls based on your documented policies.

The Policy Team

The Community Manager can take the lead in organizing the policy team, or the lead can default to the Human Resources department. Other interested parties may include Marketing, PR, Sales, Business Development, Legal, and Customer Service. This cross-functional team should review each operational aspect of your social media strategy, determine the best possible processes to achieve business goals, develop policies, implement the policies, and respond to the changing landscape. All policies should be flexible and be reviewed every six months due to the changing nature of social media environment. The lead should assign individual roles and responsibilities.

All changes must be made and approved by the policy team. The team will conduct periodic risk analysis to the related business processes that use social media, understand the technologies, and determine what operational changes must be made. The team will be responsible for disseminating the changes and ensuring the appropriate employees know what the policy requires. The policy team will be the liaison to other departments that are impacted by social media usage.

Determining Policy Response

Security monitoring of policy violations naturally requires technology managed by the IT department. Automated processes have to search for employee violations and customer and public interactions that impact the company brand over social media platforms. The policy team can determine what constitutes a violation and develop the associated appropriate responses in coordination with Human Resources. Different levels of risk can be addressed with varying levels of response. For example, Facebook does allow more information to be posted and an employee can easily and unknowingly install a malware Facebook application that's more dangerous than what you face from your typical Twitter usage, which doesn't impact network resources as much.

A response process must be in place for policy violations and related mechanisms must also be in place to actually monitor for violations. If you are looking for internal employee access, then data loss prevention tools are needed. If you are looking for external incidents, then you might need third-party monitoring services such as ReputationDefender.com. You may assign risk levels to different social media activities and apply appropriate resources based on risk to the organization. Once a violation occurs, a clear process needs to be in place to notify the right resources for a response. A fast response is vital, precisely because the real-time, instantaneous nature of social platforms accelerates the speed at which events get passed along and become viral. A plan identifies possible areas for error, minimizes risks, and provides mitigation guidelines all teams can follow on a 24×7 basis.

The level of authority that response teams have has to be defined. Like your disaster recovery plan, you should test your social media response plan for possible attack scenarios. Possible decisions when addressing violations may include:

- Identifying the issue at hand
- Responding to media inquiries
- Acknowledging the problem and responding to mentions in a timely, courteous, and professional manner on relevant blogs, microblogs, and social networks, particularly when posted by influencers
- Determining employee culpability, if any
- Implementing changes to prevent continued use of the access violation
- Isolating the technology (if any) that have been compromised
- Contacting websites that may be involved
- Recording evidence and logging a timeline of events and remediation steps taken
- Contacting the appropriate public agencies if necessary
- Notifying internal executives and legal counsel

A Sample Social Media Security Policy

Each policy varies depending on company size, industry, regulatory requirements, corporate culture, and level of engagement with customers and the public. Some companies might be more concerned with brand awareness whereas others are more concerned with sales activities. If you are a smaller company, you might not be able to field a cross-functional team from Legal, HR, Marketing, Sales, Customer Service, and IT to manage your social media security tactics: it might all fall on Marketing and IT or perhaps just Marketing. This would dictate a number of different policy requirements. But every company still needs a policy in place if it is to engage with the public in a manner that includes risk reduction tactics.

Here is a basic outline you can follow to develop your own social media security policy.

Social Media Policy Outline

1. Introduction
    i. What is this policy all about?
    a. Policy Management
    ii. Company rights to change and update this policy
    b. Effective Date
    c. Goals
        i. What are the goals of this policy (set guidelines, determine responsibilities, manage reputation, etc.)
    d. Purpose
        i. What is the purpose of this document and who does it apply to?
    e. Scope
        i. What is the applicability to the policy to technologies and employees, contractors and partners, etc.?
    f. Policy Owners
        i. Who manages this policy?

2. How Social Media Is Used

   a. Social Media Channels (Facebook, Flickr, LinkedIn, Twitter, YouTube, GoWalla, Foursquare, etc.)

   b. Social Media Benefits (marketing, sales, customer service, new product development, customer feedback, access to media, partnerships, communications, cost reductions, etc.)

   c. Community Manager Objectives

      i. Who is the Community Manager?

      ii. What is the Community Manager's role?

   d. IT Security Department Responsibilities

      i. Define role of IT Security.

      ii. Identify processes to authenticate and authorize each social media platform.

      iii. Define implementation responsibilities.

      iv. Define reporting responsibilities.

      v. Define monitoring responsibilities.

   e. Marketing Department Responsibilities

      i. Define role of IT Security to assist the Marketing department in conducting their responsibilities in a secure manner

   f. Human Resources Responsibilities

      i. Define role of IT Security to assist the HR department in conducting their responsibilities in a secure manner

   g. Legal Department Responsibilities

      i. Define role of IT Security to assist the Legal department in conducting their responsibilities in a secure manner

3. Social Media General Policies

   a. Advertising

   b. Regulatory Requirements

   c. Community Management

   d. Confidentiality

      i. What information can be shared?

   e. Disclosures

      i. What must employees disclose when using social media and what must they not disclose?

   f. Legal Issues

      i. What legal restrictions must be applied to social media usage?

   g. Level of Engagement

      i. What are the expectations of engaging with the community and what internal and external resources are required?

   h. Managing Friends of the Company

      i. Understand the dangers and opportunities posed by Friends and review endorsements, profile information that is linked and shared, and manage trust.

   i. How to Handle Negative Comments

   j. Press Inquiries

      i. Define responsibilities for dealing with the press.

   k. Third-party Employees

      i. Identify process for managing third-party relationships

   l. Restrictions on Trademarks and Intellectual Property

      i. How are trademarks, copyrights, and IP managed?

4. IT Security Policies

   a. The purpose of these policies is to establish the technical guidelines for IT security and to communicate the controls necessary for a secure network infrastructure. The network security policy will provide the practical mechanisms to support the company's comprehensive set of security policies. This policy purposely avoids being overly specific in order to provide some latitude in implementation and management strategies.

   b. Social Media Sites Authentication

      i. Define complexity of passwords for all in-house hosted application and third-party hosted social media applications.

         1. Password Construction
            The following statements apply to the construction of passwords for network devices: Eight characters, with a mix of letters, numbers, and special characters (such as punctuation marks and symbols).

Passwords should not be comprised of, or otherwise utilize, words that can be found in a dictionary, should not include "guessable" data such as personal information like birthdays, addresses, phone numbers, locations, etc.

2. **Change Requirements**
Passwords must be changed according to the company's Password Policy. Identity requirements that apply to changing network device passwords.

3. **Password Policy Enforcement**
Where passwords are used an application must be implemented that enforces the company's password policies on construction, changes, reuse, lockout, etc.

4. **Administrative Password Guidelines**
As a general rule, administrative access to systems should be limited to only those who have a legitimate business need for this type of access.

c. **In-House Deployed Social Media Applications**

i. **Failed Logons**
Repeated logon failures can indicate an attempt to "crack" a password and surreptitiously access a network account. In order to guard against password-guessing and brute-force attempts, the company must lock a user's account after five unsuccessful logins.

ii. **Logging**
Logging needs vary depending on the type of network system and the type of data the system holds. The following sections detail the company's requirements for logging and log review.

1. **Application Servers**
Logs from application servers are of interest since these servers often allow connections from a large number of internal and/or external sources. At a minimum, logging of errors, faults, and login failures is required.

2. **Network Devices**
Logs from network devices protecting the application servers are of interest since these devices control all network traffic, and can have a huge impact on the company's security. At a minimum, logging of errors, faults, and login failures is required.

iii. Log Management

    1. Log Review
Log management applications can assist in highlighting important events, however, a member of the company's IT team should still review the logs as frequently as is reasonable.

    2. Log Retention
Logs should be retained in accordance with the company's Retention Policy.

iv. Intrusion Detection/Intrusion Prevention
The company requires the use of either an IDS or IPS on critical application servers.

v. Security Testing
Security testing, also known as a vulnerability assessment, a security audit, or penetration testing, is an important part of maintaining the company's network security.

    1. Internal security testing

    2. External security testing

vi. Social Media Application Documentation
Documentation, specifically as it relates to security, is important for efficient and successful application management.

vii. Antivirus/Antimalware

viii. All application servers and end-user systems that connect to the application servers should have antivirus/antimalware software running.

ix. Software Use Policy

    1. Software applications can create risk in a number of ways and thus certain aspects of software use must be covered by this policy.

    2. All downloadable social media end-user software and applications for desktop, laptops, and mobile devices should be approved by IT Management.

x. Suspected Security Incidents

    1. When a security incident is suspected that may impact a network device, the IT Staff should refer to the company's Incident Response policy for guidance.

    d. Third-party Hosted Applications

        i. Service level agreement
Review all service level agreements with sites and application providers.

        ii. Updates
Upgrades must be in place for updates, upgrades, and hotfixes to address security concerns

        iii. Testing

            1. Third-parties must provide proof of security testing of their applications or allow the company to test the application for security weaknesses.

            2. Third-parties must provide proof of security infrastructure and policies that maintain a secure environment for customer data.

    e. Education and Training

        i. IT Security is responsible for training end users on security requirements for all hardware and software resources.

        ii. HR is responsible for policy and process training.

        iii. Hold a yearly training program and ongoing updates to alerts users of new risks and security measures.

5. Social Media Do's and Don'ts

    a. What are the major Do's and Don'ts?

    b. Social Media Do's

        i. Add value, promote the company in a positive light, educate, be a brand ambassador, respond to customers, engage in conversations, be a knowledge resource, build relationships, know the restrictions on content, understand the risks of the mediums, check all facts, provide disclaimers, gain feedback, check regulatory risk, understand legal ramifications, secure communications, secure and protect customer information, understand privacy requirements, etc.

    c. Social Media Don'ts

        i. Discuss confidential information, share private customer information, share derogatory comments, access unsecured or unencrypted channels, discuss customer activity, post internal information, associate personal life with corporate accounts, disparage competitors, disparage partners, be condescending or patronizing, etc.

6. Brand Guideline Policy

    a. What is the brand policy and what are the guidelines for discussing and promoting the brand?

7. Twitter Usage Policy

    a. Identify what Twitter should be used for.
    b. Identify objectives (access, brand monitoring, identity management, research, customer communications, media coverage, etc.).
    c. Policy Team Ownership
    d. Identify who can source and publish tweets.
    e. Content Guidelines

        i. Identify content requirements such as frequency, context, content, tone, hashtag usage, followers, following, etc.

        ii. Link shortening policy

    f. Re-tweeting and Following

        i. Focus areas: research, partners, industry news, statistics, other relevant content

        ii. Research, partners, industry news, statistics, other relevant content

    g. Product-specific Accounts Management

        i. Link accounts to products

        ii. Monitor specific accounts

8. Facebook Usage Policy

    a. Identify what Facebook should be used for.
    b. Identify objectives (brand monitoring, marketing, community engagement, partnership development, lead generation, etc.).
    c. Policy Team Ownership
    d. Identify who can use Facebook and post from company accounts.
    e. Content Guidelines

        i. What content is applicable and allowed?

        ii. Content types and sources (such as events, news, surveys, photos, etc.)

        iii. Tone of community engagement and interaction (personal, corporate, friendly, professional)

        iv. Online contest general guidelines from a security perspective

9. Company Blogging Policy

   a. Define the purpose of corporate blogging
   b. Objectives
   c. Policy Team Ownership
   d. Identify who is responsible for blogging
   e. Content Guidelines

      i. Define what content is allowed in blogs

      ii. Identify video policy for blogs

10. Personal Blogging Policy

    a. Identify how employees are allowed to use company information in personal blogs and social network posts, and when and where personal blogs can be accessed.

       i. What are the limitations?

       ii. What corporate IP can be used?

       iii. What can be said about company products and services?

       iv. Identify relevant Human Resources policies that restrict employee dissemination of company information in any form.

       v. What company confidential or other information can be posted?

    b. Approval process
    c. Disclaimer

       i. What disclaimers must employees use?

    d. Disclosure

       i. What must employees disclose and not disclose on their blogs?

    e. Endorsements

11. Employee Code of Conduct Policy

    a. Reference Human Resources handbook on code of conduct.
    b. Do not damage the company reputation.
    c. Use of inappropriate comments.

Wrap Up

Your Social Media Policy is the foundation of your operations and procedures. Constructing it is challenging, as it has to take into account new functions that many companies have not had to deal with before and has to be constantly updated. Also, departments must collaborate in ways they haven't done previously. To develop a comprehensive policy, you have to address all the major aspects of the H.U.M.O.R. Matrix. A key driver is how the different departments work together daily to achieve a baseline level of secure operations.

Improvement Checklist

☐ Is there ongoing communications and collaboration across departments?

☐ Have you defined specific policies for internally hosted applications versus externally hosted applications?

☐ Are you managing the policy on a constant basis?

☐ Did you create a new role for the Community Manager?

Human Resources: Strategy & Collaboration

W hether employees use social media platforms for personal or professional reasons, or both, the key value of social media usage is that humans are communicating with and paying attention to each other. But who's looking out for the affects social media communications can have on the company? From an organization's perspective, securing social media starts with a closer look at the human resource strategy for employee communications and collaboration using these new media tools and technologies. Human Resources manages this overall strategy for the organization, along with driving and enforcing the social media security policy with the assistance of the IT department.

The first step to securing social media is to create the social media policies, as outlined in the previous chapter. In this chapter, we review the next step: the critical role Human Resources has to play in securing social media. A human resource strategy is essential to creating procedures needed to link social media policy to existing business processes across departments, including Information Technology, Customer Service, Product Development, Legal, and Marketing. Unifying your security practices with other departments requires creating a chain of custody for remediating policy violations.

The social media policy addresses two types of employees: the Community Manager—whose job it is to participate actively on a daily basis on social networks by listening to and engaging with customers, clients, and consumers in general—and the remaining employees—who primarily use social media for personal reasons or with specific professional objectives, such as one-to-one business sales, or who should not be allowed to use social media at work but still participate. Human Resources (HR) should play a key role in identifying or recruiting personnel for the Community Manager position. HR also ensures that all existing employees and new hires have signed onto and are kept up to date with the company's evolving social media policies, by implementing social media monitoring practices and controls in conjunction with the IT and Legal departments. Human Resources is also responsible for keeping a chain of custody, cataloguing policy violations for immediate remediation when necessary.

This chapter discusses the key challenges Human Resources needs to address:

▶ Identifying the necessary business processes, regulations, and legal restrictions regarding social media usage.

▶ Defining and implementing the role of the Community Manager and enabling coordination across departments.

▶ Training the Community Manager and employees in appropriate social media usage.

We also examine the Community Manager's role in small, medium, and large companies.

Case Study: "Expensive Paperweight" Gets Fired

In April 2010, an employee of the Social Development Ministry Authority of Auckland (New Zealand) was sacked for posting on her Facebook account, referring to herself as a "very expensive paperweight," "highly competent in the art of time wastage, blame-shifting and stationary [sic] theft."[1] Her favorite Facebook post was "hey boss, can I go home sick???" The Employment Relations Authority in Auckland did not uphold a complaint from the employee that she was unfairly dismissed. Understandably, the employer had lost trust and confidence in her. Another Authority member said the employee's online comments "endorsed a stereotyped view of slothful and exploitative public servants."

Although postings alone do not automatically justify a firing, the employee's other past actions combined with the postings to get her fired. The employer was able to add the posting comments to her file and justify termination.

Unfortunately, we don't know what the Ministry did in terms of training employees regarding the proper use of social media. It is interesting to note that the employee had posted on several occasions that she wanted to go home sick. What we know the Ministry did correctly was to gather data about what was being said about the organization in public spaces. We aren't sure how long it took for the Ministry to find this post, but they are addressing the fact that attacks can come from outside the corporate firewall from areas like Facebook that are really not under organizational control.

What did the Ministry do wrong in previous cases? Was she reprimanded for her previous posts? Did the Ministry even know what she was posting up to this point? In current firings due to social media use, no mention is usually made of prior incidents, so we don't know if the employee received a warning or referral to policies or in-house social media training courses. Not having these policies and trainings in place could lead to unjustified firings. Many companies do have a policy on what it takes to get fired. But these policies are usually somewhat vague and open to interpretation, which is why there are so many lawsuits. With social media postings, the reasons for being fired can become even vaguer. We will see how this develops over the next year.

---

[1] Victoria Robinson, "'Expensive Paperweight' Fired After Facebook Posts," Stuff.co.nz Dominion Post (December 20, 2010), http://www.stuff.co.nz/national/4472229/Expensive-paperweight-fired-after-Facebook-posts.

How Is JAG Doing?

Our company JAG has gone through a process to access how the company is using social media. As a small and medium business (SMB), JAG realizes it needs to implement changes; however, resources are resources. But no matter what size the company, legal and human resource controls are a necessity. Let's take a look at the changes JAG has implemented since they did their self-assessment in Chapter 2. In the current state column, we can see tactics JAG has implemented to move the environment to an "Average" or "Best practices" stance from an initial "Poor" rating as shown in the table below.

HUMAN RESOURCES	Current State 1 – Poor 2 – Average 3 – Best practices
Human Resource Policy	
Specific social media security policy	2 – JAG has written a social media policy that will be disseminated by HR.
Social media conduct defined by HR	2 – Within the policy, HR has defined boundaries for social media usage.
Capabilities of HR to manage social media	2 – JAG is not large enough to have a dedicated Community Manager, but HR and Marketing will share these duties.
HR's dissemination capabilities	2 – JAG has made the policy available on their Intranet.
Capability to engage employees through policies and processes	2 – A yearly training program has been put in place.
Capability of HR to manage training	2 – A yearly training program has been put in place.
Capability of HR to communicate policies	2 – HR uses the company Intranet and e-mail to update employees on social media policies and risks.
Capability of HR to respond to social media breach	2 – HR has a basic incident response process as part of the social media policy.

HUMAN RESOURCES	Current State 1 – Poor 2 – Average 3 – Best practices
IT Security Policy	
Applicability of social media policies	2 – The IT security policy now refers to and integrated with the social media policy.
Social media security technology defined in IT policies	2 – IT operational policies have put specific actions in place to monitor social media security risks.
Capability to respond to social media breach	2 – IT has put processes in place for social media monitoring, including tools such as Social Mention and Radian6.
Training Regimen	
Training for employees on social media usage	2 – Employees will now participate in yearly training and receive online and e-mail alerts on social media risks and updates to policies.
Training for employees on social media security issues	2 – Employees will now participate in yearly training and receive online and e-mail alerts on social media risks.

Identifying Business Processes, Regulations, and Legal Requirements

Each part of the social media security policy must be managed through training, implementation, and monitoring. As the policy itself contains high-level descriptions of expected behavior, which are sometimes translated into friendly guidelines, the company must be able to track and measure the effectiveness of the policy, compliance with legal regulations, and compliance with the policy, which can be used as a key performance indicator; adapt the policy to changing conditions; and establish a chain of custody in problematic cases. Let's say your company accepts and keeps credit card information, your company must comply with the regulatory requirements of the Payment Card Industry (PCI) 2.0 (https://www.pcisecuritystandards.org/). The PCI standards contain a component that applies to employee training if your social media activities impact customers' personal information:

▶ *12.6: Implement a formal security awareness program to make all personnel aware of the importance of cardholder data security.*

▶ *12.6.a: Verify the existence of a formal security awareness program for all personnel.*

▶ *12.6.b: Obtain and examine security awareness program procedures and documentation and perform the following:*

   ▶ *12.6.1: Educate personnel upon hire and at least annually. Note: Methods can vary depending on the role of the personnel and their level of access to the cardholder data.*

   ▶ *12.6.1.a: Verify that the security awareness program provides multiple methods of communicating awareness and educating personnel (for example, posters, letters, memos, web based training, meetings, and promotions).*

   ▶ *12.6.1.b: Verify that personnel attend awareness training upon hire and at least annually.*

   ▶ *12.6.2: Require personnel to acknowledge at least annually that they have read and understood the security policy and procedures.*

▶ *12.6.3: Verify that the security awareness program requires personnel to acknowledge, in writing or electronically, at least annually that they have read and understand the information security policy.*

Another example of regulations that have training components is the Massachusetts 201 CMR 17.00: Standards for the Protection of Personal Information of Residents of the Commonwealth:

▶ *17.03: Duty to Protect and Standards for Protecting Personal Information*

   ▶ *(b) Identifying and assessing reasonably foreseeable internal and external risks to the security, confidentiality, and/or integrity of any electronic, paper or other records containing personal information, and evaluating and improving, where necessary, the effectiveness of the current safeguards for limiting such risks, including but not limited to:*

      ▶ *ongoing employee (including temporary and contract employee) training;*

      ▶ *employee compliance with policies and procedures;*

▶ *17.04: Computer System Security Requirements*

   ▶ *(8) Education and training of employees on the proper use of the computer security system and the importance of personal information security.*

Sharing customer data or discussing customer information in social media posts is very easy. These rules are an attempt to restrict data from being shared inappropriately.

A wide range of possible online interactions can affect separate company departments. An employee may post a great new product idea for an existing brand, or a customer may post a video or tweet (as in the case of Kevin Smith on Southwest Airlines) about an unhappy customer service experience; an employee in a publicly traded company may post content that breaks legal compliance in heavily regulated industries, such as posts about adverse effects from pharmaceutical drugs; and a customer may express her delight with her favorite brand. Each one of these social media mentions merits further follow up within the company to address the issue in question or to research and seize new potential opportunities and to educate employees about which posts are allowed and which are inappropriate or potentially firing offenses.

Companies generally have established business processes for all job functions, and processes for dealing with customer service complaints and reparations or new business development most likely already exist in the company. If not, processes must be developed. For example, perhaps you need a policy to respond to delighted customers with special treatment (e.g., bell ringer) or to include online mentions in regulatory compliance reporting and resolution. In the case of customer promotions, Federal Trade Commission (FTC) regulations concerning blogger disclosure rules must be observed.

In 2010, the FTC (www.ftc.gov) investigated Ann Taylor for providing bloggers of a marketing event with gifts.[2] The investigation was launched after Ann Taylor's LOFT division held a January 2010 "exclusive blogger preview," and the company promised that "bloggers who attend will receive a special gift, and those who post coverage from the event will be entered in a mystery gift card drawing where you can win up to $500 at LOFT!" The size of the gifts was not the problem; it was the disclosure in the blog articles that Ann Taylor paid the bloggers in gifts. The FTC's first investigation was based on its "Guides Concerning the Use of Endorsements and Testimonials in Advertising" (otherwise known as the "Guides"), which cover promoting products and services. The end result was that Ann Taylor was not fined. Although the FTC proved very lenient in this case, they took a first step in managing the social media space. Ann Taylor has since developed a policy of disclosure of all gifts to bloggers. The FTC has powers to regulate "unfair or deceptive acts or practices in or affecting commerce," including the power to issue regulations, conduct investigations, and bring enforcement actions seeking injunctive relief and civil penalties (see 15 U.S.C. §45). Basically, Ann Taylor needed to clearly define a line between marketing and endorsements. Not to mention, the company should have a

---

[2] Natalie Zmuda, "Ann Taylor Investigations Shows FTC Keeping Close Eye on Blogging," *Advertising Age* (April 28, 2010), http://adage.com/article?article_id=143567.

defined policy regarding how it uses social media. Legal and Human Resources departments should own this policy.

Once the business processes have been mapped out and developed, the Human Resource department should provide training for all employees on how to comply with the expected regulations to ensure a consistent approach to its operating procedures across all business lines. First, however, let's look more closely at new and evolving role in companies: The Community Manager.

The Community Manager: Defining and Implementing

The Community Manager is a new type of position that ties a company to its community of consumers and fans. Human resources should work with Marketing to develop this new job function and define its responsibilities. The role lies at the intersection of the community and the company, sometimes sitting in between the proverbial rock and a hard place. In other words, the Community Manager has the vital function of listening to the community and bringing messages back to the company—with the objective that the company will note and deal with the issues brought to light in these messages as well as responding to and engaging with the community according to the company's strategic objectives.

To carry out their responsibilities effectively, community managers must possess or acquire certain competencies, including good interpersonal skills, technological proficiency, and business acumen. First, the person involved in this role must be willing—and preferably enjoy—meeting, discussing, and creating relationships with strangers online. To do so, they must be able to identify who they are communicating with and be able to respond appropriately, taking care not to appear condescending or patronizing. Since people online come from all walks of life and educational backgrounds, the Community Manager must be able to moderate language to engage at all levels, while adhering to company values and principles.

Second, the Community Manager must embrace technology. We have already mentioned Dell's active engagement with social media. Dell has two key social media job functions: Social Media Listening & Engagement Operations Sr. Manager and VP Social Media & Communities. More than 5,000 employees have been trained in social media and actively participate in building communities. These roles have built processes and training practices that require more than implementing new technologies. While social media tools are becoming increasingly easy and intuitive to use, there are still a number of challenges that tools alone cannot solve. For one, Community Managers must not be allergic to listening to, evaluating, and responding to mentions! Not all Marketing employees want to interact with the general public and so might not be suitable for this role. Furthermore, there are always certain technical elements involved in posting to a blog, creating and maintaining profiles on social networks, and particularly in creating, posting, and embedding photographs and video and audio podcasts. Before hiring your Community Manager, make sure he or she has a following, has built communities, and has references from public social media communities.

Community management really involves the use of online, desktop, and mobile platforms, tools, and applications, provided by the social networks themselves or by third parties, for the ongoing management of social media communications and relationships. Your Community Manager must be as involved with delivering training for employees as in monitoring your Twitter stream in MentionMap from Asterisq.com (http://apps.asterisq.com/mentionmap/#user-mentionmap), as shown in Figure 7-1, or using other tools. The proper and secure use of these tools requires a modicum of technical proficiency that can be easily learned, but that requires an important natural curiosity on the Community Manager's part.

The Community Manager should work with IT to identify and recommend required applications for the job, including tools for monitoring social media mentions and activity, for internal collaboration and reporting, and for external communications across platforms. Depending on the need, such tools may be available for free or on a subscription basis; they may be available as cloud-based services or for self-hosting; and they may be built using open-source or proprietary

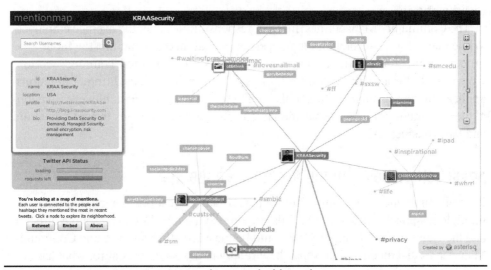

Figure 7-1   *MentionMap Twitter visualization dashboard*

technologies. Each of these configurations or combinations will pose additional social media security considerations and training.

For example, when using self-hosted systems, like a Drupal community website or a WordPress blog, you need to check regularly for the latest updates to the core and to install plug-ins and modules. These updates may not be immediately apparent when opening the dashboard for daily use, however, and users must be trained to check specific screens regularly on the dashboard. You can subscribe to mailing lists maintained by the community and containing news and updates regarding security vulnerabilities and patches. On cloud-base systems, the service provider maintains software security centrally, such as with Twitter and Facebook. Because of the vast populations of people using these platforms, security is about maintaining the integrity of passwords and observing safe practices, rather than about installing security patches. It is also advisable to devise backup systems in all cases to preserve a history of published materials, interactions, and activity on these networks. These security and backup practices are specific to each tool and platform that the Community Manager is required to use. These tools and platforms are continually evolving with new features, even as the Community Manager's tech skills and familiarity with the tools increase naturally through regular use and practice.

Finally, the Community Manager must be aware of the organization's business objectives when developing and communicating with the community. Even though friendly relationships should be built over time and the communication may be genial, business imperatives must be kept in mind to better focus the efforts and resources allocated to social media, according to predetermined objectives and security priorities.

The Community Manager has different responsibilities than the average employee. While many companies let all employees use social media—and most without proper training—the actually job responsibilities differ. In the "Training" section, we will walk through the various roles to see how each requires different functional applications to use social media tools on a day-to-day basis. First, however, we look at the Community Manager role and Human Resource challenges in small, medium, and large businesses.

Small Companies' Human Resource Challenges

In small companies, the Community Manager may be just one person juggling multiple responsibilities at work. This person may be the Human Resource director and the Community Manager. Or it could be the Marketing director and Community Manager. Social media policies may be virtually nonexistent, except for what has been applied through common sense and through personal learning. Small businesses often turn to continuing education classes and workshops about social media, online or at local colleges and universities. Often, the local chapters of marketing and PR associations, such as the Public Relations Society of America (PRSA), American Marketing Association (AMA), the SMC Social Media Club (SMC), and the Chamber of Commerce, offer monthly meetups and workshops to provide guidance on social media best practices, ethics, and case studies. Also, these trade associations may connect small businesses with social media practitioners for further training and consulting. But the small business still needs a written social media policy.

Social media security might be delegated to the providers of applications and social platforms, such as relying on Facebook security or Google to protect your GoogleDocs and Gmail. But many companies that rely heavily on these social media platforms for business have the ability to do self-hosting, which can be a more secure practice, for instance, for a company blog.

In general, secure social media practices for small business involve:

▶ Hosting applications on the company's hosting provider whenever possible and affordable; in many cases, using cloud-based applications may make more financial sense.

▶ Creating secure passwords on an individual basis.

▶ Distributing passwords securely among company principals for communications continuity in case of emergencies and unplanned absences.

▶ Identifying people in the community who act as influencers, whether positively or negatively.

▶ Keeping up to date on security flaws as well as on innovations highlighted by leading technical and social media blogs, including TechCrunch.com and Mashable.com. Each individual application you use will have security issues that you need to follow up on and be aware of when things happen.

▶ Researching each cloud platform being used and determining what security restrictions can be put in place in a hosted application. For example, every manager should know how to access and modify the Facebook Privacy settings, as shown in Figure 7-2. By the time this book comes out, we are sure these will have changed—yet again.

NOTE

Follow Bob Lord on Twitter for Twitter security-specific information (http://twitter.com/boblord).

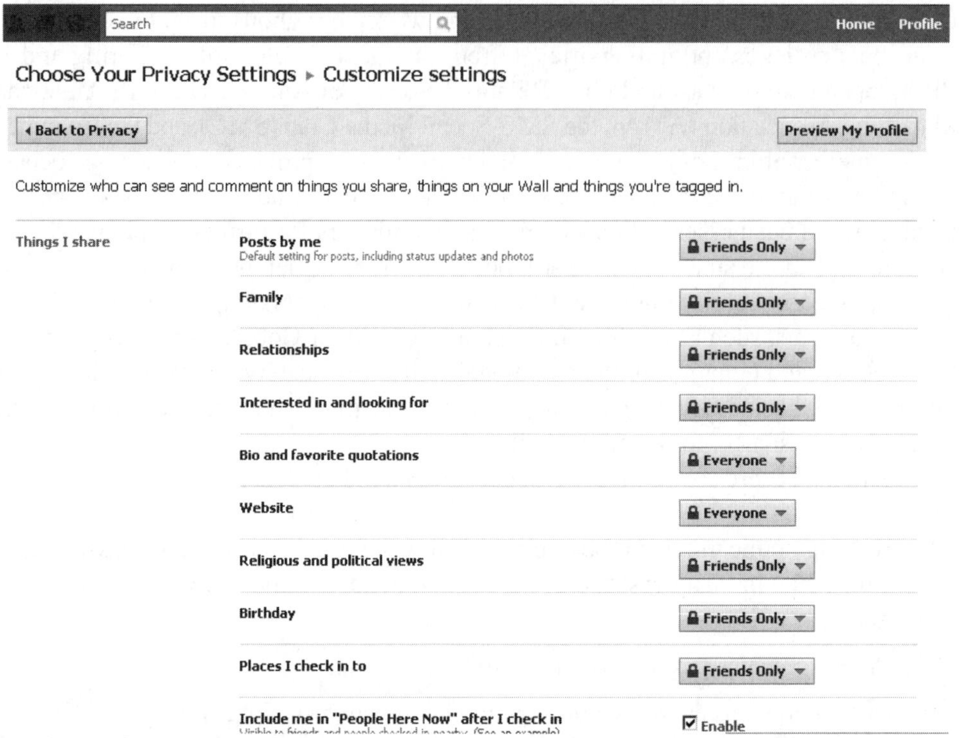

Figure 7-2   *Facebook Privacy Settings*

Medium-Sized Companies' Human Resource Challenges

At medium-sized companies, the Community Manger may be a handful of people across company functions, collaborating with each other through the use of internal tools such as wikis, social media monitoring applications, and group publishing applications, including CoTweet for Twitter. In a medium-sized company, Human Resources is usually a stand-alone department that can work with Marketing and IT on social media policy problems.

Sometimes, Community Managers are identified from the larger online community of customers and fans. Some people are naturally inclined and very familiar with their favorite brands and would jump at the opportunity to participate in social media on behalf of these brands whether they are remunerated or not. Otherwise, social media interactions can be delegated to employees who have been identified as having natural community management skills, as described earlier in this chapter, and are excited about the opportunity.

In addition to the tactics taken by a small business, a medium business may want to adhere to some additional security principles:

▶ Hosting applications on company servers to the extent possible. Some applications are only available on the cloud.

▶ Limiting access to applications to authorized Community Managers and assigning secure passwords on an individual basis and changing passwords periodically.

▶ Holding regular weekly or biweekly meetings to discuss the challenges and opportunities found online.

▶ Keeping administrative-level passwords for high-level access when necessary.

▶ Identifying key influencers, customers, and clients in the community, through a social media customer relationship system (Social CRM) that may be added on to a company's existing CRM system.

▶ Communicating through internal enterprise-wide collaboration tools, including a wiki, such as SocialText.com, or instant messaging and social networking applications, such as Yammer.com.

▶ Keeping up to date on security patches for open-source and proprietary technologies, such as WordPress, Drupal, and other types of self-hosted websites. If you host your own WordPress blog, you will have to keep it updated in much the same way you have to keep your Windows operating system updated with patches. Figure 7-3 shows an example of having to patch your WordPress application manually.

▶ Keeping up to date on security flaws as well as on innovations highlighted by leading technical and social media blogs, including TechCrunch.com and Mashable.com.

Large Companies' Human Resource Challenges

At larger organizations, the role of Community Manager may actually evolve into a dedicated team of up to a few dozen people to up to several thousand brand ambassadors using different levels of social media administration privileges, depending on the nature of the industry, with dedicated technical resources and, in some instances, dedicated areas and hardware. In a large company, Community Managers are generally recruited specifically for the job and work in their own hierarchy, even as they interface with all parts of the company. The heads of the community management team wield increasing influence in the company and may, in some cases, rise to the C-level, on a par with the CMO, CTO, CLO, and others.

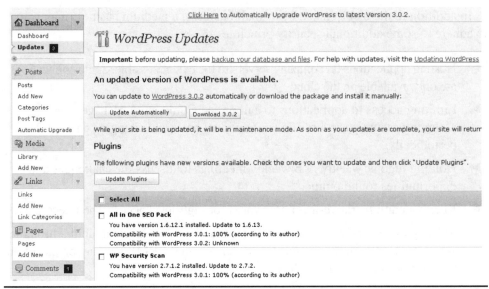

Figure 7-3 *WordPress manual security updates*

Community management is becoming a truly cross-functional occupation within more companies, as they learn to deal with issues ranging from information security policies, monitoring and reporting, marketing campaign management, sales promotions, customer (dis)satisfaction, legal issues, product development ideas and opportunities, competitive tracking, and shareholder and investor relations. As we discussed in Chapter 6, Human Resources can push out a complete social media policy and utilize the Community Manager to manage that policy and get corporate buy-in.

In some cases, large teams of people are assigned with community management roles in addition to their current job responsibilities. For example, at Microsoft and at Intel, identified engineers are trained and encouraged to create and maintain their own blogs in which they identify themselves as employees and engage their respective followers on more technical issues. Although they do not share company confidential information and are not official spokespeople for companywide issues, they help to humanize the organization and to move the conversation about product ideas and innovations forward.

In leading-edge social media management, dedicated teams are allocated specific areas and hardware within company headquarters to carry out their daily responsibilities, which includes managing or coordinating social media efforts across company divisions in other parts of the world. A leading example is Gatorade's "Mission Control" room (Figure 7-4)—an area filled with flat-screen monitors where Community

Figure 7-4   *Gatorade's Mission Control for social media*

Managers observe what people are saying about the brand across all social media sites and where they engage with consumers.

At Gatorade, a team of four full-time staffers works at the center in collaboration with the company's PR and Marketing agencies. Mentions of Gatorade, competitors, and related topics, such as "sports" and "hydration," are monitored on Facebook, Twitter, and around the Web on blogs and other sites, as shown in Figure 7-5. The Mission Control operation has engaged in thousands of one-on-one conversations with people online, helping the brand to shape the conversation around sports performance, rather than just hydration.

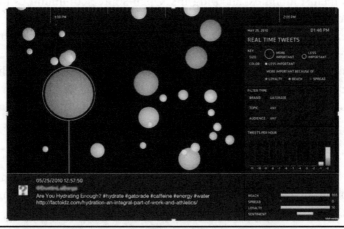

Figure 7-5   *Dashboard featuring mentions of Gatorade on Twitter*

Security issues are multiplied with each new area of participation by the community management team, and best practices for large organizations, in addition to those listed in the previous sections, include:

► Developing applications and mashups when appropriate, oftentimes applying for and using the Application Programming Interface (APIs) provided by social media platforms and mobile platforms.

► Creating and hosting a secure social network for the community based on the company's products and services. For example, the Nike Plus Running Community or the ad-hoc physician communities organized by pharmaceutical companies. Often, these communities involve mobile and/or geolocation features.

► Creating and hosting limited marketing micro-sites to support campaigns for specific promotions or product launches.

► Assigning limited administrative roles to Community Managers so they may better moderate and act as "superusers" with extended powers.

► Keeping "user 1" administrative-level passwords for high-level access when necessary.

► Communicating through internal enterprise-wide collaboration tools, including a wiki, such as SocialText.com, or instant messaging and social networking applications, such as Yammer.com. Sometimes, communication occurs through VoIP applications, in particular, the ever-growing Skype.

► Holding daily operational meetings to support company initiatives and marketing and communications objectives.

► Creating relationships with open-source communities and contributing new developments, modules, and plug-ins. Open-source communities maintain scores on reputation and are quick to respond with help to other community members known to have a history of helpful participation and contribution.

As you can see, the role of Human Resources, Marketing, and IT has changed when it comes to managing social media. These roles' key responsibilities are evolving to bridge the gaps between the Marketing, Information Technology, Human Resources, and Legal departments. The main functions we see today across these departments include:

► **Brand evangelist**   Promotes company in all social media platforms, utilizing the appropriate technologies and processes to get the message across.

► **Researcher**   Determines where the industry is going and finds the next great social media platforms.

▶ **Trainer**   Educates employees and customers when necessary, follows legal regulations and best practices, and ensures employee compliance to requirements

▶ **System administrator**   Manages technology in the social media space, defines requirements, implements, and monitors.

▶ **Content developer**   Manages company and community content about the company.

▶ **Strategist**   Develops new campaigns, decides on technologies to use, manages resources, and guides company restrictions on social media usage.

▶ **Solution provider**   Responds to company problems in social media discussions and provides answers.

▶ **Moderator**   Brings together different roles and smooths out conversations.

▶ **Social networkers**   Brings people into the company community.

▶ **Feedback expert**   Takes into account what the customers are saying and relays the challenges back to the correct departments within the company.

▶ **Policy manager**   Develops, promotes, and monitors social media policies and security policies, determines and manages policy violations, and responds quickly to threats due to social media usage.

Because of their daily work with social media platforms, tools, and applications, Community managers have additional security responsibilities, procedures to follow and maintain, and regular training to keep current. Their security responsibility bridges the human and technology elements. On the human side, they must adhere to commonsense interpersonal rules they would observe offline, while keeping the company's business and communications objectives and values in mind. On the technology side, they are responsible for keeping up to date with safe and secure practices related to the tools they are using and to distill these safe practices back to the organization in close coordination with the IT and Human Resources departments.

Training

One of the better training strategy implementations is employed at Intel. Bryan Rhoads, Senior Digital Strategist at Intel, has implemented a strategy that is based on the Intel Social Media Guidelines (http://www.intel.com/sites/sitewide/en_US/social-media.htm). He also provides training in how to use social media for business results and employees' responsible use of social media. Intel created the Social Media Center of Excellence, which is a diverse team of Legal, Marketing, PR, and Web Communications experts who together create training across social media platforms.

As opposed to employees who are specifically assigned community management responsibilities, other employees must follow another set of guidelines. Although similar in nature, standard employee guidelines differ with respect to how employees identify themselves when posting or responding to posts involving industry issues, how they report relevant social media mentions, and what they should do when social media mentions begin to escalate.

Generally, the company's Community Managers are an instrumental part of the cross-functional team that determines security policies, guidelines, processes, and training. Other members of the team determining training objectives would include the IT, Human Resources, Marketing, PR, Legal, and Customer Service departments, since most enterprise social media activity occurs within these areas.

It is important to note that social media platforms are subject to national jurisdiction regarding employment laws, even when dealing with large transnational platforms such as Facebook. For instance, in certain countries, Human Resources and company employees may not use a prospective candidate's social network profile as a reason to deny employment. In other countries, social network platforms are treated as public forums and employees have the same equal rights to free speech as they enjoy in offline physical spaces. In these cases, any company mentions made by employees to their friends during nonworking hours may not be admitted in a chain of custody case for termination.

Training Community Managers

Most likely, employees or community members identified and promoted or recruited for Community Manager–type positions will already possess the required interpersonal, technical, and business skills we discussed previously. More specific training and guidance is required, however, in the following areas:

▶ Defining communication principles, tone of voice, and personality, to fit with the online communities' changing moods, while simultaneously reflecting the company's overall marketing and communications objectives as well as with the company's brand values and culture

▶ Defining technologies to be used and associated security practices specific to each platform and application

▶ Determining reporting lines in case of emergencies or technical issues

▶ Defining business objectives and opening communication lines to key stakeholders in the company in each department for quick resolution to identified problems

▶ Creating business processes to remediate new problems and to seize new opportunities

▶ Codeveloping and refining security practices on an ongoing basis in coordination with the company's IT and Human Resources departments

Although the role of Community Manager is essentially the same across small, medium, and large companies, the way it is implemented varies widely, as discussed previously. For one, larger companies may have more at stake, particularly when they are publicly quoted and have corporate brands and reputations to maintain. Also, larger companies generally have greater resources to allocate to social media human and technology resources. Even though larger companies naturally have bigger budgets for social media community management, they can learn from the more hands-on approaches of small and medium companies, particularly with respect to community development at the local level.

The Community Manager has to interface with the IT department. The tools used by the Community Manager are implemented and maintained by IT. If these tools allow information to be sent out of the company, then data loss prevention technologies have to be in place to monitor what the Community Manager is actually doing with the information, what is being sent, and determining if it compromises confidential information. As we discussed, it's easy to break regulations if you do not understand what the restrictions are and most Community Managers are not as educated as IT security teams or Human Resources as to what data can be shared with the public and what might lead to a fine or investigation if a regulation is broken.

Training Employees

In contrast to Community Managers dedicated to advancing the company's objectives through social media platforms, employees generally use these same platforms for a mix of personal and professional reasons. Regardless of the purpose, they most likely connect personally and professionally with others online several times a week, if not several times a day.

On the personal side, most of your employees have probably joined Facebook, Twitter, Flickr, and other massive social networks to keep in touch with friends, family, and like-minded acquaintances. These interactions are generally meant for updating others about their daily life and may include the sharing of photos and articles of interest. Previously, some of this activity occurred through e-mail, but it has now migrated toward social networks. On the professional side, employees may be developing their own brand, so to speak, for enhancing their current jobs through new professional and sales contacts, developing new options for future advancement and employment, or staying abreast of industry trends in real-time. They may have joined LinkedIn with a summary of their professional history, both for identification by future employers, as well as to establish presence for current sales prospects and vendors. If they are in sales and marketing roles, they may be using the social aspects and applications included in business platforms such as Salesforce.com or on the sites of dedicated trade industry associations or networks.

Regardless of their personal or professional use of social media, noncommunity management employees must understand how their social media activity differs from that of the Community Manager and the process to follow after identifying issues that require the attention of the company's Community Manager. Particularly in cases in which an employee takes it upon her- or himself to respond directly to an issue on a social media site, the employee must understand what behavior is expected, how to identify her- or himself, and what not to do. As we stated in the policy template discussed in Chapter 6, employees should be educated about any restrictions on using the company name in posts, what can and cannot be disclosed, and what the consequences are for breaking that policy.

Employees should also be encouraged when positive results occur so you develop a culture of positive reinforcement versus negative reinforcement (which, in social media, poses far more of a long-term threat). Negative reinforcement begs rebellion in the enterprise social media space. How to handle positive versus negative posts is a critical area of social media security, as mishandled responses may escalate into larger security issues, even when done genuinely, authentically, and with the utmost sincerity. Often, unhappy customers should be dealt with individually by top-level management, while also keeping the larger community abreast of the issue and the company's response. A good example of a bad outcome was how Southwest Airlines treated actor/director Kevin Smith on a flight in 2010.[3] Mr. Smith was thrown off a plane for being too fat! He then proceeded to launch a Twitter "attack," or conversation, on the Southwest brand. His first Twitter message was simple enough but escalated quickly, as shown in his Tweets over the next day.

---

[3] Chris Lee, "Kevin Smith's Southwest Airlines Incident Sets Web all a-Twitter," *Los Angeles Times* (February 16, 2010), http://articles.latimes.com/2010/feb/16/entertainment/la-et-kevin-smith16-2010feb16; and Foster Kamer, "Update: The Kevin Smith Southwest Airlines Fat-Fight Tweakout of Epic Proportion," Gawker, http://gawker.com/5471463/update-the-kevin-smith-southwest-airlines-fat+flight-tweakout-of-epic-proportion.

Dear @SouthwestAir - I know I'm fat, but was Captain Leysath really justified in throwing me off a flight for which I was already seated?

Dear @SouthwestAir, I flew out in one seat, but right after issuing me a standby ticket, Oakland Southwest attendant Suzanne (wouldn't give..last name) told me Captain Leysath deemed me a "safety risk". Again: I'm way fat... But I'm not THERE just yet. But if I am, why wait til my..bag is up, and I'm seated WITH ARM RESTS DOWN. In front of a packed plane with a bunch of folks who'd already I.d.ed me as "Silent Bob."

Wanna tell me I'm too wide for the sky? Totally cool. But fair warning, folks: IF YOU LOOK LIKE ME, YOU MAY BE EJECTED FROM @SOUTHWESTAIR.

Hey @SouthwestAir! I've just recorded a Very Special Episode of SModcast - all for you. It goes live tomorrow night. http://www.smodcast.com.

So how did Southwest handle this "brand attack"? Southwest did respond with the following:

"I've read the Tweets all night from @thatkevinsmith – He'll be getting a call at home from our Customer Relations VP tonight.

@thatkevinsmith Again, I am very sorry for the experience you had tonight. Please let me know if there is anything else I can do.

"Mr. Smith originally purchased two Southwest seats on a flight from Oakland to Burbank—as he's been known to do when traveling on Southwest. He decided to change his plans and board an earlier flight to Burbank, which technically means flying standby. As you may know, airlines are not able to clear standby passengers until all Customers are boarded. When the time came to board Mr. Smith, we had only a single seat available for him to occupy. Our pilots are responsible for the Safety and comfort of all Customers on the aircraft and therefore, made the determination that Mr. Smith needed more than one seat to complete his flight. Our Employees explained why the decision was made, accommodated Mr. Smith on a later flight, and issued him a $100 Southwest travel voucher for his inconvenience."

But the damage had already been done. How would a $100 voucher actually make this alright? How was the employee who was handling the Southwest Twitter feed supposed to handle this without guidance? The employee who kicked Kevin Smith off the plane certainly didn't consider the social media storm that would follow, and not having a response in place shows a lack of social media policy development by the Human Resources department. They were following company guidelines. Employee education has to be a major part of human resource policies going forward, but the case can be made that, at a corporate level, the policy to remove people from the plane will always result in someone being offended. Changing that policy goes beyond the scope of what we are discussing here.

Because each company is different and employees jump between companies, a standard security training regimen should be in place. Many employees are not security inclined and are not aware of what a true risk is to the organization. With the rapid change in the security landscape with each new social media platform being launched, almost on a daily basis, no employee can keep up without help. All employees must assist the organization in protecting the security of information they disseminate in the social media space and know when there is a potential problem with how they're communicating, and be cognizant that they are part of the overall solution. Training can be done through web-based portals, webinars, posters, and reminders, monthly e-mails and more. But it has to be consistent and ongoing. Key aspects of employee training should include:

- ▶ Detecting and avoiding social engineering attacks
- ▶ Recognizing competitive intelligence probes from unknown "friends"
- ▶ Choosing strong passwords and changing them regularly
- ▶ Protecting sensitive information
- ▶ Implementing basic PC security
- ▶ Basic understanding of encrypted access to web sites
- ▶ Employing E-mail safeguards
- ▶ Recognizing and dealing with viruses, malware, and Trojans
- ▶ Reporting suspected security violations
- ▶ Reporting security vulnerabilities
- ▶ Recognizing the dangers of working on unsecure computers when visiting new social media sites
- ▶ Recognizing phishing and identity theft
- ▶ Understanding safe web surfing practices

- ▶ Understanding the risks of data leakage
- ▶ Understanding when they can get the company in trouble for regulatory noncompliance
- ▶ Understanding the dangers of sharing too much information over social networks
- ▶ Knowing software and copyright laws when posting information
- ▶ Understanding privacy concerns with their own data and customer data
- ▶ Encrypting data and data destruction
- ▶ Training on all aspects of the social media policy
- ▶ Knowing when and how to use the company name
- ▶ Knowing when to disclose information about themselves or the company

Once the social media policy has been developed and disseminated and employees have been trained, human resources has to work with IT Security to track violations and have a proper response ready when violations occur. Employees have to understand the ramifications of violating the policy and damaging the company brand or compromising customer data. The tools need to be in place for monitoring and reporting and knowing when to involve the Human Resources department for reprimand, termination, or prosecution.

Wrap Up

The Community Manager and the Human Resources department have to be the leaders in disseminating the company's social media policy. IT Security cannot enforce restrictions that have not been clearly defined by the community management team, Human Resources, Legal, and Marketing. IT's job is to implement the tools and techniques to make sure that employees follow the organization's requirements.

Improvement Checklist

- ☐ Have you mapped business processes to social media usage?
- ☐ Have you defined the Community Manager's or Marketing's responsibilities for managing social media and have you determined who manages what?
- ☐ Have you identified the tactics and procedures necessary based on how the company uses social media applications and websites?
- ☐ Are you providing social media training for employees?

Utilization of Resources: Strategy & Collaboration

D eploying resources and controls to protect the utilization of intellectual property and copyright is a huge challenge. How do you know if employees are sending out confidential information in blog posts or Twitter messages? Or, if you are Apple, how do you know if an employee has taken out the latest iPhone5 for a spin and started tweeting about the latest developments? Or maybe a nurse at your hospital, as in the case of HealthPark Medical Center, is sharing patient information on Facebook.

Companies have a hard time knowing about all the information being sent from their networks via communication channels such as e-mail or FTP or through web browsers. Add social media to the mix and it becomes an even greater challenge. Traditional security controls like firewalls and antivirus products are focused on data elements such as a SQL database or an important spreadsheet that contains customer information. These controls are easy to implement. Companies have also increased their monitoring and blocking capabilities with new technologies that can inspect every packet going into and out of the network. However, many Data Loss Prevention (DLP) tools, although available from companies such as McAfee, are not widely deployed. A new breed of products is coming on the market but we predict adoption will be slow as many companies still do not understand the risks of social media.

In our framework, Utilization of resources is about the implementation of secure social media capabilities and tactics across technologies and policies to protect intellectual property, copyrights, trademarks, and confidential data. The use of an organization's protected information on social media poses the additional challenges on which this chapter focuses. We'll look at the processes, tools, and tactics needed to prevent data from exiting your organization through social media channels.

In this chapter, we also cover the capabilities needed to secure your company's intellectual property. Many IT departments are not implementing the methods available for addressing social media concerns. We also discuss the relevant capabilities of the blocking, monitoring, and reporting tools that need to be in place.

Case Study: Inappropriate Tweets

With the right tools in place, you should be able to block, monitor, and report on social media usage. A complete process for managing social media tools should be in place for both the user of social media, such as the Marketing department, and those designated to secure social media usage, such as the IT department. Each group uses different tools. The lack of the right tools and, more importantly, the right processes can cause a lot of damage.

A good example of the lack of both tools and processes is an inappropriate tweet sent by a government employee. In March 2011, an employee of the Singapore government accidently sent a tweet using a curse word on the government's official Twitter account rather than the employee's own personal account.[1] The message said "F*** you lah, you same level as me can dont talk to me like tt?" Aside from the bad grammar and "lah" being part of the vocabulary, there seem to be numerous breakdowns in how the Singapore government handles social media.

What could technology have actually done in this case? In theory, a DLP solution could have blocked the foul language message from being sent out of the network. But if the employee accessed Twitter from a phone or at home, this technology resource would not have helped.

Next, reporting tools should have been put in place to monitor all activity related to government tweets for a faster response. How soon did the government respond? Did the government not know about the tweet until someone notified them?

From a process perspective, what restrictions were in place regarding who could access the Twitter account? Was an approval process used to determine who has access to the official account and were all tweets being sent out subject to a review process?

The process failed in several areas: there was no strict approval process for sending out data that represents the government; employees were not properly trained in appropriate etiquette; and the right tools were not in place to monitor and report on activity.

How Are Security Processes Handled?

The initial reaction of IT security is to block, block, and block some more. Blocking is a very limited capability in social media, especially if some people do and some people do not have access to certain social media websites in the organization. Implementing URL filtering technologies is easy, but that only controls employees in the workplace. What happens when they are on the road with their laptops and using a hotel's Wi-Fi to connect? What happens when they are at home? What happens when they use their company-provided, web-enabled smart phones?

---

[1] Jamie Yap, "Social Media Use Puts Business Reputation at Risk," ZDNet (March 2, 2011), http://www.zdnetasia.com/social-media-use-puts-business-reputation-at-risk-62207284.htm.

As we have mentioned, educating the user about what they put into the social media universe is part of securing that data. By combining user education about what data can be appropriately utilized (by not trampling on the rights of the actual data owner) with the right tools, IT departments can monitor and report on data usage and, in some cases, block unauthorized use. By implementing the appropriate tools, IT can execute policies that have been put in place without impeding the business use of social media platforms. For a large company, building a simple application that tracks web usage on all company-owned smartphones and laptops can be a simple solution to monitoring social media and other website usage without blocking. We'll cover monitoring and reporting in more depth in Part IV.

When tracking data across all platforms, patterns will emerge as companies gain more experience in implementing and using new monitoring technologies. Historically, IT has tracked employee usage and employee access to data with tools such as log management systems and Security Information Management (SIM) systems. Tracking how data is used should still be a priority; not only does it give you a historical perspective and help you to identify patterns, but also it leads to more efficient training and the deployment of more focused tools.

A number of security controls are available for understanding how social media is used, how it can be controlled, and how it can be monitored when employees, and even customers, are accessing different kinds of information. Our major concern here is, of course, intellectual property and copyrighted information.

Collaborating Securely

The first step in utilizing social media resources securely is to determine the best methods of collaborating over social media to conduct business. Traditional forms of communication are familiar to IT departments. When you check corporate e-mail today, you hopefully use encrypted tunnels such as VPN access or you access e-mail via websites over SSL. The channels for accessing corporate data are pretty well known. You can encrypt those channels (even if you choose not to). You can monitor data access with any of the hundreds of log management tools and block access with the many available intrusion detection programs. But social media has not matured yet in terms of having the necessary tools for security. New forms of collaboration include shared online workspaces such as internal wiki pages or shared forums for discussing projects. You have to utilize the tools you have today for IT security and implement the right processes to determine what processes should be modified to better track social media technologies. You can encrypt all communication to internal social media platforms such as wiki access, but you have less control when your company uses third-party social media sites such as Facebook Fanpages to share information or LinkedIn groups to form discussion sessions.

Many companies give their users rights to install software on their computers. But users can install a Trojan or malware using social media applications like Facebook because they don't realize what's going on in the background; many users believe technical-looking messages and prompts. For example, in November 2010, McAfee Labs discovered a malicious Java applet taking advantage of Facebook. By browsing to a specific Facebook application page, the user was rerouted to a hacker site that hosted the attacking application, which displayed the message: "Sun_Microsystems_Java_Security_Update_6," allegedly published by "Sun Java MicroSystems," as shown in Figure 8-1. As you can see, the message seems legitimate but will actually allow a hacker to access your machine. The Trojan then steals passwords and sends a password log to an e-mail account on Gmail over an encrypted SMTP/TLS connection. Giving users the ability to install whichever social media application they want is potentially fraught with danger. To counter this reality, companies should preinstall all smartphone apps like Facebook, Flickr, Twitter, and LinkedIn so they're secure and send employees approved links to update social media apps regularly. Many companies already do this on the desktop as a matter of policy; this policy should extend to company smartphones.

Utilizing Technology

In Chapter 2, we categorized the steps in the Utilization of technology under Inventory, Capability, and Policy Mapping. To implement technologies to support the requirements for best practices, follow the steps in Table 8-1. You can also see how our fictional company JAG Consumer Electronics is implementing some of these tactics to improve its environment.

Figure 8-1   *Facebook malware application being installed*

Technology Step	Action Items/Procedures to Implement	JAG's Implementation
Inventory	1. Utilize the asset management tools you currently use for IT hardware and software tracking to also track all social media sites.	1. JAG is using their IT asset management application to track their social media sites as "soft assets."
	2. Inventory all social media applications that are used and installed on company resources, such as TweetDeck and Seesmic.	2. JAG is treating social media software the same as other software licenses such as Microsoft Office. Mobile applications are installed by the IT department now.
	3. Inventory all applications installed on company mobile phones such as foursquare, LinkedIn, Facebook, Hootsuite, and GoWalla.	3. JAG can only inventory company-owned devices.
	4. Inventory social media services such as Reputation.com and Reputation Management.com for Marketing.	4. All sites are tracked by IT and Marketing and all login information is controlled.
	5. Identify groups or individuals who have rights to use social media tools and have tools installed on company desktops, laptops, and mobile devices.	5. The IT team and marketing team are coordinating who has access to social media tools.
	6. Create profiles for individuals and groups with access to social media tools.	6. A profile and group has been set up for those needing social media access.
Capability	1. Identify the capability of each tool being used. For example: • **Seesmic** Social network posting and monitoring • **GoWalla** Location-based tracking • **Hootsuite** Cross-platform social media dashboard for monitoring, results tracking, team collaboration, and information dissemination • **LinkedIn** Business profile management • **foursquare** Location-based tracking service (geolocation, but Facebook and Twitter also offer geolocation) • **WordPress** Information dissemination through blogging	1. Each tool has been documented in the asset management software.

Table 8-1 *Technology Mapping*

Technology Step	Action Items/Procedures to Implement	JAG's Implementation
	2. Identify the tools necessary to monitor different social media platforms and map each tool to a platform. For example, if you allow all employees to access Facebook from their company laptops and computers, be aware that Facebook allows third-party companies to create applications that can access your employees' computers directly and install Trojans or viruses.	2. JAG has identified each tool and categorized it by function and social media platform. IT has selected two different tools for monitoring and reporting and has purchased a third-party monitoring service to assist with tracking public mentions.
	3. Identify the skillset of employees using social media tools. Nowadays IT staff and security staff have a job profile that identifies their competencies, and social media usage for business purposes requires another set of competencies. For example, someone who is a poor writer should probably not be writing the corporate blog.	3. The Marketing department uses the tools. IT has expanded requirements for certain staff to maintain security for specific access to certain social media sites.
	4. Conduct regular employee training regarding the safe and secure usage of social network platforms and related third-party applications.	4. IT is working with HR to conduct training. The Marketing team is the first to be trained. All employees will be scheduled to be trained as budget permits.
Policy Mapping	As we discussed in Chapter 6, within your IT security policy and your specific social media policy, you have to map key components to social media usage as follows: 1. **User access** This is a key component as social media is generally freely available to all employees with access to an Internet connection. If you implement restrictions on user access, identify tools used for monitoring users and create alert mechanisms from endpoint protection devices or data loss prevention systems.	IT has identified new sections within the IT Security policy specifically to address social media security and identified sections within the IT Operations guidelines for social media usage. IT is working with HR to approve new policies. 1. The user profile created grants specific access rights to social media sites to certain employees.

Table 8-1   *Technology Mapping (continued)*

Technology Step	Action Items/Procedures to Implement	JAG's Implementation
	2. **Regulations** Just about every company is subject to regulatory requirements. Companies have to take steps to meet regulations, such as implementing encryption for HIPAA and PCI. The social media tools you use impact regulations, so a mapping of these tools is required when evaluating compliance.	2. JAG has put their Legal team to work researching what regulations must be followed when using social media. JAG knows it has to comply with PCI DSS.
	3. **Data storage** Requirements for regulations as well as for security best practices dictate storage requirements, including cloud-based storage of company data.	3. JAG does not have much control over third-party sites and their data storage capabilities. JAG is downloading their Facebook contacts and LinkedIn contacts to keep a local copy of consumer data.
	4. **Data access** In most cases, encrypted login should be a requirement for your employees to access information, whether internally or externally. Many people do not know that you can access Google and Facebook over HTTPS. The appropriate data access method must be clearly defined—restricted access on unencrypted logins, for example. If a social media platform has unencrypted login, you should understand the risks of allowing your employees to log in from a Starbucks or a hotel's open wireless, where session hijacking can easily occur over Wi-Fi. A solution is to provide VPNs for employees, so they retain the flexibility to respond quickly when needed through a secured connection.	4. JAG forces employees to use encrypted login connections where possible to social media sites.

Table 8-1   *Technology Mapping (continued)*

Technology Step	Action Items/Procedures to Implement	JAG's Implementation
	5. **Shared services** All online social media platforms are shared services. If you have a policy against using a shared service or comingling of corporate data, this will affect your social media usage. Allowing vendors or multiple employees to access your social media tools or profiles will impact your policy against shared services. This requires modifying the policy to allow for the platforms to be used and for providing vendors and third parties with access to cloud resources.	5. JAG will closely monitor activity on any account that has to be shared among multiple employees.
	6. **Business continuity** Social media platforms have to be part of your business continuity plan. If your Marketing team relies daily on using sources such as Facebook and Twitter for communication, community relations, and promotions, you should have an alternative strategy ready when an incident disrupts the organization.	6. Business continuity planning is not as relevant for JAG's use of social media sites as its business is not yet fully integrated with social media usage.
	7. **Education and training** Most IT policies contain guidelines for employee education. Some companies have online training or instructor-led training. In today's online environment, the use of social media and restrictions of its use must be added to the training manual.	7. JAG will roll out training to all employees before the year is out.

Table 8-1   *Technology Mapping (continued)*

How's JAG Doing?

As you'll recall from previous chapters, JAG Consumer Electronics started out as most companies when it comes to social media maturity; they rated themselves "Poor." After analyzing their weaknesses, JAG has changed the way they utilize resources to better implement social media security. From Table 8-1, the changes made so far would raise JAG's rating to "Average" in its use of social media security tools.

Preventing Data Loss

Social media information is hard to detect, monitor, and prevent from leaving the corporate environment. Data loss prevention is focused on intellectual property (IP). Where is IP used in social media? Whether employees send out IP consciously or inadvertently, the channels for distribution are readily available. A web-based social media application can allow employees to access Facebook via a browser and easily post confidential information and photos. Without URL filtering technology in place, an employee can easily bypass other monitoring solutions and post your information via web browsers and desktop applications. To prevent data loss, IT must implement technologies such as McAfee to monitor, block (although blocking may encourage rebellion and misuse anyway), and report on social media activity that can compromise intellectual property requirements. To manage IP data loss, you must conduct the following:

▶ **Monitoring**   Technologies have to be in place to monitor how employees and even customers are using your IP.

▶ **Training**   Make explicit to employees the policy concerning the authorized and unauthorized use of company IP.

▶ **Blocking**   If employees have no rights to utilize IP, then they should be prevented from accessing and publishing that IP.

▶ **Reporting**   If you cannot report on activity in a measurable way, you have no idea what is going on in your environment.

As we discussed in policy development in Chapter 6, you don't have the power to execute corrective actions without the ability to actually enforce the policies you have developed. In a typical IT security policy, enforcement is based on technology controls. With social media, unless you have monitoring systems in place to see who is using which social media site, knowing how the site is being used or what is being said about your company is impossible.

Enforcement has to be a key component of social media security. It's a very diverse medium. Employees can create hidden profiles or fake profiles and say anything they want about your company. The only thing you can really accomplish is to enforce your corporate policy on employees who break your social media policy and work with Human Resources to implement some form of corrective action.

However, you're fighting a losing battle unless you engage employees directly to participate in the monitoring process. Reinforcing positive usage and positive employee role models when it comes to social media usage is far more effective than banning sites or trying to catch misuse. Encouraging employees to monitor each other greatly reduces the need for corrective measures.

Determining if a policy is better enforced with processes or technology can be challenging. For example, you can employ keylogging software to capture all activity on a computer, but that would be impractical for just tracking social media activity. Or you can use Web URL filtering to inventory which social media sites employees are visiting and map this back to which employees are authorized to use those platforms. Then you can get more granular and determine what, if any, intellectual property is being disseminated over those platforms. By understanding which employees are using social media platforms, you can understand their access to IP and then implement more specific restrictions and training regarding IP leaving the environment.

Tracking data loss is much harder when it comes to copyright versus intellectual property. The nature of copyright infringement is really about abusing the rights of others in printed material. It's next to impossible to monitor, block, and report on employee abuse of copyrighted material. If your employee steals someone else's copyrighted material to use in a blog post for corporate marketing, the IT department would be hard pressed to know if the employee is actually infringing on someone else's material, particularly when the material is copied and pasted or downloaded and then hosted on the company's servers. Yet the corporation is still liable for copyright violation. Sites are available that will allow you to check for plagiarism (i.e., http://www.dustball.com/cs/plagiarism.checker/), but the IT department cannot and should not check every post Marketing puts out for copyright infringement. Neither is it feasible to check every post out there to see if your material has been stolen. At a minimum, make sure your employees are not stealing other site's material by randomly checking employee posts. See Figure 8-2 for the output of a paragraph already posted on Alex's blog. This task could fall to the Legal or Marketing department managers.

Licensing options, including Creative Commons (www.creativecommons.org), exist to allow for publishing, using, remixing, and reusing text, photos, video, audio, music, graphics, illustrations, and other artwork without infringing on copyrights. But again, IT cannot know what is and is not licensed under Creative Commons. The responsibility lies with the person or team publishing the material.

Neither the IT nor the Marketing department can be expected to be experts in copyright law. Earlier restrictions on the use of copyrighted material do not really

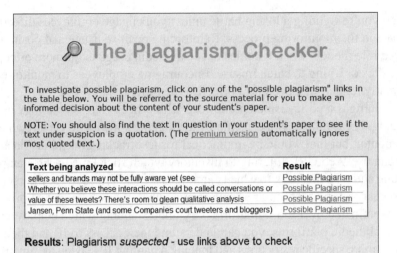

Figure 8-2 *Finding a plagiarized article*

affect today's copyright problems in the social media sphere. The basic copyright terms are listed here:

Unpublished works	Life of author plus 70 years
Unpublished anonymous and pseudonymous works	120 years from date of creation
Works made for hire	As part of a job, 120 years from date of creation or 95 years from first publication
Works when the death date of the author is not known	120 years from date of creation or 95 years from first publication
Works published by the U.S. Federal Government	Always in the public domain, no matter when it's created
Works published in the U.S. before 1923	Public domain
Works published in the U.S. from 1923 through 1963	In the public domain, unless the copyright was renewed during the 28th year following creation
Works published in the U.S. from 1964 through 1977	Not in the public domain, 95-year term applies
Works published in 1978 or later	Not in the public domain

How many of these really apply to a blog post you saw that might be useful to your company, so you copy it to post on your intranet? As far as we know, web blogs did not exist before 1977! But you may copy a reference from a newspaper article going back many years for a blog post, so knowing what is and isn't public domain is helpful.

Educating Employees

Educating employees about copyright restrictions in social media is a good way to avoid infringement by your Marketing department. Regulations like the HIPAA Security Rule (http://www.hhs.gov/ocr/privacy/hipaa/administrative/securityrule/) and PCI DSS standards (https://www.pcisecuritystandards.org/) include an education component. As a security best practice, we always want to have education programs in place. The PCI DSS standards say

> *12.6.1.a Verify that the security awareness program provides multiple methods of communicating awareness and educating personnel (for example, posters, letters, memos, web-based training, meetings, and promotions).*

HIPAA Standards require

> *(1) training each member of the workforce no later than the compliance date of the covered entity; (2) training each new member of the workforce within a reasonable period of time after the person joins the workforce; and (3) training each member of the workforce whose job functions or duties are affected by a material change in the HIPAA Privacy Rule policies and procedures within a reasonable time after the material change becomes effective.*

Your security dollar is more valuable when invested in education. Just throwing money at a problem with more technology will not give you the right controls. With education and training, you can help employees determine what is restricted content, determine what the data classification schemes are that require different levels of security, and what data can and can't be shared.

Social media requires various levels of security over different types of data. The first step is to integrate social media processes, procedures, and tools into your current data classification model. A typical data classification scheme is Secret, Proprietary, Confidential, Non-Public, and Public.

The mediums for social media dissemination are varied. This means you have to change the requirements for the types of data you have to classify. Education has to address the following:

▶ **Audio, video, and photography**   What are employees allowed to take pictures of on premises? If you're in a data center, you probably do not want employees posting pictures of the systems. But if you're having a promotional activity, you may want to post pictures of the event. This also has to apply to any vendors, customers, or visitors who come to your office. They have to be made aware, notified, or handed a policy of what audio visuals are allowed. Your practices should also cover pictures of other employees, partners, or customers. There should be an "ask first" practice before posting.

▶ **Publicly available guidelines**   Explicitly state what your guidelines are on the use of copyrighted assets. Employees, customers, or the general public can inadvertently break your rules if you do not make them obvious.

▶ **Making public assets available**   If you make specific resources available to be remixed, then you have more control over your material by creating a channel where you can manage public assets. The public will most likely infringe on your copyrights, so you may as well make certain assets available to better control those assets.

The development of processes and training regimens is the best solution for controlling how content is handled. When images or other material is included in a blog post, for example, the author of the post should inventory where the image came from and attribute the photograph to the photographer with a link back to the original source, at a minimum, and only when a Creative Commons license exists. If the Creative Commons license cannot be found with the original content, then the author must be contacted for permission, prior to publishing the content. In all cases, it is common courtesy to contact the author. These principles must be explained to employees responsible for the company's social media, and corresponding reporting or inventorying processes should be put in place.

NOTE

These issues become even more complex when material that is posted to social media platforms is lifted by the company's Marketing or Advertising team for reuse in advertising. Even when such use is authorized by the original authors of the content, best efforts must be made to contact them for permission and waivers, and it is wiser to err on the safe side.

In certain cases, the fair use doctrine in United States copyright law allows for the limited use of copyrighted material without permission from rights holders and generally applies to news reporting, research, teaching, and scholarship—not for marketing, sales, or any other commercial enterprise. All material that is borrowed from somewhere else should be clearly identified and credited in the post and linked back to the original source. (For more information, see the U.S. Copyright Office, http://www.copyright.gov/fls/fl102.html, or check another country's regulations.)

Wrap Up

Implementing controls over intellectual property and protecting copyright are very challenging tasks. IT security tools have to evolve to focus more on the content of the data traversing the network, how it makes its way into the public sphere, and what happens when it's out there. Tools have to move beyond just looking for files to helping businesses function more securely in the connected cyberspace. Blocking access is not the answer when it comes to managing IP, nor is it truly feasible.

Improvement Checklist

- ☐ Have you inventoried all your social media assets and their management capabilities?

- ☐ Have you identified social media tools and capabilities and how they can be managed?

- ☐ Have you tried to understand how policies must map back to IT security capabilities to secure IP properly?

- ☐ Have you implemented Data Loss Prevention technologies for the new social media mediums being used?

- ☐ Have you educated employees, customers, and the general public about appropriate uses of company IP and copyrighted material?

Monetary Considerations: Strategy & Collaboration

IT security budgets have not yet clearly defined the line item for social media security. And trying to retrofit the IT security budget by assuming that tools already purchased for data loss prevention will also cover all your social media security concerns won't give you enough coverage. According to the 2010 Ponemon Institute Cost of a Data Breach study,[1] data breach incidents cost U.S. companies, on average, $6.75 million per-incident and $204 per-compromised-customer record (Australia has the lowest cost per data breach incident, but even that's $1.83 million). The most expensive data breach event cost a company nearly $31 million to resolve. Several other interesting findings from the study include:

► The annual U.S. Cost of Data Breach Study tracks a wide range of cost factors, including expensive outlays for detection, escalation, notification, and response along with legal, investigative, and administrative expenses, customer defections, opportunity loss, reputation management, and costs associated with customer support such as information hotlines and credit monitoring subscriptions.

► Negligent insider breaches have decreased in number and cost, most likely resulting from training and awareness programs having a positive effect on employees' sensitivity to and awareness of the importance of protecting personal information. Additionally, 58 percent of companies have expanded their use of encryption—up from 44 percent last year.

► Organizations are spending more on legal defense costs, which can be attributed to increasing fears of successful class action suits, resulting from customer, consumer, or employee data loss.

► Third-party organizations accounted for 42 percent of all breach cases, dropping from 44 percent of all cases in 2008. These remain the most costly form of data breaches because of the additional investigation and consulting fees.

► The least expensive data breach event for a company included in the study was $750,000. The result of these breaches is the "churn" rate of customers due to data loss; the study found abnormally high churn rates in pharmaceuticals, communications, and healthcare followed by financial services.

As we've been discussing, a company's social media engagement can impact multiple vectors that impact cost, as verified by the Ponemon study's specific mentions of detection, escalation, notification, response, opportunity loss, and reputation management. If you are not managing social networks and potential data loss through

---

[1]Ponemon Institute, Five Counties, Cost of Data Breach (April 19, 2010), http://www.ponemon.org/local/upload/fckjail/generalcontent/18/file/2010%20Global%20CODB.pdf.

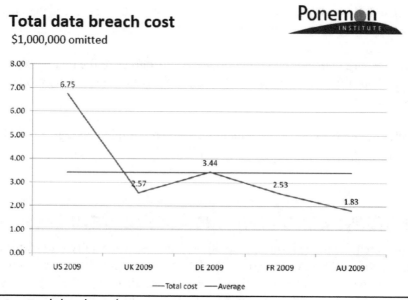

Figure 9-1 *Total data breach cost*

social networks, you will incur costs in these areas. Legal actions will become a more significant cost as social media cases make it through the courts. Figure 9-1 shows the total cost of data breaches as found in the Ponemon study.

The healthcare industry leads all industries in data breaches. Some of the key findings in the Ponemon Institute Cost of a Data Breach study regarding the healthcare industry include:

▶ Data breaches cost the healthcare industry $6 billion per year.

▶ Data breaches cost healthcare organizations an average of $1 million per year.

▶ Lack of staff and preparation (policies and processes) are blamed for most data breaches.

▶ Organizations have little or no confidence in their ability to secure patient records appropriately (58 percent).

▶ Healthcare organizations have inadequate resources (71 percent) and insufficient policies and procedures in place (69 percent) to prevent and quickly detect patient data loss.

▶ 70 percent of hospitals stated that protecting patient data is not a top priority.

► Patient billing (35 percent) and medical records (26 percent) are the most susceptible to data loss or theft.

Are companies dedicating the right monetary resources to the real problems they face? This chapter focuses on your social media security monetary strategy. Specifically, we look at

► Determining the cost of implementing—and not implementing—controls

► Determining the cost of threats

Case Study: Calculating the Cost of Data Loss

Regulations require many industries to report data loss, especially for healthcare and financial services. If you want to track the latest reported incidents, a collection of incidents can be found at DataLossDB (www.datalossdb.com). The publicly known incidents tracked by the database can be used as an example of what it might cost you in the event of a data loss. As you can see in Figure 9-2, some recent examples of data breaches are listed, the most recent being Dean Health Systems at St. Mary's Hospital (Madison, Wisconsin), where a doctor's laptop with 3,288 patient records was stolen from his home. The Hospital now has to incur the costs of responding to the incident and determine the costs of the breach itself. Data loss can happen through any medium, and posting information to Facebook can be the same as losing patient data on a laptop—and have the same regulatory consequences, in this case, violating HIPAA Security Rule regulations.

Latest Incidents		twitter / DataLossDB

RECORDS	DATE	ORGANIZATIONS
3,288	2010-12-20	Dean Health Systems, St. Mary's Hospital (Madison, WI)
760,000	2010-12-15	Ohio State University
15,000	2010-12-15	New York State Office of Temporary and Disability Assistance
2,284	2010-12-13	Mountain Vista Medical Center
1,300,000	2010-12-12	Gawker Media
20	2010-12-12	Department of National Defence Canada, Canadian Forces Base Stadacona
200,000	2010-12-12	Mesa County Sheriff's Office
23	2010-12-11	NatWest
0	2010-12-11	Unknown Organization, McDonald's Corporation, Arc Worldwide
0	2010-12-10	Genesco Inc

Figure 9-2   *Recent records stolen as listed by DataLossDB.com*

Companies are spending enormous amounts of money responding to social media breaches. As you will see in Chapter 11, Dominos had to launch a multimillion dollar campaign to combat a negative attack on its brand in the social media sphere. Dell has launched an aggressive social media command center, training over 1,000 employees in social media usage in 2010 and building a data center focused on social media tracking in 2011.

One free tool that St. Mary's Hospital can use is from Allied World, which created the Tech//404® Data Loss Cost calculator (http://www.tech-404.com/calculator.html) so organizations can calculate the financial impact of a data breach or identity theft data loss incident. This online calculator is free and automatically generates an average cost for expenses associated with data loss. Because the doctor's laptop contained 3,288 records, the average cost, as shown in the calculator in Figure 9-3, is $546,703.

Determining what went wrong in this case is easy. If the hospital had invested in hard drive encryption technology such as PGP, they would not have to incur these costs according to the HIPAA Security Rule regulations. The cost of a license is less than $200 per laptop, which is a much better deal than incurring $546,703 in incident management expenses. The second problem we can infer is the business process around how data is used and stored. Should the laptop have contained patient

Enter the total number of affected records here
(no commas ie., 25000)   3288 − +

Internal Investigation	-20%	Average Cost	+20%
Cybercrime consulting	18149.76	22687.2	27224.64
Attorney fees	18402.2784	23002.848	27603.4176
Sum:	$ 36552	$ 45690	$ 54828
Notification/Crisis Management			
Customer notification (certified mail)	33458.688	41823.36	50188.032
Call center support	23673.6	29592	35510.4
Crisis management consulting	13257.216	16571.52	19885.824
Media management	2619.8784	3274.848	3929.8176
Sum:	$ 73010	$ 91262	$ 109514
Regulatory/Compliance			
Credit monitoring for affected customers	152142.336	190177.92	228213.504
Regulatory investigation defense	56280.0384	70350.048	84420.0576
State/Federal fines or fees	119378.073€	149222.592	179087.1104
Sum:	$ 327800	$ 409751	$ 491701
Total Data Loss Expenses:	$ 437362	$ 546703	$ 656043

🌐 Graph   reset defaults

Figure 9-3   *Cost of data breach for St. Mary's Hospital*

information in the first place or should the doctor have been allowed to take the laptop home (if not his personal laptop)? Many healthcare organizations are moving to an online model for managing patient health information. If you can eliminate the need for local storage, you can eliminate some risk of data theft.

Costs of Implementing Controls

The costs of implementing controls vary by an organization's size, resources, and infrastructure. The controls put into place should address existing systems and support new products or systems as they are brought online.

Accurate costs for implementation can only be developed after you've created a detailed social media security policy, which we defined in Chapter 6.

NOTE

You can also find some additional policy resources at www.securingsocialmedia.com/resources.

Once the policy is in place, you can calculate the implementation costs of the controls you want to put into place. The costs of implementing and monitoring your social media activities can be tracked using Table 9-1. This table takes into account the monitoring and reporting tools necessary to implement employee monitoring and security reporting. For a marketing budget return on investment calculator, a number of free tools are available. One such tool is Frogloop (http://www.frogloop.com/social-network-calculator).

Table 9-1 details what our fictional company, JAG Consumer Electronics, has chosen to do regarding its budget. They have made a lot of progress from no budget to having a dedicated budget.

Social Media Implementation Costs	Costs for JAG	Notes
Setting Up Social Media Tools		
Blog	Free	Using WordPress
Twitter	Free	
Facebook	Free	
LinkedIn	Free	
YouTube	Free	
Other		
Annual Maintenance Costs	N/A	

Table 9-1 *Social Media Implementation Costs*

Social Media Implementation Costs	Costs for JAG	Notes
Training Employees		
General training	$30 per employee	JAG has signed up for an online CBT course for its employees.
Community Managers	NA	Has not hired one, using the Marketing manager as the Community Manager at this point.
Social Media Monitoring and Reporting Tools		
Data Loss Prevention tools	NA	
Media mention tools	0	Using SocialMention.
Analysis tools	0	
Training	$1,600	Hired a company to provide eight hours of training on using social media tools.
Ongoing Maintenance		
Research Costs	NA	
Policy development and maintenance	$2,000	Hired a company to develop policies.
Costs per click		
Costs per click fees	NA	
Campaign setup	NA	
Ongoing maintenance	NA	
Search engine optimization costs	$3,000	Hired a company to optimize the website.
Personnel Hours		
Number of employees engaged	1	
Hours per week	10	
Cost per hour	$25	
Cost of designing and implementing policies	$1,000	40 hours to design and implement.
Monitoring policies	N/A	Part of Marketing manager's job functions.

Table 9-1   *Social Media Implementation Costs (continued)*

Social Media Implementation Costs	Costs for JAG	Notes
Content Production		
Article/blog costs	0	Doing the writing in-house, sunk cost of salary.
Cost of posts	0	Doing the writing in-house.
Video costs	0	Doing the writing in-house.
Customer feedback messages	0	Using free tools.
Legal		
Legal review of policies	$1,000	Four hours of legal review.
lphaLegal follow-up on intellectual property infringement	NA	
Legal follow-up on employee/customer activities	NA	
Regulatory requirements analysis	NA	
Incident response management	NA	Have not designed an IR policy and procedure as yet.

Table 9-1   *Social Media Implementation Costs (continued)*

Combine the Frogloop calculations with the Data Breach Loss calculator from Tech//404, and you can estimate the return on investment figures for the implementation of technology initiatives. It is important to remember, however, that in the case of social media, threats can be triggered via online discussions, forums, and social media platforms.

Costs of Threats and Countermeasures

Once you've identified the costs of implementing controls, your next step is to estimate the costs of the threats you face based on your social media activities. In Chapter 4, we walked you through an assessment process for identifying potential threats. If you know those potential threats, you can utilize Tables 9-2 and 9-3 to analyze the potential costs of those threats and the countermeasures you put in place to counteract the threats. (See the Ponemon study for costs, http://www.ponemon.org/local/upload/fckjail/generalcontent/18/file/2010%20Global%20CODB.pdf.)

Asset/Process at Risk	Potential Incident (Threat to the Asset)	Likelihood	Severity	Estimated Risk	Annual Rate of Occurrence	Direct Cost per Incident	Total Annual Cost
Example: Confidential data loss	Employee posts information about new product design on Twitter.	Medium	Significant	High	2	$400,000	$800,000

Table 9-2   *Costs of Threats*

Countermeasures	Upfront Cost per Countermeasure	Maintenance Cost per Countermeasure	Likelihood of Utilization	Severity after Utilization	Annual Cost
Example: Data loss prevention tool to monitor posts from company-owned systems	$20,000	$4,000	High	Medium	$20,000
Social media mention monitoring service	$600	$600	High	Medium	$600

Table 9-3   *Costs of Countermeasures*

CAUTION

Social media monitoring tools can only monitor public posts. And social media commentary can go viral within Facebook's walled garden before it ever spreads to the public Internet.

These tables allow you to analyze assets and potential threats and to calculate the likelihood of occurrence and what the cost of an occurrence may be. You can also analyze the costs of countermeasures you want to implement. You can apply some objective data to this by researching industry metrics and baseline costs you have incurred in your organization. But some subjective analysis is involved as well, in the areas of Estimated Risk and Severity.

Wrap Up

Social media security threats should be viewed separately from other IT threats such as virus attacks and hacker attacks; dedicated tools have to be identified and purchased and specific social media budgets developed to manage social media risk correctly. All monetary requirements have to address threats, vulnerabilities, and the cost of response.

The threat assessment process identifies the ease of exploitation, impact, and mitigation tactics necessary to reduce risk. The overall costs of modifying your typical IT security tactics have to be implemented into your budgeting process. Because social media poses a risk of uncontrolled threats, such as customers posting on blogs and Facebook, you have to redefine your acceptable risk standards and shift budgets to reputation management, employee training, and crisis control rather than more traditional direct software and hardware tools. As social media tools and cloud services change almost on a monthly basis, your budgeting process has to be more flexible than the typical yearly cycle of most IT security budgeting processes.

Improvement Checklist

- ☐ Have you developed a tracking matrix for all costs associated with social media usage?

- ☐ Have you implemented specific budget line items dedicated to social media security tools?

- ☐ Have you identified threat tactics and costs to address different kinds of threats and countermeasures?

- ☐ Have you implemented a process to budget for new social media tools and threats on a quarterly basis?

Operations Management: Strategy & Collaboration

Your Operations Management strategy outlines the implementation of the tools and techniques needed for everyday maintenance of your social media activities. The social media policy outlined in Chapter 6 includes numerous steps to execute regarding new processes and technologies. IT system administrators need to have the right tools in place for real-time centralized management of activities. The Marketing and Human Resource departments need to know how to integrate their campaigns and policies into IT's operational guidelines. The Community Manager needs to understand the business rules, workflows, and processes involved in updating Customer Relationship Management systems with social data.

In this chapter, we discuss the IT department and other departments' management of social media technologies and processes. We cover the challenges of determining who owns the tools and defining responsibilities. We discuss creating a centralized process for managing social media that allows you to direct users; effectively monitor, report, and prioritize events; and determine risk requirements and the impact to both data and brand assets; and implementation auditing capabilities.

Case Study: Military Cyberprofiles

An extreme example of a centralized social media operation is the revelation in March 2011 that the U.S. military's Central Command (CENTCOM) is developing software with a company called Ntrepid and implementing tactics to manipulate social media sites for military purposes.[1] A concerted effort across departments is aimed at creating fake online profiles to influence the conversations on sites, gather information, and spread specific messages. These false personas, known as *sock puppets,* are being developed and managed by a third-party for the military.

CENTCOM spokesman Commander Bill Speaks said, "The technology supports classified blogging activities on foreign-language websites to enable CENTCOM to counter violent extremist and enemy propaganda outside the US." U.S. personnel can manage multiple profiles and track potential enemies. General James Mattis said the process "supports all activities associated with degrading the enemy narrative, including web engagement and web-based product distribution capabilities."

What can corporations learn from this? Well, there are some negatives and positives. First, it's probably not really a good idea to get into the business of creating fake profiles and spreading fake marketing messages. You eventually get found out and there goes your reputation. A government agency is probably better at doing this. Second, there is a lot of value in centralizing your social media efforts across

---

[1] Nick Fielding and Ian Cobain, "Revealed: US Spy Operation that Manipulates Social Media," *The Guardian* (March 17, 2011), http://www.guardian.co.uk/technology/2011/mar/17/us-spy-operation-social-networks.

How's JAG Doing?

What can JAG Consumer Electronics learn from this? Well, it pays to be a military contractor. But that's probably not what the company takes away from this. JAG does, however, need to put into place the ongoing operational steps to implement a consistent social media presence. At the beginning of this book, JAG had no tools in place, no consistent activities to manage their social media strategy, and no way to monitor and report on activities. As you'll see, by the end of this chapter, JAG will have tools to manage social media assets, implement steps for day-to-day activities, communicate across departments, audit and test their implementations of social media tools, and comply with industry standards where necessary for their business.

departments. And third, using the right tools for the job is always a good idea. Numerous innovative tools are being developed that can be a boom to your social media security strategy.

Operations Management Strategy

Your Operations Management strategy provides a way to correlate information about your day-to-day activities in the social media landscape. By compiling information from all departments using the centralized tools we discussed in previous chapters, such as Radian6, SocialMention, or Addict-o-matic, you can manage and respond to threats that come through social media channels, limit damage to the company, and reduce your risk. In this section, we look at who is responsible for various operations, what assets need to be managed, the training necessary to conduct operations and communications, as well as network management, access controls (both physical and logical), compliance management, and security testing processes.

Roles and Responsibilities

Operations Management strategies have to be companywide and also applied to the contractors and partners you use in your social media campaigns. The purpose of this guideline is to manage day-to-day social media usage to handle any adverse events in which some aspect of security is threatened, including loss of data confidentiality, disruption of data or system integrity, or disruption or denial of availability.

The IT department. the Community Manager, or both, are responsible for developing and maintaining the social media policies we discussed in Chapter 6. Specific responsibilities for Operations Management include

▶ Developing and maintaining the company social media security program

▶ Developing information risk analysis, assessment, and acceptance processes for all tools being used

▶ Promoting awareness and training for the new processes and policies put in place

▶ Educating personnel as to the implementation of the social media security program

▶ Serving, or assigning a direct report, as a member of any technical advisory committees to evaluate new technology resources

▶ Collaborating with other business units regarding their changing business goals to ensure that social media security issues are addressed early in marketing campaigns

▶ Consulting with senior management early on in any social media security crisis

An annual periodic information security risk assessment and review of implemented security controls should be performed. In addition, ongoing self-assessment can be part of the security processes. In a larger organization with its own security team, this audit can be handled internally. With a smaller team, this review may have to be outsourced. The review and assessment ensures that the existing guidelines and controls adequately address changes to business requirements and priorities and consider new threats and vulnerabilities to the company as social media evolves.

Asset Management

IT should maintain an inventory list of all the tools used in managing social media usage as a subset of the IT general inventory—by department and by responsibilities. Every application, whether hosted by a third party or internally, should be part of this asset management system. All systems that have installed applications should be secured, just as you would secure any other installed application, and if social media data is stored locally, it should be encrypted. Data management of third-party applications and storage becomes more difficult because it is distributed on sites you don't control.

Information and data stored on laptops, mobile web-enabled devices, and portable computers and third-party applications must be backed up regularly. If you store customer data in third-party applications like Facebook, keep a local copy of all the customer contact data offline. With the assistance of the IT department, authorized Facebook users should ensure that backups take place on a regular basis. For example, if Marketing uses Facebook to manage customer interactions, there should be some method of downloading and storing contacts and e-mails from consumers who are following the company on Facebook. This backup process is not as simple as backing up a server in your data center. You can do a manual download of your Facebook information by selecting the Account option in Facebook. Then select Account Settings and Download Your Information. Third-party applications, such as SocialSafe (www.socialsafe.net), are available as well.

As covered in Chapter 8, the company's intellectual property is also an asset. IT, along with Marketing and Legal, should check for potential infringement of this asset. For example, the company's brand name might be stolen by someone on one of many social media sites. Your company may have registered a page or a profile on Facebook, Twitter, Foursquare, and Flickr, but how about on Slideshare, MySpace, Tagged, bebo, hi5, Tumblr, or others? In Figure 10-1, you can see how using a tool such as Knowem allows you to see how your name is being used in a number of social media applications. In this example, the name "KRAASecurity" is taken in Twitter, Digg, YouTube, and LinkedIn, but not yet taken in MySpace, Flickr, or Tumblr, among others. What if someone had registered this name on those other sites and posted a page that made the company look bad? This is why it's a good practice to register your company name with as many of these sites as possible to eliminate some risk of brand damage. We'll talk more about Reputation Management in the next chapter.

Figure 10-1   *Using Knowem.com to check your registered name*

> **NOTE**
>
> *If you haven't registered your name but it has been taken, in some cases, you may be able to work collaboratively with the site to get your name back. In other cases, you may have to explore legal action with the platform or with the squatter to recover your brand name on a particular social media site.*

To the extent possible, it is better to reserve the company's brand name across the most important current and emerging social networks, establish an official profile, and monitor engagement on those sites. Whether the company is active or not on these other social networks, monitoring for brand mentions is important. The volume and sentiment of mentions will largely determine the engagement or corrective actions that the Community Manager must take to respond to consumer interest or concerns.

Security Awareness Training

The company should train its own personnel and third parties in information security when dealing with company data on social media sites. Training can be accomplished through a variety of methods: Webinars, PowerPoint presentations, policies, live training, and so on. Training should cover all platforms that may impact brand management or customer relations. When new social media platforms and sites are created, the company should provide regular and relevant information security awareness communications to all staff through various means, such as electronic updates, briefings, and newsletters, as well as via social media sites such as corporate wikis.

If any business unit uses third-party companies to manage social media, especially when managing customer information, your social media security guidelines must be formally delivered to the third-party company prior to the commencement of any provision of services, and you must ensure that they understand your security protocols and requirements. Key goals of the operational training program include:

- ▶ Providing specialized training based on applications and job functions
- ▶ Training according to policies that are in place, such as your IT security policy
- ▶ Providing training on the differences between business and personal social media functions and where the line gets crossed (such as posting personal anecdotes on the corporate Twitter account, which is just meant for corporate posts)
- ▶ Providing risk classification and information disclosure training
- ▶ Providing guidance on how to communicate with the public
- ▶ Providing training on specific regulatory requirements relevant to your business
- ▶ Providing knowledge of threats in the social media sphere

> **NOTE**
>
> *As part of training, ensure all company personnel understand that they have a responsibility to report incidents affecting security through appropriate management channels. Every IT security policy should include steps for incident response; these guidelines should also be followed in the case of a social media incident. If you do not have an Incident Response policy, you are definitely not up to best practices! Any incident, event, or circumstance that might reasonably be expected to adversely impact any individual, or the security of the company, its data, interests, or operations must be reported to IT security or to the Community Manager or other designated staff.*

Physical Security

If applications are hosted in-house, appropriate physical entry controls should be in place to ensure that only authorized personnel are allowed access to data facilities. All computer premises must be protected from unauthorized access using an appropriate identification system—such as card key access to server rooms or password protections to company laptops and desktops—to identify, authenticate, and monitor all access attempts.

When using third-party hosted platforms such as WordPress, you can request a SAS 70 report on the security measures they follow. Most reputable vendors will have a report on their security procedures, which includes physical security.

Communications

Document operating procedures for all tools and processes used to manage social media campaigns and communicate these procedures appropriately. At a minimum, you want to have procedures for

- ▶ Handling company restricted or confidential information as appropriate
- ▶ Scheduling requirements, interdependencies with other systems, job start and completion times
- ▶ Instructions for handling errors such as inappropriate posts
- ▶ Support contacts for each social media site for assistance in problems such as unavailable access or lost passwords
- ▶ System recovery procedures in the event of hosted application failures

Change control procedures should also be in place when changes occur, whether regarding the tools or hosted sites used, marketing campaigns, or the back-office tools for monitoring the environment and employees activities. If new staff is authorized to access the company social media accounts, create a change control form to track that access.

The challenge of managing change control on third-party hosted tools is significant. You cannot dictate what functions will change or even know ahead of time what's coming from the site you are using. Facebook seems to change its privacy functions every few months. At best, you can monitor all the sites you use for updates and analyze those updates quickly to determine if they have any adverse effects on your usage or customers or employees. Utilize formal change control procedures for all major changes to production applications and software that you do control in-house, and then communicate those changes to staff.

Part of the change process should be a notifications process when there are any threats to the software being used. If a worm or virus is spreading through a Facebook application, the IT staff or Community Manager must convey the danger to users through e-mail notifications or company wiki websites or shared forums. Company employees should be made aware of the danger of unauthorized or malicious software and of detection, escalation, containment, and eradication procedures when malicious software is discovered.

Network Management

Access to information and actual social media sites and tools should be strictly controlled. If possible, log all access to these sites and tools. With third-party sites, logging will be difficult. But you can provide some logging by monitoring all access to these sites from a company-owned computer or smartphone. Enable security auditing on all critical applications that are hosted in-house. You should log:

▶ Authorized access, including user ID, date and time of key events, types of events, accounts accessed, and program/utilities used

▶ Unauthorized access attempts, including failed access and login attempts, access policy violations, alerts, and system failures

Network management should follow best practices for network security for any systems managing and hosting social media applications within your control:

▶ Establish hardened operating systems.

▶ Enable strong encrypted authentication and communications especially across different networks.

▶ Follow best practices in application and operating system patch management.

▶ Use the latest patched web browsers.

▶ Provide black lists and white lists for social media site access.

▶ Create authorized user access control protocols to specific sites and applications.

▶ Implement web content filtering to monitor and manage all network access.

▶ Implement data loss prevention technology to block and report on content.

Employees should have no expectation of privacy when using company resources. As we mentioned in Chapter 3, the U.S. Supreme Court ruled in favor of companies being able to monitor their employees. Other countries may have a different legal stance on this topic, and if your business is international, you should be aware of the local country's data privacy laws and human resource laws. According to a 2010 Trend Micro survey (http://uk.trendmicro.com/uk/about/news/pr/article/20101102170926.html) of corporate and small business Internet users, 50 percent admitted to revealing confidential information using unsecured web mail or social media accounts and 60 percent of mobile employees admitted to sending out confidential information. The survey also revealed that one out of ten users admitted to overriding their company's security systems in order to access restricted websites.

The company should reserve the right to investigate any information with the company's systems. Some situations may require access to personnel files, such as complying with a court order, subpoena, lawsuit, discovery request, or other authorized request from a government agency investigating an incident. The IT department and the Community Manager (if one is in place) have to document and update all operational security procedures.

Access Control

Access to software tools should be controlled based on business and security requirements. When implementing new campaigns or tools, observe the following protocols:

▶ Security requirements for business applications and supporting information systems and processes.

▶ Assigned roles and responsibilities for managing business application security and supporting information systems and processes. A Community Manager may have more rights than someone in marketing to post to the company blog or a regular employee may be barred from mentioning the company name without permission.

▶ The classification level of information handled by the in-house and third-party hosted social media tools and the definition of the type of data being handled—generally acceptable classifications are Confidential, Privileged (do not distribute), and Public.

▶ Relevant legislation and contractual obligations regarding protection of access to data or services being used in applications.

The IT department or the Community Manager should require a formal user registration process for granting access to social media accounts. This process should include the following:

▶ Assigning unique user IDs so users can be linked to and made responsible for their actions

▶ Ensuring access levels (privileges) are implemented in a least-privilege manner

NOTE

Least-privilege *means employees are only given the bare minimum access needed to do their jobs, in accordance with each role and responsibility.*

▶ Ensuring appropriate management/data owner authorization is obtained prior to granting access to customer information

▶ Ensuring employees are aware of their security responsibilities and the terms and conditions for their access to social media

▶ Reviewing user access rights on a quarterly basis

Because many social media platforms are hosted by third parties, reviewing access rights frequently is extremely important. If an employee leaves, he or she can easily log into the company Facebook account and cause trouble, if the password hasn't been changed.

As with all systems that require a login, a good password policy and process must be in place. This process must include both newly assigned and reset passwords. An ideal password management process must:

▶ Ensure that users are aware of their responsibilities for maintaining the confidentiality of their passwords.

▶ Ensure users are provided initially with a secure temporary password.

▶ Require that the temporary password must be changed immediately.

▶ Ensure verification of a user's identity prior to providing a temporary password.

▶ Require password expiration every 180 days (this works only for internal sites and applications you host, third-party hosted applications generally do not have password expiration).

Access to application systems must be based on an individual's roles and responsibilities and on the underlying business application requirements. Functional roles, such as the Community Manager, should be defined based on the job requirements, and IT should grant application access based on these roles and requirements.

Access to hosted social media sites from non-company-owned systems should be restricted if possible. For example, if the employee is at a hotel and using a public kiosk, you may not want him or her logging in to your accounts. You don't know if a keylogger might be running on that public machine and capturing all data typed. If your employees are using your company systems to access a site, you have some comfort level in knowing you have antivirus and firewalls running to protect the computer and minimize the risk of a hacker gaining the login ID and password. If you allow access from distrusted systems, the risk of compromised login credentials increases exponentially. It is very hard to programmatically restrict access from only certain devices; you have to use policies to enforce this type of behavior.

Application Development and Testing

If you will be hosting your own internal social media applications such as a wiki, you should follow best practices in software development. You have to build in security as you design the application and its functions. You should also consider adding controls and audit trails of activities that can be easily monitored and logged. Follow basic applications testing procedures even if you use open source applications internally. Testing can include reviewing the following:

► **Input data validation testing**   Test if the application accepts only valid types of data and not corrupt or garbage input data.

► **Data integrity controls**   Verify that legitimate data is entered.

► **Message authentication**   Verify who is sending the message.

► **Application hosting facility**   Test the security posture of the servers hosting the applications.

► **Cryptographic controls**   Verify that data is sent and used over encrypted channels.

► **Security of system files and directories**   Verify that the operating system files can't be compromised to allow unauthorized access to application data.

► **Application of operating system security patches**   Verify consistent patch management for known weaknesses.

► **Backup processes and version control**   Verify consistent backup processes are in place.

► **User access controls**   Verify that only authorized users can access the applications.

Developing in-house application for social media is low on the list for most companies since using a free application such as WordPress and internal wikis or an installed application such as HootSuite is much easier. If this is the case, application testing will focus on ensuring that the systems hosting the application are secure from attack and that the application installation does not have any weaknesses. For IT departments, conducting a routine application security assessment or host security assessment should be a part of ongoing security processes.

When using third-party applications, you can only really rely on their SAS 70 reports. You can't conduct testing of third-party sites without explicit permission, which is usually hard to get. You have to rely on your own research into the reputability of the site, reviewing their posted policies and privacy information and publicly available testing such as using Google Safe Browsing diagnostic. With this free service, you can see if a site is known to be malicious or host malicious applications, as shown in Figure 10-2. The site "maharath.com" is reported to be potentially harmful to your computer.

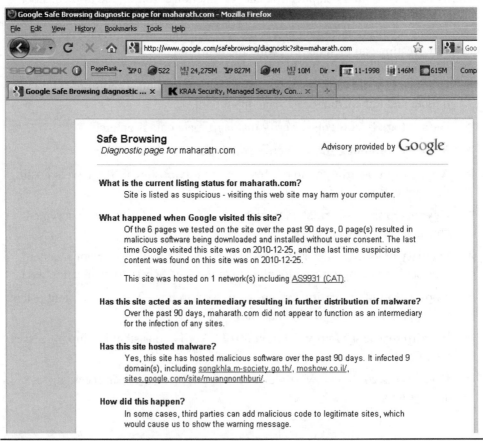

Figure 10-2   *Testing a site with Google Safe Browsing for malicious activity*

Compliance

Every company faces some form of compliance restrictions. IT cannot be solely responsible for making sure systems meet all the compliance standards. Legal and Human Resources must work with IT to make sure the right controls are in place to meet all regulations that impact the company. For each application being used for social media campaigns, have the legal department review how data is handled, contracts with any third-party providers, and what data may impact regulations.

International law also poses a challenge to social media. Many sites you use may not be hosted in your home country. You might be impacted by privacy laws if you are transferring customer information from the European Union to the United States. In Europe, for example, consumers have to give permission for a company to collect personal information and the consumer can review that information; employers cannot read workers' private e-mail; companies cannot share data across borders without consumer permission; and checkout clerks do not have the right to ask for your phone number. The European Union Directive on Data Protection of 1995 creates a Data Protection Authority to protect citizens' privacy.

If you operate in a country that blocks or attempts to block social media sites, such as Uganda or China, then your marketing policies have to take this into account. You have to be aware of what access consumers will have to your social media platforms and the data you provide through those platforms.

The users of social media platforms also have to be informed and trained regarding intellectual property rights, copyright laws, and the proper use of media licensed under the Creative Commons regime. It's easy to copy articles into blog posts or share information you find on the Internet, but it's also easy to infringe on someone else's rights. You have to implement the right tools to verify compliance with these standards, including monitoring of programs and data on company computers and communication equipment with data loss prevention techniques.

Personal use of social media during standard business hours can lead to a loss of productivity. If you implement data loss prevention tools, you can easily monitor what employees are doing and see when they are spending too much time on personal activities. Before monitoring, review with Human Resources to determine what the company prohibits, which might include any or all of the following:

▶ Engaging in any communication that is unlawful or breaks company policy

▶ Using someone else's passwords to access other resources

▶ Installing personal software on company assets

▶ Communicating too much information about the company over social media sites

▶ Impacting the company's reputation

▶ Viewing prohibited sites such as those involved in gambling, adult material, or other illegal sites

▶ Conducting personal business

Controls Auditing

Once you have implemented your social media policy and have controls in place, you need to know if you are following best practices and determine if employees are adhering to your policies and if IT and the Community Manager are actually following your processes. As you would for any other security process, you must have consistent auditing in place.

An economical solution to keeping your compliance costs reasonable and a growing trend is to adopt a Control Self-Assessment process for management. Control Self-Assessment is a methodology where management evaluates their own risks and controls over any set process. For purposes of monitoring compliance with the company's social media policies, management could create a series of control questionnaires listing out the guidelines/objectives of the policies. The surveys are then distributed to all those affected by the policy. The results of the survey should be tallied by an independent party. These results can be easily converted into a risk assessment, which we discussed earlier in this chapter. We provide a more granular view of the risk and threat assessment methodology in Chapter 4.

Each hosted application or software used in social media, whether a site to launch marketing campaigns or a site to monitor social media usage, should have an auditing process in place. This ensures compliance with company policy. You can categorize the tools into those used by IT security or by the Community Manager to audit employees' use of social media (at work and offsite) and then audit the capabilities of actual business processes. Those business processes that use social media can be further audited, for instance, to make sure a marketing campaign is in compliance with the social media policy requirements or state regulations. Following are two separate processes for auditing social media sites.

Auditing Steps for Internal Security Tools and Social Media Sites

Follow these steps to audit internal security tools and sites:

1. **Process management** Review procedures for integrating social media into the IT security model.

2. **Monitoring** Review procedures for monitoring public and employee social media mentions.

3. **Reporting**   Review reports generated on social media activity.

4. **Incident management**   Review activity and procedures to handle incidents on social media sites.

5. **Employee education**   Review procedures for educating employees on the dangers of social media.

6. **Research**   Review research processes that allow for continuous updates to social media tools and knowledge of the changing landscape.

7. **Policy**   Update policies annually on social media security practices.

8. **Inventory**   Assess all software tools and sites used in social media business practices periodically.

9. **Software**   Test all application software applications for vulnerabilities that may allow hacker access.

10. **Site audit**   Research and report on all changes to third-party hosted applications that are in use by the business.

11. **Code review**   Review and test all code on in-house applications used for social media.

12. **User access**   Audit all user access to social media tools.

Auditing Steps for External Social Media Sites

Follow these steps for auditing company use of external social media sites:

1. **Profile information**   Review all company profiles and messages being disseminated from official company accounts.

2. **Company search**   Search all available profiles to ensure no fake company profiles are being used.

3. **Data accuracy**   Review all data posted by the company for accuracy.

4. **Branding**   Review all material about the company to ensure it meets all branding and marketing requirements for design elements.

5. **Content**   Review content and how it's displayed to ensure it meets company standards.

6. **Posting**   Review processes for posting, authorizations needed to post, and approval processes for posting.

7. **Feedback**   Review how feedback is handled and the responses sent for content, accuracy, and timeliness.

8. **Tools** Review new technologies and sites that could impact or change business processes.

9. **Customer notification** Review how customers are notified and the availability of policies and information the customer may need regarding company social media usage.

10. **Tracking** Analyze data from tracking tools to ensure appropriate data is being managed and captured regarding social media campaigns.

11. **Research** Review research processes that allow for continuous updates to social media tools and processes for learning about the changing social media landscape.

12. **User access** Audit all authorized personnel for social media postings.

Wrap Up

Social media operations have to be managed like any other application operations. All applications, whether hosted by a third party or in-house, have inherent technology weaknesses. Employees using these applications have to be aware of the dangers posed by these different tools or websites. IT, the Community Manager, Human Resources, Marketing, and Legal must collaborate to ensure that the tools being used meet not only the business's functional requirements but also good security practices requirements.

Improvement Checklist

☐ Are you monitoring employee and public mentions with the right tools?

☐ Have you put an approval process in place for all tool usage?

☐ Do you educate the employees on the tools they use in the social media sphere and how they should be used?

☐ Do you audit social media platforms as you would any other software tool?

Reputation Management: Strategy & Collaboration

The opportunities and freedom of the Internet is wonderful. But it also comes with the risk of anyone with a camera and an Internet link to cause a lot of damage, as in this case, where a couple of individuals suddenly overshadow the hard work performed by the 125,000 men and women working for Domino's across the nation and in 60 countries around the world.

—Tim McIntyre, Vice President of Communications at Domino's Pizza

Social media is an ever-increasing force in marketing, whether companies like it or not. The rapid spread of damaging mentions about a company's product, services, or practices in social media is a viral phenomenon. The opposite of word-of-mouth marketing, where people positively recommend brands to each other, negative mentions can spread and create havoc on a company's hard-earned reputation and brand in mere hours. What, if anything, can be done to protect a company's brand from such risks? In this chapter, we discuss steps that you can take to actively manage the controls around your reputation. The tools we have discussed so far can only provide you with information. Now you have to take steps to utilize that information to defend your brand equity and keep abreast of all the attacks against your company name. In this chapter, you'll learn how to

▶ Distinguish between logos and brands

▶ Actively manage your reputation

▶ Engage with your online community

▶ Manage a crisis

▶ Use incident management to reduce risk to your reputation

Case Study: Domino's Reputation Attack

In April 2009, two Domino's employees published four short videos to YouTube that showed them mistreating food about to be delivered to customers.[1] Overnight, the videos spread virally through social media channels and the company was thrown

---

[1] David Kiley, Domino's Pizza YouTube Video Lesson: Focus on Standards and Pack Your Own Lunch, Bloomberg BusinessWeek (April 15, 2009), http://www.businessweek.com/the_thread/brandnewday/archives/2009/04/dominos_pizza_youtube_video_lesson_focus_on_standards_and_pack_your_own_lunch.html; and Taly Weiss, Crisis Management: Domino's Case Study Research, TrendsSpotting (April 22, 2009), http://www.trendsspotting.com/blog/?p=1061.

into a public relations crisis as widely read blogs like *The Consumerist* relayed the story, which was quickly picked up by mainstream news media. In one day, the videos had about 1,000,000 hits on YouTube. Domino's reputation came under the magnifying glass, with people attacking the quality of the company's food and service. Domino's had to act quickly to restore consumer confidence and to repair their lost brand equity. According to Domino's Earnings Call for the Second Quarter of 2009, the company experienced a short-term hit to sales in the weeks following the incident, estimated to cost between 1 and 2 percent in domestic same-store sales for the quarter.

What Went Wrong?

Domino's had little control over what employees could do on social media sites. The first thing Domino's should have done was come out with a stronger response. Their initial communication said that the employees were tracked down, fired, and had warrants for their arrest sworn out. Even though they tried to have the video taken down, once material is out on the Internet, it is pretty much there to stay. The firm Ad Age reported a hit to the "buzz" ratings of Domino's as measured by BrandIndex. Buzz fell from 22.5 points to 13.6. Domino's quality ratings fell from 5 to minus 2.8 temporarily.

The second key problem was the timing of Domino's response. More than a day went by before the company started to respond. In the social media world, that's a day of over 1,000,000 bad impressions of your company on YouTube and probably more on Twitter. Where was their social media monitoring to report immediately on any mention of the brand? Monitoring should have been in place to immediately notify the company of what was happening.

The third problem was due to internal controls. Could training regarding the proper use of social media have influenced the employees to not post the videos? We can't answer this question, but the underlying problem of poor behavior might have been avoided, in theory, with better internal training and communication. We do not know if the video was posted onsite or offsite. If it was posted from a mobile phone, the company couldn't have done much to block outgoing videos to sites such as YouTube. If the posting was from a corporate computer (in this case, probably unlikely), they could have potentially blocked access to sites such as YouTube.

What Did They Do Right?

Eventually, Domino's did do several things correctly in responding to this reputation attack. First, the company launched a Twitter account to start positive coverage—dpzinfo—and to get their messages re-tweeted. Second, it did make an aggressive attempt to get the video taken down from YouTube. The postings were quickly found by the company and the crisis management team got to work defending the company and addressing the problem. Third, Domino's did not try to hide from the problem. It tackled the issue head on and worked through social media channels to engage with customers and make customers aware of what it was doing to address the problem. The president of the company came out with his own video addressing the issue. And fourth, Domino's put together mitigation tactics to rebuild its reputation. The company launched a new feedback campaign discussing the quality of its product and ingredients and addressing customer concerns about food safety, demonstrating that they were listening to customers.

Attempts to Ruin Brand Equity: From Logos to Brands

In Chapter 8, we addressed protecting a company's intellectual property, trademarks, and copyrights, including its logos. Here, we make the distinction between a *logo,* which is the identification of a company's brand, and the *brand* itself, which is what embodies our collective concept of a company.

From a customer's perspective, logos and jingles help identify the products and services that a company sells. As one of the world's longest standing and most recognized logos, The Coca-Cola Company's logo—white cursive letters on a red background—is recognized by most people. Some global mobile phone manufacturers, like Nokia and Motorola, have set the default ringtone to play their own signature sound. Logos are useful because they help current consumers, prospective customers, shareholders, employees, the media, and other stakeholders to identify a company's products and services.

A brand, on the other hand, is your concept of a company or product, built up by a commitment to delivering quality products and services throughout the history of your interactions with the company. Your brand perception is further motivated by the company's advertising and what you hear about it from the media and from your friends and family. Prior to the Internet, we primarily experienced brands through just a few touch points, mostly through in-store purchases, television ads, print media, or phone surveys. The Internet added new touch points, including company websites and affiliate merchants. Social media has further multiplied your touch points with companies, including corporate Facebook pages, Twitter accounts, blogs, YouTube channels, support forums, and idea marketplaces. In addition, social media provides exposure from individuals posting to forums, blogs, Wikipedia, Twitter, photo-sharing sites like Flickr, and review and recommendation sites like Yelp.com and TripAdvisor.com.

Individuals can now share their experiences with brands, both positive and negative. In 2010, Southwest Airlines removed actor-director Kevin Smith from one of its flights in accordance with their "customer of size" policy. Little did Southwest know he would unleash his anger on Twitter to his 1.4 million followers (http://abcnews.go.com/WN/kevin-smith-fat-fly/story?id=9837268). Also, in 2010, when Nestlé created a Facebook Page for KitKat, the Company was caught off guard by environmental activists, who used social media to wage their war against the company regarding its purchases of palm oil for use in the candy bars (http://online.wsj.com/article/SB10001424052702304434404575149883850508158.html). A Comcast technician fell asleep on a customer's sofa in 2006 while on the phone waiting for Comcast's own customer service line to respond; the resulting video has been seen by millions over the years. Nothing on the Internet ever goes away. Whether on their blogs, Twitter streams, Facebook accounts, or elsewhere, individuals are talking about brands and are certainly not shy about sharing their negative experiences.

Actively Managing Your Reputation

Once the damage is done, the first consideration should be whether the content should be removed from the Web. On the one hand, leaving the content online while publicly addressing concerns and fixing the problem can turn a bad situation into a large positive win. Domino's Pizza did just that through a combination of public contrition and a crisis management campaign and by supporting material changes to the company's operations, including improved training, compliance, and monitoring tools to drive quality throughout the organization. The company's market capitalization doubled in 18 months following the event.

On the other hand, there may be good cause to request removal of the offending content, which may be done by contacting the authors of the post, notifying the owners of the social media platform, using legal recourse, and using Search and Social Media Optimization to bury negative mentions.

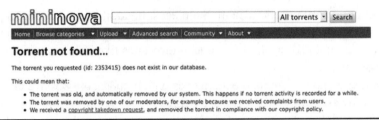

Figure 11-1   *Removed torrent from Mininova at http://www.mininova.org/com/2353415*

Contacting Post Authors and Domain Owners

When the Comedian Louis CK found a bootlegged torrent of a new routine, he quite simply contacted the person who uploaded the content with a kind message:

> HI. I'm Louis CK. Can you please take this down? This show is a work in progress and was not intended to be passed around the internet. I have absolutely no problem, personally, with file sharing, and if you take everything I have on the market on DVD, CD, and put it up for free downloading, I don't care. But this is an artistic and personal request. Please take this torrent down. thanks.[2]

In many cases, such courteous contact is well received and can lead to a cordial and informed discussion resulting in the removal of the material, as you can see in Figure 11-1. In some cases, nothing will happen, or worse, the situation might turn acrimonious with follow-up posts by the author or the domain owner. However, in every case, the first call should probably not be from a lawyer or with a cease-and-desist letter (more on this in "Resorting to Legal Recourse").

If your company has a good case with facts to back up your own claims about the material, then it is worth at least posting an official rebuttal comment on the offending post to indicate you are listening and addressing the issue.

Requesting Content Removal

In many cases, when the author of the offending post refuses to remove it, contacting the owners of the social media platforms and requesting removal may prove worthwhile. Services such as Flickr, YouTube, Blogger, WordPress, Twitter, LinkedIn, Wikipedia,

---

[2] Mike Masnik, "Comedian Louis CK Gets BitTorrent Removed by Asking Nicely," TechDirt (April 20, 2009), http://www.techdirt.com/articles/20090420/0246494561.shtml.

Yahoo!, Google, and others have made their policies explicit and are providing processes for removing material. In Figure 11-2, a user is trying to find a way to remove offending content (http://www.google.com/support/forum/p/youtube/). Unless the content meets YouTube's criteria for inappropriate material, getting the content removed might be difficult. These policies are often specific to the platforms, according to the type of content that is likely to be offensive.

For example, Blogger.com will remove content deemed offensive, harmful, or dangerous, such as hate against a protected group, adult or pornographic images, promotion of dangerous and illegal activity, content facilitating phishing or account hijacking, and impersonated user identity. On the other hand, Blogger.com requires court orders to remove material that represents personal attacks or alleged defamation, parody or satire of individuals, distasteful imagery or language, and political or social commentary.

Wikipedia describes several reasons for deleting an article (http://en.wikipedia.org/wiki/Wikipedia:Deletion_policy):

▶ Copyright violations and other material violating Wikipedia's non-free content criteria

▶ Vandalism, including inflammatory redirects, pages that exist only to disparage their subject, patent nonsense, or gibberish

▶ Advertising or other spam without relevant content (but not an article about an advertising-related subject)

▶ Content forks (unless a merger or redirect is appropriate)

Figure 11-2   *User concern over allegedly defamatory video*

► Articles that cannot possibly be attributed to reliable sources, including neologisms, original theories and conclusions, and articles that are themselves hoaxes (but not articles describing notable hoaxes)

► Articles for which thorough attempts to find reliable sources to verify them have failed

► Articles whose subjects fail to meet the relevant notability guideline

► Redundant or otherwise useless templates

► Categories representing over categorization

► Files that are unused, obsolete, or violate the non-free policy

► Any other use of the article, template, project, or user namespace that is contrary to the established separate policy for that namespace

► Any other content not suitable for an encyclopedia

Wikipedia also suggests a number of alternatives to deletion, including editing, merging, redirecting, discussing, incubating, including in other Wikimedia projects, and archiving of the offending content. The Wikipedia definition illustrates that the strategy and process for requesting that the service owner delete material is specific to the service itself and requires a customized approach.

When acting to request the removal of content online by the author or by the platform owner, speed is of the essence because readers and viewers often download content to edit, remix, and publish it in a newly modified version.

Resorting to Legal Recourse

If courteous contact with the author fails and if the platform owner refuses to remove the content, then you might consider legal recourse. For instance, Canon U.S.A., Inc., sent a takedown demand for the Fake Chuck Westfall blog at fakechuckwestfall .wordpress.com, which is hosted on WordPress.com.

Legal recourse is an option. However, before contacting either the author or the platform owner using legal means, it is important to understand that often such attempts to suppress content online can lead to the unwanted effect of drawing more attention to the offending material. Sometimes authors post cease and desist letters that they

receive or send them to the Chilling Effects Clearinghouse (http://www.chillingeffects
.org/), an online clearinghouse that studies legal complaints and threats regarding online
activity:

> The Chilling Effects aims to support lawful online activity against the chill
> of unwarranted legal threats. We are excited about the new opportunities the
> Internet offers individuals to express their views, parody politicians, celebrate
> favorite stars, or criticize businesses, but concerned that not everyone feels
> the same way. Study to date suggests that cease and desist letters often silence
> Internet users, whether or not their claims have legal merit. The Chilling
> Effects project seeks to document that "chill" and inform C&D recipients of
> their legal rights in response.

Legal recourse may not always work, unless of course it is accompanied by a
court order carrying the weight of the law and forcing compliance. It remains to be
seen whether certain whistle-blowing websites, most notably WikiLeaks.org, will
comply with court-ordered takedown notices.

Utilizing Search Engine Optimization

A separate and parallel way to manage negative mentions online is to take active
control of the Search Engine Results Pages (SERPs) for relevant keywords. The
objective here is to own the first page of search engine results for the keywords by
securing the top ten search results through active Search Engine Optimization (SEO)
and Social Media Optimization (SMO).

This process entails identifying which keywords are most important and creating
new content or new blogs and bumping up existing pages that have positive mentions.
Adding new domains, subdomains, and top-level domains and adding positive
content to external websites with strong authority may be useful. Build links to the
new content by requesting them from reputable external websites. Creating and
managing new social media profiles can supplement SEO efforts by adding new
websites that are well-indexed. For example, well-managed profiles and content on
Twitter, Yelp, YouTube, and corporate blogs can easily rise to the top of search
engines for selected keywords. To gain a better understanding of SEO, refer to
Wikipedia (http://en.wikipedia.org/wiki/Search_engine_optimization) or a good
paid resource such as SEOBook (www.seobook.com).

Zen and the Art of Social Media Strategy

In 1974, Robert Pirsig wrote a philosophical novel about a 17-day journey on his motorcycle from Minnesota to California. *Zen and the Art of Motorcycle Maintenance* explores the meaning of quality and aims toward a perception of reality that embraces both the rational and the romantic sides of the world. This means developing one's scientific understanding as well as embracing one's creative and intuitive bursts of wisdom. "The book demonstrates that motorcycle maintenance may be dull and tedious drudgery or an enjoyable and pleasurable pastime; it all depends on attitude."[3]

In much the same way, successful online reputation management entails a similar qualitative approach that includes constant monitoring of activity about your company as well as the finesse to understand how to engage and respond to opportunities and perceived threats in the right manner. We covered several tools for tracking activity in Chapter 10. What you do with that data is really the end result of reputation management.

Most often, the continuous delivery of excellent products and services leads to a passionate community of users who are ready to carry the company's flag and who are ready to forgive mistakes by the company. If product and service delivery fails too often, however, then the company must take an active approach to improve its processes, accompanied by being transparent in terms of the steps the company is taking.

The alternative to such a qualitative approach to social media is to instead conduct and operate in a "fire-fighting" mode, where the company overreacts to even the slightest negative mention. Furthermore, the company may take too much of a scientific approach, which risks alienating and distancing the online community.

When Marketing Campaigns Go Wrong...

McNeil Consumer Healthcare had a problem: their marketing campaign was received with great hostility by some vocal individuals in their target segment, mothers with young children. Their new advertisement for the pain-reliever Motrin was cleverly worded to help mothers deal with back pain associated from carrying their babies. Instead, some mothers with popular blogs and YouTube channels strongly expressed the opinion that they took offense at the new ads, feeling they were being patronized by the company. In short, they felt Motrin, not their babies, was the new cause of headaches. Motrin quickly responded by contritely removing the ads.

Of course, advertising campaigns are critically important and most companies should not simply switch all their promotional activities to social media. The difference is that it pays to be aware of the presence of a community of users online who are interested in your brands. Not only that, it also pays to engage with the

---

[3] Wikipedia, http://en.wikipedia.org/wiki/Zen_and_the_Art_of_Motorcycle_Maintenance.

online community, particularly when such engagement occurs through a company's established social media presence. By establishing a history of rapport with individual consumers online, you can open up new lines of communication and test ideas before committing to them. You can also turn to these individuals, if and when things start going wrong, for authentic advice and public support. This type of engagement will also prevent you from conducting promotions that are perceived as too aggressive, since you'll already have a pulse on the community's reaction.

When establishing close rapport with the community, observe the company's values in all communications by complying with legal regulations, such as HIPPA laws in the healthcare industry, and by observing professional etiquette. Boundaries between customers and the company must be clarified and understood so as not to disappoint passionate community members. While engagement is indeed desirable, people should never feel they are being taken advantage of.

The fields of marketing, advertising, and public relations are becoming increasingly digital and technical. This means the IT department is being consulted more regarding setting up new types of interactive platforms, including promotional games, product blogs, and even branded social networks for consumers. This provides an excellent opportunity for IT to manage security risks while advising on the capabilities and limitations of emerging digital technologies.

Creating Your Own Social Network

Most promotional activity in social media follows predetermined timeframes from beginning to end. Promotions may involve sweepstakes through Facebook pages, mini-sites, or games, or they may occur through regularly communicated discounts, such as on the Dell Outlet account on Twitter (http://twitter.com/delloutlet). A company with a limited budget can set up its own network with a service such as Ning.com or Socialgo.com, which are automated services that ease the pain of creating a social media platform yourself. With such services, you can create your own community with minimal technical knowledge.

The SocialGO administrator interface is shown in Figure 11-3. As you can see, you can pull together functions and widgets for your customized social network, such as blog capability, improve your SEO capabilities, create RSS feeds, customize your layout design, and select profile questions, and have it up and running within a day. Whether you get users is a different issue.

A longer-term commitment involves the creation of a branded community, or dedicated social network, for consumers. Launching your social network with a service such as SocialGO does not generate a user base. You have to create awareness. Associations and nonprofits, as well as some large companies in the retail, media, and other industries, are setting up such communities. Examples include

Take control in your Admin Center

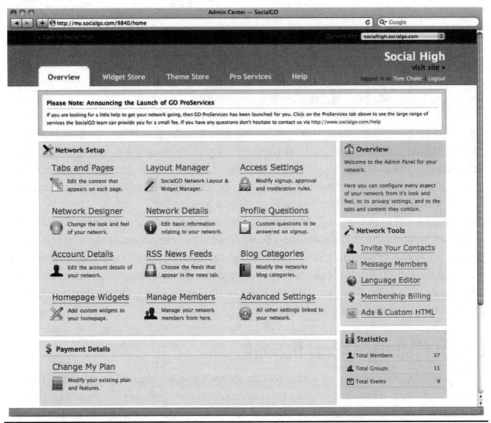

Figure 11-3   *SocialGO's customized social network creation platform*

RunEasy by Reebok, Nike+, MarthaStewart.com, MyStarbucksIdea, and Think by MTV. As you can see in the Think by MTV example shown in Figure 11-4, the MTV platform connects community activity with the ability to make purchases and generate revenue and it also links to MTV's Facebook page.

Such websites can be complex to conceive, design, and implement—both technically and creatively. A small or medium business can use Ning or SocialGO for a minimal cost, whereas companies such as Reebok and MTV have the resources for dedicated development. The most successful dedicated social networks are closely aligned to a company's products and values, giving users a real sense of connection with like-minded people.

The risks are high with customized social networks, however. Examples abound of poorly conceived social networks that users have abandoned. Google Buzz is a

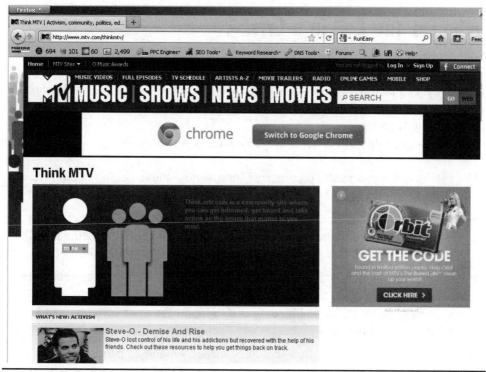

Figure 11-4   *Think by MTV's customized social network*

very public example of a social network that did not take off, even with the backing
of the behemoth Google—although Google+ launched in July 2011 as the newest
iteration of Google's foray into social media and has over 20 million users thus far.
Let's check back in a year and see how it's doing. Friendster.com is another example
of a social network that didn't make it even though it was a precursor to Facebook.
The reasons for failure are various: either the platform did not provide creative value,
since there was no real facility or reason to connect with others, or the website made
it difficult to connect and communicate with others because of poor user interface
decisions, too few or too many features, or slow page loads. Before creating your own
social network, consider any legal implications regarding eligibility to participate;
user privacy; posting and moderating content; storing, delivering, and archiving
content; and storing user details, especially with users from other countries with
strict database laws. Finally, security considerations are paramount when dealing
with consumers and the content they create, and leaks and other breaches can deal
a serious blow to any company's reputation.

Who Do You Call in a Crisis?

Social media crises are unique to each industry and each company, as situations can arise out of nowhere. Because consumers can so easily publish their grievances, even by just taking a picture or shooting a video and posting it from their mobile phone to Facebook or another site, each situation will be different, which is why companies must constantly follow online mentions.

Some commonalities in crisis management exist, however:

▶ Establish a social media presence as soon as possible to begin building rapport with consumers online.

▶ Respond immediately to a problem with a frank acknowledgement that the company is aware of the situation and will follow up quickly (within hours) with more information.

▶ Keep communicating about the situation; don't wait till more information is available, but respond that you are looking into the crisis, explain how, and as soon as more info is available, deliver it. Support the open communications effort with real business processes and decisions.

▶ New lines of communication should be made available to people who wish to contact the company privately with their concerns, observations, questions, and suggestions.

▶ Individual consumers with legitimate concerns deserve the company's attention, recognition, and problem resolution.

Reducing Reputation Risks with Incident Management

Risks to reputation generally occur when consumers publish their concern over defective products, poor service, or grievous customer service. This also means that most issues can be controlled—or avoided altogether—by implementing business processes that ensure consistent quality in the delivery of products, services, and customer service through social media channels with quality engagement before, during, and after the crisis.

A company can identify failures in service and customer service at the delivery point, *before* a consumer has had time to post their grievance. Most problems can be resolved on the spot by empowering employees to identify and resolve issues *during* a crisis—before the customer goes home and writes a blog post or tweets from a smart phone. Often, negative customer service can be turned into a positive customer experience through immediate resolution. The third moment for incident management occurs *after* the crisis when a company identifies a social media mention by an aggrieved consumer.

Each of these three moments implies different types of business processes and incident management responses. The second involves training, empowering, and monitoring employees to make sure they act in the best interest of consumers. The third involves online vigilance for mentions of company brands, with accompanying problem resolution mechanisms. Appropriate responses to security incidents include, but are not limited to:

▶ Rapidly identifying and classifying of the severity of the crisis for any social networks that are involved in the incident

▶ Continuous monitoring for any data or events related to the incident

▶ Determining the actual risk to the data or information shared on the social network

▶ Repairing, patching, or otherwise correcting the condition or error that created the security incident

▶ Retracing how the incident was allowed to occur, or if outside of corporate controls, retracing timelines

▶ Determining if the security incident rises to the level of a reportable breach under any particular regulation

▶ Mitigating any harmful effects of the security incident

▶ Fully documenting security incidents, along with their causes and your responses

▶ Expanding your knowledge base of security incidents to prevent future occurrences, improving training and awareness programs, and changing procedures

Wrap Up

This chapter addresses the potential risks to a company's reputation and the techniques and processes for incident management and problem resolution. When negative mentions are posted online, a company can explore many successive avenues to address the problem and minimize the negative impact. However, the best way to build and protect your reputation is to consistently deliver high-quality products and services.

Improvement Checklist

- ☐ Do you have a plan in place for addressing an online crisis?
- ☐ Do you have tools in place to monitor when your brand is being mentioned?
- ☐ Do you have a process in place to learn from incidents to improve your response?
- ☐ Do you have a process in place to work with your community to defend your reputation actively?

Monitoring & Reporting

Human Resources Monitoring & Reporting

I n the previous parts of the book, we covered how to assess your current
environment for social media weaknesses, methods for determining the threats
to your reputation and security, and the tools and techniques for implementing
operational guidelines. In this part of the book, we cover the monitoring and
reporting tactics that you have to implement so you know what's going on within
your company and in the public sphere. If you can't measure your activities, you will
never know if you are making any progress toward social media security nirvana.

As we discussed in Chapter 4, companies face numerous threats via social media
channels. These threats basically concern the loss of confidential information, allowing
access to hackers via network security weaknesses in social media platforms,
intellectual property challenges, and customer relationship issues. We reviewed
a number of controls in Part III and now we turn to how to effectively monitor and
report on social media activities in Part IV.

The first step in the monitoring and reporting process is, of course, the Human
Resources part of our H.U.M.O.R. Matrix. Monitoring tracks confidential data loss,
compliance to industry regulations, and enables reputation management. Requirements
and departmental responsibilities have to be clearly defined, and the social media
policies defined by HR have to be implemented and managed as the environment
changes.

According to a Job vite Survey in 2009, companies use LinkedIn 75 percent of the
time for background checks, Facebook 48 percent of the time, and Twitter 26 percent
of the time (http://recruiting.jobvite.com/news/press-releases/pr/jobvite-2009-social-
recruitment-survey.php). For recruiting purposes, companies use LinkedIn 95 percent
of the time, Facebook 56 percent, and Twitter 42 percent. Although social media can
be used by the HR department as a force for good, many HR departments see social
media as a loss of productivity and view it as a source of liability. According to the
Ethos Business Law/Russell Herder Social Media Survey in 2009, 51 percent of
companies fear productivity loss, 49 percent fear reputation damage, and 80 percent
fear social media is a liability. To ensure social media security, Human Resources
has to integrate monitoring as part of their daily practice for everything from tracking
time wasters to illegal activity.

Seeing as HR uses social media as a tool to hire and fire employees, a better employee
monitoring process needs to be in place. In this chapter, we discuss how Human
Resources plays an active role in developing your company's monitoring and reporting
solutions, including setting up the criteria for monitoring employees and compliance
measures the company has to follow, defining the baseline requirements for what
employees can and cannot do in social media, and disseminating policies to the
organization.

Case Study: Facebook Posting Leads to Firing

In one recent March 2011 case, a Yorktown School District in New York State fired five employees for a "practical joke" Facebook post.[1] The five tied up, shrink wrapped, and photographed another employee on school grounds. They then posted the picture on Facebook, and administrators found out about the incident when a message was sent to the head of grounds and maintenance. It was not flagged with any type of monitoring software. Even though no charges were pressed, as the tied-up employee was in on the joke, the employees were still fired. One is trying to get his job back. Since the tied-up employee was not being harassed or hazed, they probably thought it was not a problem, but the district thought differently.

A number of issues here are subject to interpretation. In this case, the HR department was not proactively monitoring for incidents associated with the school. What they could have done better was have proactive monitoring solutions in place rather than relying on word of mouth to notify them if something inappropriate was happening in the social media sphere that needs to be addressed. HR cannot rely on ad hoc methods. They could also have had a social media policy that defines how any details or connections to the school can and cannot be used on social networks. The employee trying to get his job back could challenge the district on not having in-depth social media current policies in place. Were there any written policies that defined appropriate behavior and were employees given training about the rules and regulations of the job?

Social network–based information has been more prevalent in the news in regards to both hiring and firings. It is still not clear what constitutes a firing offense or what postings may hinder a person from being hired.

Monitoring by Human Resources

IT should be able to provide the right tools for monitoring employee activity and monitoring public information regarding your company. We discussed a number of tools in Part III that you can use. The company's reputation is directly tied to employees' activities. The line is undefined when it comes to what employees do during off hours. The challenge is when an employee types a message on the job and then posts the message on her Facebook page when she gets home. In August 2008, a Burger King employee uploaded a video to YouTube and MySpace that showed

---

[1] Plamena Pesheva, "One of Four Yorktown School District Employees Fired After 'Practical Joke' Seeks Reinstatement," *Yorktown Patch* (March 25, 2011), http://yorktown.patch.com/articles/one-of-four-yorktown-school-district-employees-fired-after-practical-joke-seeks-reinstatement.

him taking a bath in the restaurant sink.[2] The health department and Burger King's management got involved and the employee was fired. However, Burger King also had to respond to the public to protect its brand. Burger King's initial response was "We have sanitized the sink and have disposed of all other kitchen tools and utensils that were used during the incident. We have also taken appropriate corrective action on the employees that were involved in this video. Additionally, the remaining staff at this restaurant is being retrained in health and sanitation procedures." The comments about the story on different news websites show a negative response to Burger King initial response.

If an employee's personal posting about a company could be considered defamatory or is targeted at a customer or competitor, HR has to know what actions to take. Laws already cover the social media posts of employees when it comes to things like defamation, confidentiality, and intellectual property theft. Some level of monitoring of employee posts when they are not at work should be in place to track what is really being said. This can be accomplished by general tracking of online mentions of the company name and key words related to the company. In Chapter 14, we go into detail about the monitoring capabilities of specific tools. If employees have company laptops, you can track laptop usage and all data sent from that laptop, as it is corporate property. You may cross the privacy line, however, if you target specific employees by monitoring their specific social media accounts. The courts have not yet determined what is legally crossing the line in social media monitoring.

An example of a company definitely crossing the line is when Hewlett Packard hired subcontractors to conduct private investigations of employees in 2006.[3] The investigators used *pretexting,* a controversial method of obtaining phone records and personal information under false pretenses to gain phone information. AT&T informed Thomas Perkins, an HP director, that someone had gotten an AT&T customer-service representative to send Perkin's phone records to an e-mail account at Yahoo!. This type of information tracking and gathering goes far beyond monitoring public social media postings. It could have potentially violated the Telephone Records and Privacy Protection Act of 2006, which makes pretexting—the obtaining of phone records under false pretenses—a federal crime. Several employees either resigned or were terminated over using poor judgment in handling employee monitoring. If the company had placed the correct monitoring tools in place beforehand, it may not have had to go down this very questionable path.

---

[2] "Burger King Worker Fired for Bathing in Sink," MSNBC/Associated Press (August 12, 2008), http://www.msnbc.msn .com/id/26167371/ns/us_news-life/.
[3] Patrick Hosking, "Snooping on HP Board a Pretext for Disaster," *The Times* (September 9, 2006), http://business.timesonline .co.uk/tol/business/article633447.ece.

Employees must be made aware of any monitoring activities. Through training and distributed written policies, they should know that the company will be monitoring staff for confidential and proprietary information disclosure and activities such as defamation. As we discussed in Chapter 7, employees have to be made aware of the policies regarding the corporate brand image, intellectual property, who they befriend, who they endorse, customer information, and other confidential information.

Compliance

Human Resources also has a responsibility to monitor employee activity if the company is under any type of regulatory requirements (such as HIPAA privacy rules). For example, if an employee in a healthcare company posts any information about patients, then that employee is breaking HIPAA rules and the company can be fined. In June 2010, Tri-City Medical Center in Oceanside, California, had to fire five nurses for discussing patients on their Facebook accounts.[4] This goes against HIPAA regulations and the hospital had to report the incident to the California Department of Public Health, which then conducted an investigation. HIPAA violations are more prevalent as the law actually can be applied very quickly to initiate firing.

In the financial world, banks and other financial institutions must comply with regulations on advertising. These regulations can be violated by those in the financial industry advertising deliberately or inadvertently over social media. Regulation Z (Truth-in-Lending) and Regulation DD (Truth-in-Savings and Overdraft Protection) advertising rules apply to advertising in any form, including social media. Other restrictions that can impact the use of social media include:

- ▶ **Traditional advertising compliance rules** Financial firms are very restricted in terms of advertising.

- ▶ **Unfair and Deceptive Acts or Practices Act (FTC Act)** If a company changes its privacy policies without warning or makes changes retroactive, the company could be in violation of this act. Social networks that collect and sell without informing users could also be in violation of this act.

- ▶ **Telephone Consumer Protection Act** Part of this act restricts SMS text messages received by cell phones, and with social networks integrating texting into their platforms, this could cause problems for companies.

---

[4] "Oceanside Nurses Fired for Facebook Postings," San Diego 6 News (June 10, 2010), http://www.sandiego6.com/mostpopular/story/Oceanside-Nurses-Fired-for-Facebook-Postings/2grZXIQTR0my9tYMH73ZqQ.cspx.

▶ **E-SIGN Act** This act regulates the validity of electronically signed contracts.

▶ **State laws** Many states have their own variation of the FTC Act plus additional laws that can impact how social media is used in business.

An example of how new forms of communications outside traditional monitored channels can lead to these laws being broken is the case of vFinance Investments, Inc. A chief compliance officer violated Section 17(a) of the Securities Exchange Act of 1934 and Exchange Act Rules 17a-4(b)(4) and 17a-4(j) by failing to preserve and promptly produce electronic communications.[5] The compliance officer used instant messages and nonapproved e-mail accounts to communicate financial information, which violated the law. Social networks all have communications capabilities that can be used to circumvent monitored channels such as corporate e-mail systems.

With the Truth-in-Lending and Truth-in-Savings acts, posts that are intended to promote a bank or its products and services are advertisements that are subject to compliance disclosure rules. If you have to disclose the official advertising statement about FDIC membership, tweeting all that in 140 characters is kind of hard. Certain regulatory agencies, including the FDA among others, have yet to determine a set of policies for corporate use of social media, despite strong demand by interested parties. As a result, some companies are exploring social media very conservatively and avoiding all possible risk by severely limiting their communication and promotional activity over these channels.

HIPAA Security rules are focused on privacy restrictions but the rules are actually vague on how to implement controls to control private data. Companies turn to external third parties for help in implementing security controls and many look to the American Medical Association for help. But guidance from the American Medical Association is just as weak in providing details on how to actually implement security controls over social media postings. Their new "AMA Policy Helps Guide Physicians' Use of Social Media" is pretty generic. The new policy only "encourages" physicians to conduct processes but without offering specific implementation capabilities:

▶ Use privacy settings to safeguard personal information and content to the fullest extent possible on social networking sites.

▶ Routinely monitor their own [physicians'] Internet presence to ensure that the personal and professional information on their own sites and content posted about them by others is accurate and appropriate.

---

[5] Bill Singer, "Significant New SEC Ruling: Compliance Officer Slammed Over Emails and Instant Messages," BrokeandBroker.com (July 19, 2010), http://www.brokeandbroker.com/index.php?a=blog&id=488.

▶ Maintain appropriate boundaries of the patient-physician relationship when interacting with patients online and ensure patient privacy and confidentiality are maintained.

▶ Consider separating personal and professional content online.

▶ Recognize that actions online and content posted can negatively affect their [physicians'] reputations among patients and colleagues and may even have consequences for their medical careers.

Focus of Monitoring

External monitoring by HR should focus on what employees are saying to customers and each other and posting in general public forums. Marketing should take the lead in focusing on customers' positive and negative mentions. Marketing has to manage interactions that relate to language and social media etiquette used with the public, including any potential personal attacks on customers, content of messages, and methods of contact and follow-up with customers and potential customers. On the other hand, Human Resource monitoring, using tools provided by the IT department, should focus on:

▶ **Defamation** Employees saying anything that could be considered defamatory about customers or competitors

▶ **Misinformation** Employees posting misleading information about the company or competitors

▶ **Attacks** Negative statements posted by employees that might reflect poorly on the company

▶ **Accuracy** Employees being honest and accurate with the public about the information they share about the company

▶ **Confidentiality** Employees breaking any confidentially restrictions on company information

▶ **Disclosure** Employees providing the correct disclosures about how they represent the company on posted messages

Can HR Ban Activity?

There are many pros and cons to banning social media activity. A 2009 Robert Half Technology survey found that approximately 54 percent of companies ban social media activities at work. Another survey by an IT service firm, Telindus, found that 39 percent of 18- to 24-year-olds would consider leaving a company if they were not allowed to access applications like Facebook and YouTube. Whether this is a good or bad policy is yet to be determined. If you ban activity, you have different reporting challenges when using data loss prevention technologies. You will focus more on monitoring employees' public profiles to see if they are talking about the company or your customers when they get home. The only way to really monitor home activity is if they use a company-issued computer on which you've installed monitoring software or by performing public searches for the company name and key words regarding the company and perhaps key employee names. Employees are pretty tech savvy, however, and they may find other ways around the bans; one obvious way is by accessing social sites and applications on their personal and corporate mobile devices. If you are not monitoring activity, you lose an opportunity to correct behavior that you have no idea is going on.

If you allow social media usage in the workplace, your monitoring and reporting rules are different. You can monitor activity and then train employees on appropriate use of social media at work. Hopefully, your employees will take those practices home with them. Engaging employees in how to interact properly with customers and the public, as we discussed in the policy section in Chapter 6, rather than the outright banning of social media is deemed to be the more positive, "employee friendly," and realistic approach.

How to Monitor Employee Usage

Do you get involved in the personal lives of your employees? Have you conducted an analysis of the effort required to monitor your employees' off-hours social media usage? How does a company determine where to draw the line and at what cost and then how does a company actually conduct the monitoring?

If you determine that you should be monitoring employee usage, you then need to determine what risks you are trying to mitigate and how you will mitigate those risks. As we have been discussing, you do have the tools to monitor employees, both free and paid. What you monitor is for an individual company to decide. If you monitor employee Twitter accounts, assuming you find out what employees' user names are, you might find something like the tweet shown in Figure 12-1, in which an employee is complaining about his or her job and may be looking for a new job!

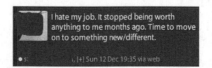

Figure 12-1   *Example of an "I hate job" post on Twitter*

Figure 12-2   *Profiles with and without company name mentions*

Unfortunately, it is rather difficult to find out employees' Twitter names. If you do a search for your company name, you may come across employees referencing your company. Monitoring is nowhere near an exact science at this point. As shown in Figure 12-2, Gary does not have his company name associated with his profile information but Alex does have UMiami and BarCampMiami associated with his profile. If employees do not have company names associated with profile descriptions, you can probably get results based on links or mentions in the actual tweets if a company name is used.

Monitoring can be very different across all industries. While the financial and pharmaceutical industries have many specific requirements that must be monitored, the retail world is generally more open ended. Regulations are constantly evolving. Human Resources has to identify the specific types of data that should be tracked and work with IT to develop the right search criteria using the tools we've discussed to implement the management requirements.

Once you've defined the requirements for monitoring, you need to assign roles and responsibilities regarding who will undertake the actual monitoring and reporting. When should IT get involved versus Human Resources versus Legal or Marketing? Who owns the tools needed to do the monitoring and who is responsible for using the tools? Who has the time to monitor 24/7? Specific filters need to be in place to help you look for what is important to your company; otherwise, you will waste a lot of time reading through useless search results. In Chapter 14, we get into more depth about how to set up your monitoring filters. If you are an information-based company, then you are looking for specific confidential data being posted. If you are a Legal firm, then you might be more concerned about your client's information being spread around inappropriately. You can't really anticipate and set up a search for "employee takes bath in restaurant sink." What is important to you?

Monitoring for Potential Legal Action

What happens when you have to sue an employee or ex-employee or build a case for termination? When you do monitor for potential legal action, there are several key activities you should consider (but first seek legal advice on this, of course):

► What are all the employee's social networks and what has the employee posted publicly (you may need investigators to help on this)?

► What steps are you taking to ensure social media evidence is persevered?

► What tools can you rely upon in reviewing chain of custody of data?

► What kind of communications will you have with the target of the investigation?

► What are the key search terms and evidence you are actually searching for?

A few words of caution:

► Do not delete any sites/accounts the company controls without first collecting evidence.

► Do not fake any kind of access or "friends" with the target that may compromise your case, as HP did when pretexting.

► Ensure you have the appropriate policies in place before you get to the point of legal action.

How to Use Social Media to Monitor Prospective Employees

In August 2009, Careerbuilder.com conducted an interesting survey about hiring practices and using social media. Forty-five percent of employers said they used social media to research potential employees and 34 percent used that data to make a decision not to hire someone. Key pieces of information included:

► Drinking/drug photos

► Displaying poor communication skills

► Badmouthing previous employers

► Confidential information being shared

► Inappropriate photos

► Lying about qualifications

Because you cannot ask anything directly about a prospective employee's social life that touches on age, sexual orientation, religion, national origin, disability status, or personal health information, you will have trouble finding this information without social media. However, social media is not 100 percent accurate. And monitoring for inappropriate activity can easily cross over into spying. As in the case of HP, pretexting, over-aggressive searches, and monitoring could lead to a violation of privacy laws or other protection laws. Case law hasn't worked out all the details yet regarding what is permissible, but this will definitely make it through the courts in the next few years. In the meantime, do your best to avoid any form of discrimination based on the social media activities of prospective employees.

Recruiting employees is a different matter than actually researching what they do on social media. Social media sites such as LinkedIn, Facebook, and Twitter can be a unique way of finding candidates, particularly for new media jobs. For example, you can use Twitter with appropriate hashtags for the skills you are looking for. There are actual Twitter job search engines, including Microjobs, TwitJobSearch, and TwitHire, that you can use. See Figure 12-3 for an example of TwitJobSearch. It's kind of funny that when you search for "social media security" no real jobs are yet out there targeting social media security.

Figure 12-3   *TwitJobSearch results*

Baseline Monitoring and Reporting Requirements

HR, IT, and Legal should agree on a baseline set of monitoring requirements. This list of requirements includes:

► Defining the necessity and scope of monitoring of social media usage by Community Managers and employees

► Understanding and updating security threats to social media platforms used by the company and monitoring employee activity on affected platforms

► Monitoring reaction and change in behavior based on training

► Monitoring sites that mention the company most often

► Tracking tools used to monitor employees on social media

► Monitoring activity of other organizations in your industry

► Monitoring and reporting on what online communities are saying about your company

► Tracking the influencers in your industry and those specific to your brand

To set the baseline requirements, all departments that have a stake in social media have to be brought in to determine monitoring and reporting needs. The Community Manager, who is essential to coordinating and monitoring activities, can be the lead in collecting the necessary requirements for monitoring. You need to understand what each department does in the social media sphere and what their concerns are regarding how social media impacts their business processes. What tools are they using that require assistance from the IT department to manage and monitor? In Chapter 15, we will cover some operational tools in detail.

How are you monitoring actual usage, authorized usage, and productivity loss versus productivity improvements? How can HR work with Marketing to follow a specific strategy? The Community Manager can coordinate training programs over time for social media usage, and gain an understanding of the staff's digital capabilities. Define specific monitoring and reporting goals such as determining who is using social media, if policy restrictions are being broken, and how to identify and avert risk scenarios.

Monitoring internal usage of social media can be easy. Because all the data is on your network, you can monitor and track all data communications. Using standard intrusion detection systems for monitoring is already part of many IT department tool sets. Examples of internal usage for social networks are wikis, SharePoint boards, intranets, Twitter backchannels, informal employee Facebook groups, and so on.

We have discussed a number of tools such as SocialMention.com to monitor external mentions of your company name. Internally, you might have a forum where

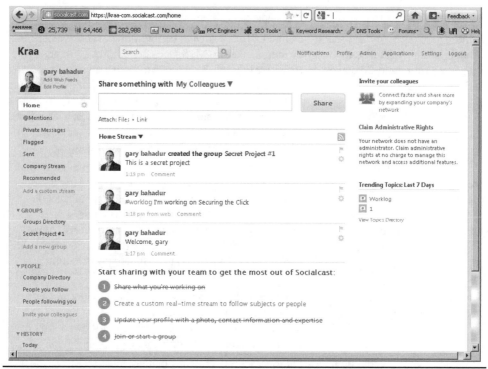

Figure 12-4   *Using SocialCast for monitoring an internal social network*

employees discuss the company. You can use a tool such as SocialCast.com for internal social networking management. Figure 12-4 shows an example of using SocialCast to manage an internal social network. Since you have complete control of your internal networks and any software installed on your servers, tracking usage is easy. Whatever tools you use internally, you should have the capability to allow IT security and Human Resources to monitor and report on what is being said.

How JAG's Doing

Let's revisit our fictional company, JAG Consumer Electronics. JAG has been making steady progress in changing how it handles the challenges of social media. JAG does not have a large HR department; actually one person runs HR. So the company has to be very efficient in monitoring and reporting on employee activity. JAG has addressed the baseline requirements for monitoring and reporting, as shown in the following table. With a limited staff and budget, JAG has still been able to move from a "Poor" rating in their original assessment of how it employs social media monitoring to an "Average" by making changes to its environment.

Baseline Activity	JAG Implementation
Defining the necessity and scope of monitoring social media usage by Community Managers and employees	Defined a list of sites to be monitored, such as Facebook, Twitter, LinkedIn, MySpace, Bebo, Flickr, Friendster, Hi5, LiveJournal, Blogger, WordPress, Plaxo. Defined threshold of types of incidents that management will review, for example, employee posting negative comments about company, other employees (management), posting confidential documents, talking about customers. Worked with IT to implement monitoring tools.
Understanding and updating security threats to social media platforms used by the company and monitoring employee activity on affected platforms	Developed a list of threats that IT can help monitor and report on for social media, such as changes to major network privacy policies, Trojan/malware attacks on popular social networks, latest hacked sites. Prioritized social media activities based on risk to the company: regulatory compliance (HIPAA Security rules or SEC rules), posts about customers, distributing nonpublic documents.
Monitoring reaction and change in behavior based on training	Training will be conducted every six months and surveys taken after each training course. Monitoring of activity will be strictly followed after each training session to determine changes in behavior.
Monitoring sites that mention the company most often.	Put together a list of sites that are most active for the industry and that mention the company, including sites that employees use most that mention the company name JAG, such as LinkedIn.
Tracking tools used to monitor employees on social media	Worked with IT to implement several tools to track employee activity, including Specter360, SocialMention, and Radian6. (We cover these in more detail in Chapter 14.)
Monitoring activity of other organizations in your industry	Tracking key competitors mentioned on social media sites, including the use of Topsy.com and Compete.com.
Monitoring and reporting on what online communities are saying about your company	Implemented a process with IT to monitor blog posts with Blogsearch.google.com and Icerocket.com (see Chapter 14).
Tracking the influencers in your industry and those specific to your brand	Using tools such as Google Blog Search and Radian6 to determine who to follow and interact with who may impact the brand.

Policy Management

The policies developed by Human Resources set the boundaries for what is acceptable for employees to do. An IT security policy may be written by the IT department, but HR and Legal must still sign off to authorize the policy. A social media policy may be written by Marketing, the Community Manager, and IT, but HR still has to approve it. And social media policies need to be updated more frequently as the landscape changes so quickly.

HR also needs to create a separate public-facing policy, as we discussed in Chapter 6. The public policy is a basic summary of what the detailed internal policy states about social media usage. The key concepts in the public policy should include the following:

▶ Define the limitations on what the company is allowed to do.

▶ Provide transparency in all the company's social media activities.

▶ Define the responsibilities of employees.

▶ Show how the company develops relationships with customers.

The public policy should be simply communicated and friendly in tone.

As the landscape evolves, HR has to be responsible for monitoring changes in how employees use social media with assistance from IT that provides the necessary tools to monitor employee activities. Once that activity has been analyzed, HR must then update policies to reflect the necessary changes. There is a lot of work involved in monitoring and reporting on any kind of activity within a company. In the past, this has been pushed off onto the IT department. With social media, so much of the information is confidential that the information posted can lead to lawsuits. The issue is in such a gray area that IT needs the guidance of HR and Legal for this monitoring to occur. Remember, however, completely trying to restrict or ban social media in the workplace will most likely not work.

Wrap Up

This chapter covered the key responsibilities HR has in monitoring all the social media activities to keep the company out of legal trouble and reduce risk to the company's reputation. HR is responsible for building the policies and maintaining them and ensuring that they serve a practical purpose. With the right controls and tools in place, you can monitor, track, and correct inappropriate activity. Once you have implemented your threat assessment processes and installed controls to defend your company over social media channels, HR has to determine if they have implemented key monitoring capabilities.

Improvement Checklist

- ☐ Can you track employee activity?
- ☐ Can you track customer and public sentiment?
- ☐ Can you track compliance with regulatory requirements?
- ☐ Can you track compliance with appropriate hiring practices?
- ☐ Do you update your social media policy as the landscape changes?

CHAPTER 13

Utilization Monitoring & Reporting

Throughout this book, we have discussed a number of tools that can be used for tracking activity across social media platforms. Once you have made your purchases or have selected one or more of the free tools that are available, your process for consistently monitoring and reporting social media activity must be put into place. We will address these basic questions throughout this chapter, integrating them into our three Utilization metrics of technology, intellectual property, and copyright:

▶ *Who* will you monitor?

▶ *What* will you look for and what tools need to be in place?

▶ *Where* will you search for posts?

▶ *When* will you do the monitoring?

▶ *How* will you accomplish the monitoring?

Case Study: How Not to Respond

In November 2010, *Cooks Source* magazine lifted a story from a blogger's post and put it into their magazine.[1] However, the blogger, Monica Gaudio, was never paid for authorizing the reprinting of her material. When she contacted *Cooks Source,* the magazine's editor, Judith Griggs, allegedly responded and Monica Gaudio posted the editor's response:

> *Yes Monica, I have been doing this for 3 decades, having been an editor at* The Voice, Housitonic *[sic]* Home *and* Connecticut Woman Magazine. *I do know about copyright laws. It was "my bad" indeed, and, as the magazine is put together in long sessions, tired eyes and minds sometimes forget to do these things. But honestly Monica, the web is considered "public domain" and you should be happy we just didn't "lift" your whole article and put someone else's name on it! It happens a lot, clearly more than you are aware of, especially on college campuses, and the workplace. If you took offence [sic] and are unhappy, I am sorry, but you as a professional should know that the article we used written by you was in very bad need of editing, and is much better now than it was originally. Now it will work well for your portfolio. For that reason, I have a bit of a difficult time with your requests for monetary gain, albeit for such a fine (and very wealthy!) institution. We put some time into rewrites, you should compensate me! I never charge young writers for advice or rewriting poorly written pieces, and have many who write for me... ALWAYS for free!*

[1] Rob Pegoraro, "*Cooks Source* Magazine Masters New Recipe: How to Annoy the Internet," *Washington Post* (November 4, 2010), http://voices.washingtonpost.com/fasterforward/2010/11/cooks_source_masters_new_recip.html.

This response by the magazine led to their Facebook Page and their reputation being attacked within a day in news stories, blogs, and Twitter posts, and even caused some attacks by hackers. Clearly, the magazine editor did not understand copyright laws and chose to respond without consideration to the effort that went into the original work. Advertisers pulled out as well, which directly affected the magazine's financial bottom line. The end result was that the magazine went out of business! If you do a Google search, all you get are articles on all the negative things about the magazine and the incident. Even if the magazine stayed in business, how long could you last if the first page on Google contains only negative stories?

Who, What, Where, When, and How?

Many companies may be shy about monitoring employees, but the federal Electronic Communications Privacy Act in the United States makes it clear that a company-provided computer system is the property of the employer. Employees should have no expectation of privacy when using the system to transmit e-mail, surf the Web, blog, text, or engage in any other form of electronic communication. In the Europe Union, the Data Protection Acts allow for employee monitoring, but the laws are more restrictive than the US laws. The Article 29 Working Party emphasizes preventing the misuse of company resources with means other than monitoring.

CareerBuilder found that 45 percent of employers review social media sites for job applicants. One search that doesn't seem too obvious but can impact how you might view a potential employee is if you research a job applicant on Facebook and you see them posting items such as "I am not going to work tomorrow," as shown in Figure 13-1. As a potential employer, you may suspect that the potential employee is going to call in sick and skip work, impacting your productivity level.

Once the employee is hired, companies are more willing to monitor their activity on the internal network with network data loss prevention tools. So "Who" will you monitor? Employees. You can only monitor externally for activity from customers, not what the customers actually do. As social media usage expands, companies will have more choices to expand their capabilities by utilizing new tools to track employee activity in the office.

Not going to work
Not going to work tomorrow:]
May 12, 2010 at 1:10am

Figure 13-1   A Facebook post: *"Not going to work tomorrow"*

"What" you monitor for will be different across companies and industries. Banking may be more concerned with financial advice and regulations. Healthcare is more concerned with patient information being shared. Retail may be more concerned about brand damage. With employees not fully educated about the potential consequences of their posts, you have to set up a variety of tools to capture the information you're looking for and then narrow down the scope. Once you have implemented a training program, however, employees won't have an excuse for breaking the rules.

In Chapter 2, we defined three categories of Utilization metrics: technology, intellectual property, and copyright. Table 13-1reiterates those categories. So to answer our "What" question, within each of these categories, once you identify the tools that best fit your needs (see Table 13-2 later in the chapter), you can now identify what data to search for.

"Where" you monitor is limited. You obviously can't monitor employees in their homes or when they are surfing from their mobile phones using their social media applications. Well, okay, theoretically, a company can put monitoring software in stealth mode to monitor a laptop at home, but that gets a company into more trouble than it's probably worth. A company may then be violating employee privacy at home. For mobile phones such as the iPhone, apps for just about all the popular social media sites—LinkedIn, Twitter, and Facebook—can be installed and cannot really be monitored easily.

Category	Description	Data to Search
Technology	What are the technologies that are used in distributing social media content and in monitoring social media activity, both from employees and from customers?	With the technologies in place, you can then search for specific data. As we have discussed, you search for mentions of your company brand name, competitors names, and so on.
Intellectual property	How does a company track its intellectual property in today's social media universe, which easily shares restricted information?	Search for any company confidential data. Look for intellectual property, research & development information, and data that should not be made public.
Copyright	Using social media can easily compromise corporate copyright information as well as protected material from other companies. How does the company track infringement of copyright information?	Search your own postings to ensure your team is not plagiarizing. Search other posts for infringement of your material, your images, or blog posts or articles you put out. Look for sites that might be copies of your site or feature copies of your products.

Table 13-1 *Utilization Categories*

The "When" of monitoring is pretty much 24/7/365—all day, every day. The monitoring of job applicants before they are even hired has grown with social media. It is fairly easy to find prospective employees' Facebook pages, LinkedIn accounts, Twitter feeds, and blog posts to see how they conduct themselves and how that may impact the company's reputation. According to a survey by the recruitment agency MyJobGroup.co.uk,[2] 40 percent of UK employees admit to criticizing their employers on social networking sites like Facebook and Twitter. Other interesting findings include:

▶ 20 percent of employees admit to "lambasting" their employers online

▶ 53 percent would support disciplinary action against fellow employees for online activity

▶ 60 percent of employees would change online posts if they were aware of their employer reading their posts

▶ 70 percent had no idea if their employer had a social media policy

To answer the question "How" will you accomplish the monitoring, you will evaluate your situation and assess which tools we've discussed will best meet your needs. One example of a tool is Spector360.com. This tool can show you what an employee is doing on the office computer. You can track his or her keystrokes and see exactly what he or she may be posting to social media sites. If the employee takes the laptop home and uses it for personal reasons, you can also track that usage. You may not want to do that if you are very concerned about privacy infringement. You need appropriate technology to accomplish your goals. You might need something as detailed as Specter360 or perhaps you can get by with public monitoring tools such as Google Alerts. What tools you select are specific to your company goals.

Technology

In Chapter 6, we outlined a number of processes that need to be present in your social media security policy. In actually managing your tools to enable secure utilization of social media, you are faced with the same challenges that you face with any other tools you use for other security activities, such as monitoring for malware or Trojans. You can utilize these tools to track "Where" this information is being used. From an internal perspective, you can track "Where" employees visit and the sites they use to post information.

---

[2] Online Workplace Critics—UK Businesses Urged to Address Social Media HR Policies, MyJobGroup (May 21, 2010), http://www.myjobgroup.co.uk/media-centre/press-releases/online-workplace-critics-21052010.shtml.

URL Filtering

Since just about every social media site will be accessed via a web page (even internal wikis), URL filtering is a necessary component in your toolkit to monitor, block, and report on employee activity. (Sites like Foursquare.com are a bit different for now, being mobile application driven.) Utilizing technology for external web filtering does serve a dual purpose because you can use URL filtering to manage incoming data as well. By controlling what data leaves your network and what data is inbound, you have some granular control over employee activity.

The key component of URL filtering is to require employees to go through a proxy server for outbound connections. You can control where the employees are allowed to go with the proxy, stop Trojan horse attacks from sending out data to a hacker website, and monitor what employees are doing. You can use free tools such as Squid Proxy (http://www.squid-cache.org/) and commercial tools such as McAfee WebWasher. You can create your block list and continuously monitor for employees trying to access inappropriate sites and, therefore, enforce your social media policy.

The added benefit of filtering inbound links comes from stopping hacker programs that try to take advantage of an employee clicking a link on a malicious website and installing code on the employee's machine. Whenever any code tries to execute via the browser, the URL filter can analyze it and block it, if necessary. Protecting against malicious pages on some social media sites is just another part of your overall security strategy. According to the Verizon 2010 Data Breach Investigation Report (http://securityblog.verizonbusiness.com), malware attacks are a significant portion of all attacks, as shown in Figure 13-2. If you can block employees from going to malicious social media sites or stop them from installing infected apps like those that might be distributed within Facebook, you will reduce malware infections on your systems.

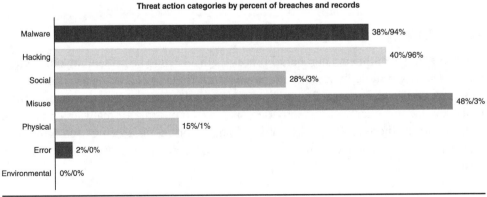

Figure 13-2   *Verizon 2010 Data Breach Report*

Searching and Analyzing Data

Social media monitoring tools help you search and analyze data. You have to automate the methods of cleaning and categorizing the social media data because there is too much data to do this manually. By selecting the best search terms, you can find the conversations that impact your company negatively and positively. Each social media application will have some of the information you need. Correlating all the different mediums in which your employees and customers communicate will provide the complete picture of what you have to monitor. As we discussed in Chapter 2, your tool assessment process has to correlate your technologies to the function needed to monitor and report on social media activity. The IT department is responsible for managing the monitoring applications as it does with most other applications a company uses. As an example, you can categorize your tools as shown in Table 13-2.

Software/ Service	Data Storage Location	News, Articles, Mentions	Employee Office Monitoring	Software/ Service Location	Support Provided	BCP (Business Continuity Plan) Capability	User Access	Tool Owner/ Manager
Addict-o-matic Tracking mentions	Cloud	X		Cloud	Yes	No	X	Marketing
Compete.com Search	Cloud				Yes	Yes		Marketing
Facebook Social networking	Cloud	X		Cloud	No	No	X	Marketing
FireEye Security controls	Internal		X	Internal	Yes	Yes		IT
Google Alerts Tracking mentions	Cloud	X		Cloud	No	No	X	Marketing
IceRocket Tracking mentions	Cloud	X		Cloud	Yes	No	X	Marketing
LinkedIn Social networking	Cloud	X		Cloud	Yes	No	X	Marketing
McAfee DLP Security controls	Internal		X	Internal	Yes	Yes		IT

Table 13-2   *Categorization of Monitoring Tools*

Software/ Service	Data Storage Location	News, Articles, Mentions	Employee Office Monitoring	Software/ Service Location	Support Provided	BCP (Business Continuity Plan) Capability	User Access	Tool Owner/ Manager
Meltwater Tracking news	Cloud	X		Cloud	Yes	No	X	Marketing
Plagiarism Detect.com Search	Cloud			Cloud	No	No	X	Marketing
Radian6 Reputation management	Cloud	X		Cloud	Yes	Yes		Marketing
Reputation Defender Reputation management	Cloud	X		Cloud	Yes	No	X	Marketing
SocialMention Tracking mentions	Cloud	X		Cloud	Yes	No	X	Marketing
Spector360 Monitoring	Internal		X	Installed	Yes	Yes		IT
Squid Proxy Security controls	Internal		X	Internal	No	Yes		IT
Topsy.com Tracking mentions	Cloud	X			No	No		Marketing
TweetDeck Messaging	Internal	X		Internal	No		X	Marketing
Twitter Messaging	Cloud	X		Cloud	No	No	X	Marketing
WebWasher Security controls	Internal		X	Internal	No	Yes		IT
Wiki Information sharing	Internal			Installed	No	Yes	X	Marketing
WordPress Information portal	Internal			Internal	No	Yes	X	Marketing
Yahoo! Pipes Search	Cloud	X		Cloud	No	No	X	IT

Table 13-2 *Categorization of Monitoring Tools (continued)*

With these tools, it doesn't matter "When" employees are being monitored on the job. The challenge is using the right tools to monitor when they aren't at the office but post information you need to know about. Table 13-2 gives you some tools you need in order the address the "How" portion of monitoring your employees. There are internal tools and cloud-based tools that give you the capabilities necessary to manage and protect your company's intellectual property from employees who may be inappropriately sharing it. Having these tools in place ensures that you address the following key points of monitoring:

▶ Identify the types of information that might be relevant or useful, such as your company and brand names, competitors, your research & development project code name, or even confidential filenames

▶ Create (and constantly modify) filters to sift out the majority of unimportant, noninsightful data, for instance, filter by

  ▶ Region or subject for influencers

  ▶ Specific combinations of terms such as "company name" + lawsuit

  ▶ Event your company is holding

  ▶ Hashtag

  ▶ Location, such as country-specific searches

  ▶ Community or specific platform

  ▶ Specific language

  ▶ Public news articles

▶ Identify stakeholders for different data sets; this will mostly apply to Marketing, Legal, and Human Resources

▶ Identify the most useful ways to report to each stakeholder. For instance, Marketing is concerned with the number and location of website hits after a new ad campaign is launched, but IT might be concerned with an uptrend in attacks against the company Internet IPs when that same new ad campaign is launched if it offended some group of people.

▶ Define clear steps for follow-up processes for the data you uncover (see "Incident Management" later in this chapter).

How JAG's Doing

As we discussed in Chapter 12, our fictitious company JAG Consumer Electronics has been making steady progress in upgrading its capabilities. JAG has gone through this exercise and has chosen the following tools and software services and categorized them, as shown in Table 13-2:

- ► Compete.com for search
- ► Facebook for social networking
- ► Google Alerts for tracking mentions
- ► IceRocket for tracking mentions
- ► LinkedIn for social networking
- ► Radian6 for reputation management
- ► Spector360 for monitoring
- ► Topsy.com for tracking mentions
- ► Twitter for messaging

The company has covered many areas with these newly implemented tools, moving JAG from a "Poor" stance to an "Average" stance.

Intellectual Property

Intellectual property (IP) can take many forms, as we have discussed throughout the book. Determining where your IP ends up and how it got there requires a diverse toolset for monitoring and reporting. You have to monitor sites that can host your information, such as LinkedIn, but you also have to monitor news articles, video stories, and offline press items, in addition to the typical social media monitoring. For all the mentions from news articles, you can utilize paid services such as CyberAlert.com, Meltwater.com, Newsnow.co.uk, and Cision.com. To make it useful, you need daily alerts and specific searches on topics of interest to your company.

Laws in the United States that could arguably apply to social media searches and monitoring include:

- ► **The Federal Electronic Communications Privacy Act**   Concerned with the sharing of personal data without permission

▶ **The National Labor Relations Act**   Employers are prohibited from interfering with an employee's rights to organize for collective bargaining purposes or to engage in protected concerted activities.

▶ **Anti-Cyber Squatting Protection Act**   A trademark owner may bring a cause of action against a domain name registrant who (1) has a bad faith intent to profit from the mark and (2) registers, traffics in, or uses a domain name that is (a) identical or confusingly similar to a distinctive mark, (b) identical or confusingly similar to or dilutive of a famous mark.

▶ **The Digital Millennium Copyright Act**   Deals with copyright infringement.

▶ **ICANN's Uniform Domain Dispute Resolution Policy**   International dispute resolution procedure that enables trademark holders to challenge trademark infringement.

▶ **State statutes**   Many states outlaw adverse employment action for engaging in off-work activities.

IP theft usually falls into three categories: first, when it is used to form a new competing business; second, when an employee takes the IP to a new company to get a better position and give the new company a competitive advantage; and third, when a competitor or third party looking to sell the information engages in corporate espionage. Once you have your tools in place, you will need to implement an incident response program in case you find information that is damaging. If you come across a third-party hosted site that you have no control over, removing a post that contains your IP may prove to be difficult. If the incident is one where your employee is disclosing confidential information, saying inappropriate things about your product or service or company, or engaging in similarly unacceptable behavior, you have a better shot of managing the incident and reducing your exposure. If the attack is someone trying to break into a secured database, you can rely on your perimeter security devices such as firewalls, intrusion detection, and intrusion prevention systems. Your last recourse could be legal action.

Employees should know they are being monitored, and you should set the boundaries that require monitoring. Specific policy violations that may trigger your incidence response process include:

▶ Transmitting or posting any material in violation of any federal or state copyright law without the permission of the copyright owner

▶ Transmitting or posting information that may cause reputation harm to the company or partners or customers

▶ Attempting to "hack" or break into any systems

▶ Conducting unapproved business activities from company premises

▶ Transmitting or posting confidential information that has not been authorized

▶ Intentionally introducing any computer virus, worm, Trojan, or malware that adversely impacts company resources

▶ Representing your company as a third party or misrepresenting a company representative

Prior to taking legal action, you have to follow your incident response program to monitor any further activity, block activity, and report on all actions taken by those stealing your IP. See the "Incident Management" section for details.

Copyright

Copyright problems are not just caused by people on the Internet stealing your company information. Your own staff or even management team can cross the line, as you learned in the case study at the beginning of this chapter.

To monitor your articles and blog posts for copyright infringement, you start with monitoring for online mentions of your company name. As we have already discussed, the basic free service provided by Google Alerts lets you do this. To get more granular, you have to monitor for particular titles of articles and posts to discover if your material may have been stolen. You can also use plagiarism-checking software to look for lifted material online. Services can scan the Internet for similar material and notify you. For example, Figure 13-3 shows how you can use PlagiarismDetect.com

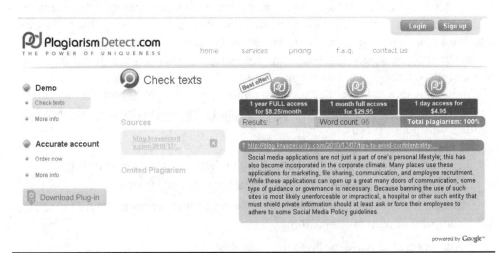

Figure 13-3   *PlagiarismDetect.com searches for copied material.*

(a commercial site) to see if your content is being used somewhere. (We, the authors, took a blog post from our own site and searched for it as a plagiarized work.) The results show the one place where the same material was found and reported that plagiarism was rampant for our post. You can also use one of the free checkers, such as Dupli Checker athttp://www.duplichecker.com/, to search for your content.

Once you have a firm grasp on the tools needed to manage and protect intellectual property and copyright, you need a process for utilizing your tools to respond to any potential incident.

Incident Management

As discussed in Chapter 3, the threat landscape is diverse when it comes to social media. A well-thought-out incident response program is necessary to manage this changing landscape. An incident, as it relates to the company's information assets, can take one of two forms:

► Electronic
► Physical

Electronic incidents range from an attacker or user accessing the network for unauthorized/malicious purposes, to a virus outbreak, to a suspected Trojan or malware infection, to the posting of disparaging comments and lies. *Physical* incidents include theft or loss of a device such as a laptop, mobile device, PDA/smartphone, portable storage device, or other digital apparatus that may contain company information.

With your complete toolset in place for managing and monitoring social media activity, you can now track and report on the problems. The most important preparation work, outside of a robust education regimen, is maintaining good security controls that will prevent incidents. Prior to an incident, you should have identified potential scenarios that could create an incident and responsibilities for responding to different types of incidents. IT Security, Marketing, and Legal should coordinate their efforts to ensure an appropriate legal and customer-centric response. Legal is especially important because they can make sure your response is in adherence to any regulations that affect your company.

When you suspect a loss of data or brand attack is being launched against your company, your tools and alerting mechanisms should allow you to respond quickly. If you have Google Alerts set up as a manual check, you would receive an e-mail about a potential attack if you have the right keyword searches in place. Incident management includes a number of basic steps that are usually taken. In Table 13-3, we have detailed the minimal number of steps and how our fictional company JAG could respond to a potential incident, after putting some of the right processes in place. JAG's marketing manager inadvertently posted a list of customer names and addresses on the company website as an attached PDF to a blog post, when the attachment should have been a product overview sheet. Incorrect files are sent out pretty frequently, as is the case with this JAG post.

Incident Management Steps	JAG's Response
1. Define your response scenarios before the incident even occurs.	JAG had not actually built any scenarios for incidents so was caught unprepared for this particular incident.
2. Determine if it is an internal or external problem.	It is as external problem because data left the organizational boundaries.
3. Determine if it is an attack on company systems and data or a brand and reputation type attack.	Since this was not really a hacking attack, it falls under reputation damage. JAG's monitoring tools have been tuned to alert on any new mentions of customer record loss or negative postings about data breaches and the JAG name.
4. Report the incident to the right owners/responsible parties.	JAG sent a letter to all customers whose information was given out in the blog post.
5. Physically secure any compromised systems.	There is no need to secure the web server physically; it's at a hosted facility.
6. Determine any chain of custody requirements that may be necessary for prosecution.	Not really a criminal act, but JAG has identified the marketing person responsible for the mistake. JAG will send their marketing team to extra training regarding security procedures and data confidentiality protection steps.
7. Create a detailed log to document all activity.	JAG is tracking each person who is responsible for responding to customer complaints, removing the data, searching the social media space with the tools SocialMention and Radian6.
8. Determine the source of the attack and take steps to block or reduce risk if it was a data loss problem.	While not an attack, it was determined that the marketing manager should not have had lists of customers easily accessible on a laptop, lists that can inadvertently be sent out.

Table 13-3   *Incident Management Steps and JAG's Response*

Incident Management Steps	JAG's Response
9. Notify relevant authorities.	Each customer was notified. Since no credit card data was sent, no PCI restrictions were broken. But JAG has customers in Massachusetts, so the Mass 201 CMR 17.00 regulation was broken and must be addressed. Every company doing business with state residents that collect certain types of data must have extensive security policies in place and actually implement security technologies to protect consumer data from being stolen.
10. Create a lessons learned process to reduce potential future risk.	After the incident management was complete, JAG scheduled a session to understand what went wrong and how it could be avoided in the future. All department managers are required to attend and a training process will be developed in response to the incident.

Table 13-3   *Incident Management Steps and JAG's Response (continued)*

Reporting Metrics

Every company has different requirements and priorities about what is important. Your particular industry may require more regulatory monitoring, e.g., healthcare and financial services. Once you have the tools in place, you can prioritize what needs to be routinely reported to management from what needs to be escalated immediately as a real threat. In Chapter 3, we defined the baseline list of threats that have to be monitored and defined the threat assessment process in Chapter 4. With your tools in place, prioritize this list and develop basic requirements for reporting measurements:

▶ **Copied sites**   Determine how often you look for fake sites.

▶ **Negative posts**   Measure negative posts and determine sentiment about your brand.

▶ **Misleading information**   Determine the threshold for when a response is necessary.

▶ **Fake profiles**   Catalogue all of your company profiles and look for fake profiles on those social media sites and on social media sites where you have never set up a profile.

▶ **Trademark/copyright infringement**   Catalogue your employees infringement of other company material as well as infringement of your own material.

▶ **Bad news coverage**   Daily searches for bad news and news in general about your company.

▶ **Confidential documents disclosure**   Daily searches for any of your internal documents that make it into the public sphere. You can do this with tools such as Google Alerts.

▶ **Complaint sites**   Identify customer complaints, whether real or fake.

▶ **Competitor attacks**   Daily searches of your competitor's brands in association with your company name; again this is easily done with a free tool such as Google Alerts or with commercial tools such as Radian6.

▶ **Hate sites**   Catalogue any sites that are specifically targeted to your company or your industry such as Facebook pages dedicated to "Wal-Mart" hate posts.

▶ **Employee personal scandals**   Report on your employees' activities as they relate to your company name.

▶ **Corporate scandals**   Report on any negative scandal that could affect your reputation.

▶ **Industry perceptions**   Report on overall industry metrics and sentiment.

Wrap Up

Social media requires a diverse toolset to monitor how employees and customers and competitors use your information and what potential threats they pose to your reputation. By analyzing the information and business processes you need to conduct social media campaigns, you can determine the necessary tools to monitor activity, determine where the dangers lurk, and report back to management all necessary data to reduce your risk.

Improvement Checklist

☐ Have you identified what key search terms you will be monitoring?

☐ Have you selected the technology software necessary to conduct monitoring and reporting?

☐ Did you define the data that needs to be tracked in the social media landscape?

☐ Have you implemented a response scenario to use when faced with a theft of intellectual property or other form of social media attack?

☐ Have you developed the metrics you need to report to management on the capabilities of your tools?

In today's marketplace, there are a number of tools, both free and commercial, for monitoring social media. Google provides a number of powerful free tools for monitoring social media conversations, blog mentions, trending topics, and searches, providing you with real-time alerts and forecasting tools. Whether you are a small to medium-sized business (SMB) or a large corporation, there are a suite of tools and processes that you can implement to manage social media effectively and securely. According to the Altimeter 2010 140 Global Corporate Social Strategists survey (http://www.altimetergroup.com/how-corporations-should-prioritize-social-business-budgets), large companies spend, on average, $833,000 on social media. In theory, if you do not have that kind of budget in place, you won't be able to develop a robust process. However, social media does not have to be expensive! The best way to maximize the benefit from your social media spending is to connect your Finance department to the Marketing and IT departments to monitor the value to spend ratio. A number of free resources are available that will let you develop a social media security strategy that meets your budget.

In this chapter, we discuss how to implement a social media security strategy on a budget that fits your organization. We'll look at several of the free and paid tools available. For different types of organizations, processes will differ and the capabilities of the tools necessary will differ as well.

NOTE

Whether you're an SMB or a global corporation, have a tiny budget or a budget in the hundreds of thousands, the Appendix lists many social media and social media security resources and you can also see our website — www.securingsocialmedia.com — for more tools.

Case Study: The Budgetary Challenge

In February 2011, MerchantCircle's quarterly Merchant Confidence Index survey[1] found that local merchants are moving to online marketing with sites like Facebook and Twitter to expand marketing capabilities, but they have not fully committed to significant marketing budgets. One of the major reasons is cost. Of 8,500 small and local business owners surveyed, many are still leery of using newer marketing

---

[1] Social media continues to gain traction in marketing strategies, Lawn and Landscape Magazine (February 22, 2011), http://www.lawnandlandscape.com/ll-022211-Social-media-marketing-strategy.aspx.

techniques such as mobile marketing and group buying with sites such as Groupon that market their products at a steep discounted.

The survey also found that half of local merchants spend less than $2,500 a year on marketing. The cost of marketing is very significant in small businesses and the ability to manage marketing is a significant challenge, with lack of time and resources being the complaint for 37 percent of those surveyed. Facebook is used by 70 percent of small businesses surveyed as an advertising vehicle. Facebook Places tops Foursquare with 32 percent adoption as of this writing.

In many cases, these merchants have only really considered the marketing aspects of social media and have not considered the security challenges posed by social media. In larger corporations, the adoption of security, in general, is more accepted because IT has been pushing security for years. Smaller businesses are more inclined to launch their product and services first and consider security implications second.

How JAG's Doing

JAG Consumer Electronics now has a budget item for social media and for security tools. JAG has used the processes identified in this book and started implementing a security framework around the H.U.M.O.R matrix; they have now dedicated a budget to address both the marketing and security aspects of social media. As an SMB, JAG does not have a huge budget. Fortunately, a huge budget is not a required! Within the IT budget, JAG now has a line items for

▶ Social media monitoring tools

▶ An online security training program that trains employees on security issues related to social media (JAG discovered an online computer-based training (CBT) portal, http://www.kraasecurity.com/social-media-security/online-training-portal/)

▶ Purchasing standard policy templates for social media

▶ Reputation management tools

JAG is moving from a "Poor" rating, as we defined in our matrix, to an "Average" rating for Monetary considerations.

Social Media Security on a Limited Budget

So what can a small business do on a limited budget? The answer is the same as what they do to market their products: access free resources! Free or inexpensive resources are available that can help the small company monitor the impact of their social media campaigns, whether they engender positive mentions or negative attacks against the brand name or perhaps even instigate hacker attacks. Recall from Chapter 3 the example of the hacktivist group "Anonymous," which was incited to attack and disrupt business for MasterCard based on the credit card company's refusal to process donations to WikiLeaks. If a campaign results in negative mentions, or an ex-employee makes derogatory comments about you or your business, using a free tool such as Google Alerts, you will quickly be notified so you can respond accordingly without having to hire an expensive PR firm to clean up the mess. In a recent lawsuit, Harrisburg restaurant Cafe Fresco owner Nick Laus is suing an ex-employee for defamation.[2] He claims the ex-employee falsely stated in a Facebook conversation that he uses illegal drugs. With the right alerts in place, any public mentions can be quickly tracked. If the SMB follows a strict process, the business can, with a very minimal budget, have a robust response capability almost as good as a large company.

Google Alerts

Based on your choice of query or topic, Google Alerts allows you to create alerts and monitor the Web for the latest relevant Google results (Web, news, etc.). These alerts track blog posts, news articles, videos, forums, and real-time discussions. Keyword-based alerts can be set to once a day, once a week, or as-it-happens. Google Alerts notifies the user via e-mail as results happen. Common examples of Google Alerts queries include a person's name, a particular topic, and even a specific company, all based on selected search terms. In Figure 14-1, we set an alert for the phrase "social media security" and the results are shown. A company would typically tailor this alert to the company name, competitors' names, and key phrases about its products, staff, and industry.

---

[2] Matt Miller, Harrisburg Restaurant Owner Sues Ex-employee for Defamation over Comments on Facebook, *The Patriot-News* (February 14, 2011), http://www.pennlive.com/midstate/index.ssf/2011/02/harrisburg_restaurant_owner_su.html.

Figure 14-1   *Google Alerts set for the phrase "social media security"*

Google Trends

Google Trends allows you to compare the world's interest in your favorite topics. Enter up to five topics and see how often they've been searched for on Google over time. Google Trends also shows how frequently your topics have appeared in Google News stories and in which geographic regions people have searched for those topics most. The information provided by Goggle Trends is updated daily, and hot searches are updated hourly. One recent example of an attack on a brand is the hacking and theft of customer data in the Sony online PlayStation network. In April 2011, hackers stole customer data and credit card information after breaking into the Sony online PlayStation network. With the right tools in place, Sony could track what people are saying about the hacking incident, track the attacks on the brand name, and understand the damage that the company has to be repaired (see Figure 14-2).

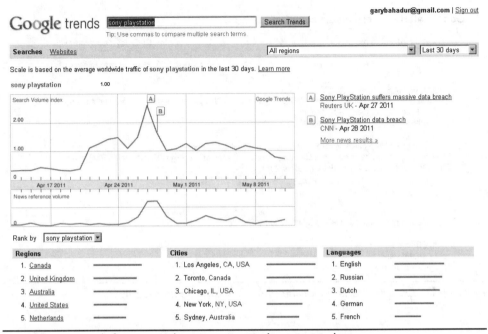

Figure 14-2   *Trends for "Sony PlayStation" over the past 30 days*

Google Blog Search

Google Blog searches help users explore the blogging universe more effectively. You might have customers who will write great things about your company and products in their personal blogs but then there are those who will attack you or even post confidential information from anonymous sources from your company. Every company, large or small, should conduct daily searches. You can use both Google Alert and Google Blog searches to find this data. You select the time frame for the posts and set up alerts.

Create search terms relevant to your company. In Figure 14-3, we did a Google Blog search on "KRAA Security," Gary's company. The interesting result is highlighted. Gary is definitely not speaking at the Mumbai security conference as stated in this post. So is someone using the KRAA Security name? This false post needs to be investigated by KRAA Security.

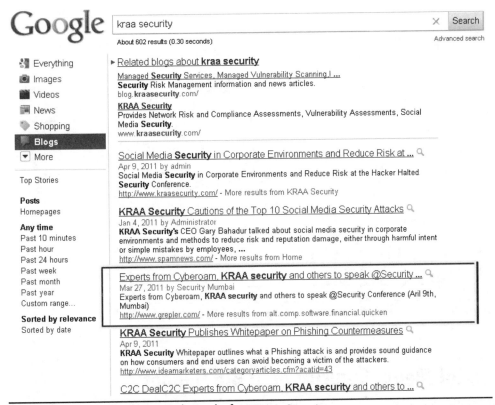

Figure 14-3   *Google Blog search results for KRAA Security*

Google Insights for Search

Google Insights for Search analyzes a portion of search volume patterns across specific regions, categories, time frames, and properties. For a company like JAG, it gives you the ability to find out what your customers are searching for to better understand your audience. Since JAG is in consumer electronics, a search term such as "Sony PlayStation" may provide some insight as to consumer interest, as shown in Figure 14-4. These results were over the last 30 days. Doing market research for free is a very powerful option for those on a limited budget. JAG can see what might impact its selling Sony products or might see an increase in returned PlayStation purchases over the last 30 days.

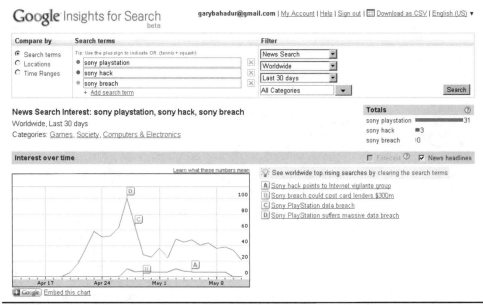

Figure 14-4   *Google Insights for Search results for "Sony PlayStation"*

Social Media Security on a Big Budget

In addition to the free resources, the following are examples of paid services for implementing several forms of social media services that help securely manage the data flows about your company. The main reason for using these paid services is that there is a large landscape to track when a company is bigger and has more interactions in the social media sphere. If a large company is using only Google Alerts, all the e-mails it receives are not being managed properly. A better filter is needed and some of the more robust paid services can greatly assist in managing this data. We will examine three services in this section. The Appendix lists many tools that you can also explore.

When you do select a paid service for monitoring, ensure the product offers

▶   An understandable user interface

▶   Integration into other tools, such as SalesForce.com

▶   Easy-to-generate metrics

▶   Comprehensive search of numerous sources

▶ Extraction and export data capability

▶ Real-time analysis

▶ Filter and summary dashboards

▶ Push capabilities

Radian6

One of the most popular monitoring tools on the market, the Radian6 software platform (bought recently by Salesforce.com) allows organizations to listen, measure, and engage in conversations across the social web. Radian6 tracks mentions on over 150 million social media sites and sources and returns the results for exploration, understanding, and action. Like most tools in this category, it can monitor blogs, tweets, news sites, video sharing sites, and discussion boards.

For a company that might be overwhelmed with a lot of data, the analysis, reporting, and filtering functions are very important in these paid monitoring services. Figure 14-5 shows an example of the Radian6 dashboard.

Cost   Radian6's volume-based plans have a starting price point of approximately $600 per month for 10,000 "posts" (as of this writing).

Figure 14-5   *Radian6 dashboard*

Lithium (formerly Scout Labs)

Rebranded as Lithium Social Media Monitoring, Scout Labs was recently acquired by Lithium. Lithium lets brand owners track what's being said about those brands on social media sites. The platform allows you to create persistent searches, giving you real-time access from the minute you log on. The automated sentiment feature gives you an "on-the-fly" look at the tone and sentiment of your social customers.

Another Lithium feature is Buzz Tracking. Buzz Tracking gives you real-time metrics around how much buzz is out there, how much of it is yours, how much of it is your competitors' and what's buzzing industry-wide. Saved Items lets you share bookmarks, notes, and social media mentions with the entire team or select recipients. Some potential differentiators from the Radian6 platform include:

- ▶ Automated sentiment
- ▶ Quotes showing you what your customers are passionate about
- ▶ Frequent words analysis
- ▶ Buzz Tracking

Cost   Lithium's monthly plans start at $99 for smaller organizations and up to $749 for a large customized solution.

Reputation.com

Reputation.com monitors what's being said about your organization online for a monthly fee and will have specific content "destroyed" or removed. Determining what data points need to be destroyed and where those data points need to be prevented from showing up is a very difficult process The platform offers three distinct services: MyPrivacy, MyReputation, and ReputationDefender. MyPrivacy seeks out and removes your personal information from the Web. MyReputation monitors search results, highlights potential problems, and promotes the biography that you push out. ReputationDefender increases positive content and actively combats false, misleading, or irrelevant Google results for businesses and business owners. This service is more about your reputation than content monitoring tools like Radian6 and Lithium. It addresses threats to your reputation by trying to manage public content actively.

Cost   Plans start at $4.15 a month. Reputation.com also offer customized business solutions.

Training Costs

When businesses think about investing in social media technology platforms, they should also consider training costs and allocation of resources. As with most security processes, good training pays more dividends than just buying a tool. Most regulations, such as PCI DSS and the HIPAA Security Rule, include a training component that has to be in place to meet the requirements. Several different training are available to a company.

▶ **Documentation**   This is the very basic training process of sending out documentation to your employees that they have to read. While documenting policies and distributing them is important, relying on documentation alone is the most inconsistent training method. You don't know if employees are actually reading and absorbing the material and there is no real great way of incrementally updating the training material. It is very difficult to obtain any reliable data from this type of process to report on training activity. Costs to send out written material are negligible. But creating the material can be costly.

▶ **CBT**   Online, or CBT, training is better and can target hundreds or thousands of employees easily. CBT training is probably the best use of resources to get the information out to a wide audience and, at the same time, verify the audience is absorbing the material by testing them at the end of the online course. You can develop reports on users who have taken the course and passed the tests. Typical online courses can run from $15 per user and upward.

▶ **Instructor Led**   Classroom instructor-led training is the best, but it is much more expensive and not very scalable. It is probably the best way to convey the material, but instructor-led training is usually reserved for courses like sexual harassment or detailed technical courses. You can develop reports on users who have taken the course and passed the tests. You can expect costs to range from $1000 per day and upward.

Depending on your budget, you have to follow one of these paths. The H.U.M.O.R. Matrix has taught you to know the answers to these questions:

▶ Do you have a policy in place that defines training requirements?

▶ Who will manage the workload or training?

▶ What is the cost of implementing and managing the training program?

Wrap Up

IT security budgets have not yet clearly defined line items for social media security. Trying to retrofit the IT security budget and assume tools already purchased for data loss prevention will cover all your social media security concerns is not going to give you enough coverage. Social media security threats should be viewed just as other IT threats, such as virus attacks and hacker attacks, are viewed; dedicated tools and budgets must be identified to manage the risk. Whether you use free online tools and resources or paid resources, you have to address the costs of both threats and responses.

The threat assessment process identifies the threats and, for each threat, its ease of exploitation, impact, and the mitigation tactics necessary to reduce risk. The overall costs of modifying your typical IT security tactics have to be implemented into your budgeting process. With social media, there is a high risk of uncontrolled threats, such as customers posting on blogs and Facebook. You have to redefine your acceptable risk standards and shift budgets to reputation management and crisis control rather than direct software and hardware tools. As social media tools and cloud services change on an almost monthly basis, the budgeting process has to be more flexible than the typical yearly cycle used for most IT security planning processes.

Improvement Checklist

☐ Have you developed a matrix to track all costs associated with social media usage?

☐ Have you identified specific budget line items dedicated to social media security tools?

☐ Have you identified threat tactics and costs to address different kinds of threats?

☐ Have you identified resources required for countermeasures?

☐ Have you implemented a process to budget for new social media tools and threats on a quarterly basis?

Operations Management Monitoring & Reporting

Effective operational monitoring and reporting requires implementing and utilizing various tools that prevent data loss before information is leaked. Companies are also being required to provide operational guidelines for protecting information based on the industry they serve; these guidelines vary across industries and across regulatory requirements. In this chapter, we cover

▶ The types of monitoring that should be in place to ensure security procedures are working properly

▶ Data loss management practices

▶ Monitoring and management tools

▶ Social media security and employee usage

Case Study: Social Media Success

One company that has been in the forefront of social media usage is Dell. We mentioned them previously as being a leader in the space. Rather than restrict employee use of social media, Dell has put in place a process to actively encourage use, both for employees and customers.

Dell engages with over 80,000 employees in using social media. They want to make discussions and information more transparent. There are internal blogs and forums for employee education. Employees can share ideas and suggestions, vote on major topics, and interact more openly using social media.

For customers, Dell has created the Social Media Command Center (http://www .youtube.com/watch?v=w4ooKojHMkA). They are actively listening to and engaging with customers. They are gathering real data on the ROI of social media and coordinating customer mentions to the brand. The statistics are proving whether the conversations actually lead to sales, as they can actually track sales from their Twitter stream.

Dell uses third-party tools such as Radian6 and Bazaarvoice to engage customers, track and report on activity, and respond in a more focused manner. By tracking over 25,000 daily conversations, the company gains insight into customer services, reputation, new product development, and marketing strategies. Dell can monitor activity, respond, record actions, and change tactics based on all these data points.

But Dell does not blindly allow social media usage. They have a detailed Social Media Policy (http://content.dell.com/us/en/corp/d/corp-comm/social-media-policy.aspx) and all employees have access to it and are aware of the consequences of breaking the corporate policy. The main points covered in the policy about social media usage by employees are

- ► Using information technology resources effectively
- ► Speaking on behalf of Dell
- ► Ensuring ethical conduct
- ► Ensuring transparency of origin
- ► Disseminating accurate information
- ► Protecting confidential information
- ► Ensuring accountability

The policy has a specific section for Procedures and Training, Reporting and Investigation, and Discipline. These operational guidelines are provided to employees to educate them on the possible consequences of using social media inappropriately.

The operational tactics Dell has put in place provide for a robust monitoring and reporting infrastructure. They have invested in tools to manage their social media usage, have provided employees with training in appropriate use, have a specific policy in place, and can gain detailed insight about all of their social media activities, both by internal employees and external customers.

Although many companies do not have the resources available that Dell has for such an expansive operation, but, as we have discussed throughout the book, there are many affordable solutions and best practices you can put in place to move the needle to a more secure operational stance.

How JAG's Doing

Our fictional company, JAG Consumer Electronics, doesn't face any particular regulatory challenge like those faced by financial companies. The company has also shifted the PCI requirements to their payment gateway, as many companies are now doing. But JAG employees have Internet access, and JAG does need to monitor for reputation impact. A malicious tweet by an employee can be bad for customer acquisition. JAG needs not only to monitor key employees who are in Marketing and PR but also to implement monitoring tools to verify that employees are not spending too much time on social media sites while at work. JAG has decided to use the service HowSociable to monitor mentions, and EventTracker to log all employee activity that happens on the corporate network, track all websites visited, and keep a secure backup log file of activity that can be referred to in the event of an incident.

If you refer back to JAG's original evaluation in Chapter 2, you can see how the company has progressed to increase its security posture when it comes to operations management. The following table shows how JAG has progressed in implementing operational guidelines.

OPERATIONS	Maturity Level Desired Within Six Months 1 – Poor, 2– Average, 3 – Best practice
Operations identified for social media	2—JAG has defined the steps that the company takes to operate social media platforms and action items for implementing secure operational guidelines.
Operations responsibilities clearly defined by department	2—Each department, IT, Marketing, Human Resources, and Legal, has clearly defined social media roles.
Operations mapped to social media policies	2—A social media policy has been developed and necessary steps to meet policy requirements are being put in place over time.
Active monitoring of social media threats	2—JAG has monitoring tools such as HowSociable in place to track company name mentions but has yet to fine-tune the tool.
Asset management of social media sites being used in the company	2—All social media platforms are now clearly tracked and managed by the Marketing team.
Track usage by employees allowed to use social media	2—Several tools have been implemented to track employee usage.
Education of operators that manage social media security tools	1—Unfortunately, JAG has not rolled out a complete training package for day-to-day operations, though JAG is working on it.
Process for determining data usage and storage in social media sites	1—This is a difficult task for JAG, as some social media sites are not helpful when it comes to sharing how they are managing company data.
Recovery process for restoring information from social media sites for business continuity plan	2—JAG is keeping a local copy of all customers' and marketing list information offline.

Types of Monitoring to Ensure Security Practices Are Followed

Most companies face the challenge of employees not using the Internet appropriately. It's easy for an employee to update a personal blog, send out Twitter messages, or update Facebook during the day. Employees will invariably bend the rules unless they understand there is a credible possibility of being caught. Just as policies without enforcement are like speed limits without tickets, operational monitoring and reporting serves the key purpose of maintaining functional policies and identifying areas where the policy may need adjustment.

In addition to supporting internal policies, operational monitoring plays a key role in ensuring your company adheres to federal, industry, and agency regulatory compliance requirements. In the U.S., regulatory agencies including the Federal Trade Commission Safeguards Rules, the Gramm-Leach-Bliley Act (GLBA), and the Health Information Portability and Accountability Act (HIPAA) require companies in related industries to implement information security processes and systems. HIPAA requires healthcare organizations to ensure patient information remains confidential. In the financial sector and for financial reporting in general, GLBA and the National Association of Securities Dealers (NASD) require that written and electronic correspondence with customers be archived, while the Sarbanes-Oxley Act is designed to prevent the destruction of data, including electronic data. For just about every industry, the Payment Card Industry (PCI) standard sets guidelines for protecting consumer information. In these and other industries, legislation mandates keeping records of correspondence and transactions in the event of an audit or legal action. Enforcement of these regulatory acts and legislation include penalties, litigation, and revocation of licenses.

The financial industry is required to have operations monitoring and reporting in place. Recently, InvestmentNews.com reported that the Securities Exchange Commission (SEC) in the United States requested financial advisors provide social network usage for 2010. From the letter sent out, the SEC required[1]:

> *1. All documents sufficient to identify [Adviser]'s involvement with or usage of social media websites, including, without limitation: a. Facebook; b. Twitter, including, without limitation, AdvisorTweets.com; c. LinkedIn; d. LinkedFa; e. YouTube; f. Flickr; g. MySpace; h. Digg; i. Reddit; RSS; and j. Blogs and micro-blogs;*
>
> *2. All documents concerning any communications made by or received by [Adviser] on any social media website, including, without limitation, snapshots of documents responsive to Item 1, above;*

---

[1]"What the SEC Is Requesting from Advisers on Social Media," *Investment News* (February 16, 2011), http://www.investmentnews.com/article/20110216/FREE/110219945.

3. All documents concerning [Adviser]'s policies and procedures related to the use of social media web sites by [Adviser], including, without limitation:

a. All policies and procedures concerning any communication posted on any social media website by [Adviser]; b. All policies and procedures concerning any prospective communications to be posted on any social media website by [Adviser]; and c. All policies and procedures concerning any ongoing monitoring or review process related to communications posted on any social media website by [Adviser];

4. All documents concerning [Adviser]'s policies and procedures concerning a third party's use of any social media website maintained by [Adviser], including, without limitation: a. All policies and procedures concerning any communication posted by a third party, including, without limitation, actual or prospective clients of [Adviser], on any social media website maintained by [Adviser]; b. All policies and procedures concerning any approval processes for prospective communications to be posted by a third party, including, without limitation, actual or prospective clients of [Adviser], on any social media website maintained by [Adviser]; and c. All policies and procedures concerning any ongoing monitoring or review processes related to communications posted by a third party, including, without limitation, actual or prospective clients of [Adviser], on any social media website maintained by [Adviser]; (and it goes on and on)

The SEC is already anticipating the damage that can be done if financial advisors are not controlled in how they use social media. For financial advisors, any communications or solicitations to clients are highly regulated. This means the right processes have to be in place to monitor and report on any employee interactions on social media that can be used to discuss financial advice.

Data Loss Management: Tools and Practices

As you saw in Chapter 10, your company's operations management strategy outlines the implementation of the tools and techniques needed for the everyday maintenance of your social media activities. These social media activities should be in accordance with your corporate policies, which are also discussed in Chapter 6. Monitoring compliance with internal policies and with regulatory requirements is a daily tactical activity. The three principal methods for data loss protection involve a combination of alerting systems, usage trend tracking, and log file archives.

Alerting Systems

As much as possible, monitoring systems should involve automatic processes that scan the content of the information that is published online, including data posted by employees, and send alerts to designated managers when company-defined keywords or phrases appear. Some alerting systems, such as the freely available Google Alerts, send notifications only after a mention is posted online. This and other systems are the best that can be done in terms of data posted by the general public, as you obviously cannot monitor and prevent the publication of that data before it is posted on the Web.

However, in the case of employees using company-provided equipment, systems should be implemented that alert the employee and those monitoring employees when certain keywords or phrases appear, or when employees attempt to access blocked sites. For example, if you use a web filter such as Websense, when an employee goes to a site blocked by company policy, he or she will get a message saying the site is blocked. Or if the employee sends an e-mail with the term "SSN" for social security number, the filter on the e-mail gateway would block it. These keywords and phrases may pertain to any data that is deemed to be sensitive, including intellectual property, trademarks, and possibly brand mentions. For instance, if a customer sends an e-mail to your help desk with customer-sensitive information such as an account number or social security number, the employee might reply to the e-mail and inadvertently send out that confidential customer information. That would be breaking the rules of most regulatory requirements. An alert should prevent the employee from sending out that e-mail. Such alerts serve to remind employees about potential breaches to agreed-upon corporate policies. Alerts are the first line of defense in data loss protection by acting as an immediate reminder of potential danger or misuse.

Usage Trend Tracking

In addition to alerts, data should be tracked for patterns related to social media websites, third-party applications, and keywords and phrases. By establishing a benchmark acceptable baseline, statistically significant deviances can be identified at the individual user level and rectified.

Usage trends also highlight how different departments and groups of employees use these sites and services, which should reflect their job responsibilities. For instance, it would be expected that communications-related staff, including roles related to Marketing, PR, and Advertising, would have higher usage rates for social media. These patterns should also reflect marketing campaigns and communication initiatives, including activity related to mainstream media reporting of company news. You may also want to track inappropriate access to websites. Usage trend data can serve to identify information leakage by helping determine where the volume of transactions and conversations are occurring.

In order to actually track this information, you have to have a software solution in place to track all activity proactively. We have mentioned several data loss prevention solutions already. For example, if you install the Specter Pro monitoring solution, you can track all employee activity, as shown in Figure 15-1.

Log File Archives

Log files may be easily overlooked in daily operations, but they are critically important in terms of compliance with auditing and regulatory requirements. Records of transactions, conversations, and social media activity must be logged and archived to facilitate the identification of how problems and breaches occurred. Log files can also be tied to alerting systems, which notify key personnel when certain types of predefined activities occur; for instance, you may want to log all failed login attempts to social media sites that you block, track all blog posts from within the company,

Figure 15-1   *Tracking employee usage and monitoring activity*

track all IM conversations in social media forums from within the company, log all visits to social media sites, log the amount of time spent on social media sites, look at key search terms being used by employees, and track all software that might be downloaded and installed on company-owned resources. Finally, log files can be mined for data relating to longer-term trends that may not be picked up by more tactical tracking mechanisms and real-time dashboards, such as what content sites employees are visiting most, what search terms are being used to find social media content, and what employees may be doing that breaks company policy regarding social media usage.

When logging, the ideal is to store logs on a protected system that cannot be easily accessed or easily modified. There are a number of logging applications such as EventTracker, LogLogic, Splunk, and LogRhythm. These tools can log just about all network activity, including posts to social media websites. New logging services such as Actiance's Socialite software as a service and Q1 Labs QRadar target specific social media activity. Socialite's key features include the following:

- ▶ **Identity management**   Establishing a single corporate identity and tracking users across multiple social media platforms

- ▶ **Data leak prevention**   Preventing sensitive data from leaving the company, either maliciously or inadvertently

- ▶ **Granular application control**   Enabling access to Facebook, but not access to chat or allowing the downloading and installing of any applications in the gaming category

- ▶ **Moderator control**   For Facebook, LinkedIn, and Twitter, controlling content that must be preapproved by a corporate communications officer or other third party

- ▶ **Activity control**   Managing access to features, such as who can read, like, comment upon, or access nearly a hundred features

- ▶ **Log conversation and content**   Capturing all posts, messages, and commentary made to Facebook, LinkedIn, and Twitter in context, including exporting to an archive of choice for eDiscovery

Monitoring and Management Tools

While data loss management tools serve to prevent possible information leaks by company employees, monitoring and management tools act to identify recently published information that may be of interest to the company. By monitoring the publication of mentions related to keywords and phrases, it is possible to identify where these mentions have been posted so you can more fully understand the context in which they were published.

Even though these systems may point to potential security breaches and policy violations, gaining a full understanding of the context around which these mentions occurs is always necessary, as discussed in Chapter 11. For example, it may be entirely legitimate and laudable for company staff to adopt an apologetic and humble tone in public communications in cases where individual customers feel they have been wronged.

CAUTION

Monitoring systems generally return very specific conversations and transactions without providing the larger communication context, which may have to do with longer news cycles and events. When using monitoring systems, don't be too quick to judge and always give others the benefit of the doubt; individuals deserve a chance to be heard before they are condemned for alleged misdeeds.

Monitoring Mentions

Over 150 solutions and counting exist for monitoring mentions online, including free and paid services. Some of the free services include Google Alerts, HowSociable, Addict-o-matic, Livedash, StatsMix, Buzzstream, Samepoint, Trendrr, and Social Mention. Figure 15-2 shows activity for "KRAA Security" using HowSociable. As you can see, a paid professional version is also available.

Compared to free services, paid systems offer more advanced features, including more powerful customization options, more robust reporting facilities, better customer support, integration into company platforms and workflows, and more privacy. Paid services range widely in price. A paid service will provide additional functions that many of the free services do not have. They also may report the same data but have more developed tools around the functionality and display of that data. Several of the paid services include SocialMetrix, Heartbeat, Radian6, Brandwatch, Biz360, WhosTalkin, VocusPR, Sprout Social, BuzzLogic, Scout Labs, Meltwater, Reputation.com, My BuzzMetrics, Trackur, Dow Jones Insight, and Alterian SM2. Some of the paid services include free trial periods.

NOTE

For an updated listing of monitoring tools, including reviews, please consult our website: http://securingsocialmedia/onlinemonitoring.

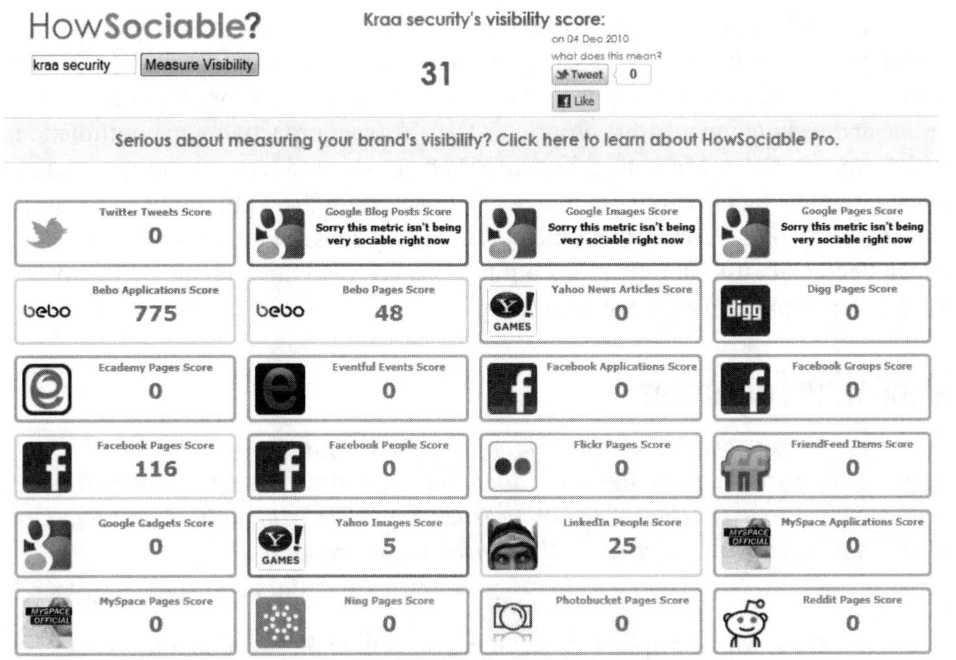

Figure 15-2   *HowSociable monitoring "KRAA Security" mentions*

Monitoring solutions provide a full set of features that continuously evolve as social media tracking becomes more sophisticated. These new tools are designed to facilitate teamwork among staff assigned social media responsibilities, including such functions as:

▶ Monitoring keyword and phrase mentions across millions of blogs and social media platforms

▶ Boolean search capability and filtering of mentions by geography and language

▶ Authority tracking and key influencer identification and following

▶ User management and user activity logging

▶ E-mail notifications and alerting for predetermined incident types

▶ Filtering by content source and social media platform

▶ Community interaction and publishing features

▶ Daily, weekly, and monthly digests of activity

Some brands, including Gatorade and Dell, have created social media management control rooms that display a wide set of monitoring dashboards and trackers. Community management and customer support staff spend their day observing the conversations online and responding when appropriate. They also act proactively in coordination with Corporate Sales, Marketing, IT, and PR objectives, and serve as the eyes and ears of the company by providing immediate feedback from the community. We expect these types of control centers to proliferate among top consumer brands that experience a high degree of customer mentions online. You can read more about Dell's Social Media Command Center in the case study.

Monitoring Employees

Security managers don't like to talk about it, but one of the greatest threats to business computer systems, networks, and data isn't from hackers or competitors. It's from employees, partners, and other trusted insiders with authorized access to a company's networks, systems, and proprietary information.

—*George V. Hulme,* InformationWeek[2]

Do you know which employees spend the most time on social media websites and applications while at work? Which ones spend their day on Facebook chat and instant messaging applications? Which employees are divulging sensitive company information through seemingly innocuous or offhand remarks made online?

By implementing tools that help you answer these questions, such as Specter Pro or Radian6, which Dell uses, you will also be acting to increase employee productivity by eliminating wasteful activities, enhance the company's ability to conduct investigations and catch wrongdoers, enforce your organization's acceptable use policy and standards, reduce legal liability, reveal false accusations, and protect the corporation from insider theft and data leaks.

As mentioned earlier in this book, employees should have no expectation of privacy when using company resources. As discussed in Chapter 3, the U.S. Supreme Court ruled in favor of companies being able to monitor their employees. Other countries may have a different legal stance, and you should be aware of local country data privacy laws and human resources laws when doing business in those countries. For its own business continuity protection, a company must reserve the

---

[2] George V., Hulme, "The Threat from Inside," *InfoWeek* (April 14, 2003), http://www.informationweek.com/news/8900062.

right to investigate any information with the company's systems. Also, potential situations involving court orders, subpoenas, lawsuits, and legal discovery requests may require access to personal files. The IT department is responsible for collecting, archiving, and providing access to electronic records, in collaboration with the company's attorneys and senior executive team.

What are the most common types of activities that employee monitoring tools uncover? The possible breaches range widely, including the following and more:

► Participating in communication that breaks corporate policy or is unlawful

► Divulging too much information about the company in social networks

► Installing unauthorized social media applications on corporate computers and smartphones

► Mentioning corporate brands or displaying logos in unauthorized ways

► Using other peoples' passwords to access online resources

► Viewing illegal websites

► Spending too much time on social platforms for personal reasons

The fear of being caught is perhaps the best deterrent to employee misbehavior. By establishing a competent and credible monitoring system that you clearly explain to employees, you are acting both ethically and responsibly in ensuring a productive and professional online experience. The log management tools and monitoring tools listed previously, such as EventTracker or LogRhythm, provide key capabilities for employee monitoring including:

► Collecting a persistent record of employee activities online, including URLs visited, applications used, and time spent

► Creating impartial proof through secure transmittal, central storage, and observance of best practices and security industry standards regarding evidence collection

► Preventing unauthorized access to reading and editing of archived recordings to protect integrity

► Sending real-time notifications of predetermined security incidents and breaches

CAUTION

A word of caution may be in order here. It is possible to go overboard in employee monitoring and create an environment that decreases morale and even creates a "hostile workplace," which may subject the company to lawsuits. Avoid situations where employees feel harassed by too stringent monitoring policies that curtail their ability to work comfortably. Ultimately, your company's intellectual capital may decide to walk out the door on their own two feet.

The implementation of monitoring tools for online mentions and for tracking employee activities on the Web comes at a financial and human resource cost. It takes money and time to integrate and maintain monitoring systems.

The Use of New Social Media Tools by Employees

By now, most of your employees have at least created a profile on a social network, and many of them are maintaining an active presence on one or more of these networks for personal or professional reasons. As these social networks grow their user base and evolve their feature sets over time, new ecosystems of partnering services emerge to plug into these social networks. Between the new services offered by the networks and those offered by third-party companies, people are being tempted to use an ever-growing number of applications that facilitate their social networking. These new tools, which are often created by lone developers or by small firms, will invariably contain security flaws in their early versions. It is, therefore, important to understand that employees will attempt to use new social media tools, and that these tools may present new security threats to the corporation.

Some tools, such as HootSuite, a Twitter management dashboard, are run primarily from within the browser. Other tools are downloaded and executed as executable files on PCs or as disk image (DMG) or Mac installer package (PKG) files on Mac OS X systems. Other applications may run within Adobe Air or Microsoft Silverlight rich Internet application platforms. Finally, there are countless social networking applications available through smartphone operating systems, including Android, Symbian, Blackberry phones, and the iPhone, as well as tablets.

As discussed earlier in the book, the policies you create should clearly outline what software and services employees are allowed to use. This includes applications that may need to be installed or cloud services that need no installation but could still pose a threat to the environment. Each service and application should be authorized and then monitored with the tools we have just discussed.

Tracking Employee Usage

As social media matures and gains wider adoption by the world's population online, employees will come to terms with the fact that their activities are being monitored while at work. In most cases, it is not possible to use social media all day and remain productive at work. There are exceptions to this rule, however:

▶ You are a Community Manager or Customer Service Representative responding to and engaging with your community of customers and fans.

▶ You are an Search Engine Optimization (SEO) professional trying to backlink to content legitimately as well as increase the page rank of Twitter profiles through quality posts.

▶ You are running promotions like @delloutlet and Dell's whole family of Twitter accounts (http://www.dell.com/twitter).

▶ You are conducting research for your work or for a story you're working on and gleaning new information from the responses.

▶ You are following a relevant set of professionals in your domain whose posts are adding to your level of knowledge and awareness of your industry by keeping you on the leading edge.

▶ You are developing business for the company by increasing your authority through relevant and useful posts, mixed with relationship building online.

▶ You are periodically taking a break from work and are getting "connected" and motivated by engaging with others online, especially if you're working alone from a home office.

There may be other cases, but generally speaking, most people find that too much time spent on social networks throughout the day drains their productivity and they will accept that their employers monitor for such activity.

Benefits of Tracking Employee Usage

Earlier in the chapter, we mentioned some of the key activities you can track with a log management system. If you begin to track these actions, when do you really want to report on that activity? And why would you need to report on employees' social media activity? The key reasons are really first, good business practices, and second, regulatory requirements.

As we have seen through Dell's positive example, real revenues from social media are possible, and the ability to understand what both your employees are saying in addition to customers is critical. One of the great potential threats is employees time wasting. If you do not track how much time your employees are spending on social media sites, you might lose real dollars in wasted hourly salaries. Employees can communicate over social media with you and about you, so knowing what they are saying may help you improve your business, train employees better, and impact how employees work.

The regulatory requirements of tracking employees cross just about all industries. Privacy laws will expand and crackdowns begin on what companies are doing with customer data. Employees are a major source of breaking regulations. We have mentioned several cases throughout the book on the dangers of sending out a tweet or a picture of a customer, especially in the healthcare industry. As we mentioned previously, the SEC rules on social media use will have a wide ranging impact in the financial industry. Employees have to be tracked to ensure your compliance to regulations.

Dissemination of Policy Changes

Social media policies will change over time as new types of social platforms come into existence and as existing ones change in functionality. These changes may take time to develop and to implement throughout the organization with new procedures and monitoring tools. However, any new policies and procedures should be widely communicated when they are updated: not only is this the correct ethical stance for a corporation, but also communicating about social media policies acts as a deterrent to misbehavior in itself. Some companies have even taken the additional step of making their social media policies available to the public at large, so that everyone, including employees and customers, understands the company's position and values regarding social media.

Following the Social Media News

The social web is a quickly evolving ecosystem of websites, applications, cases studies in success and failure, personalities, and other types of events, situations, and incidents. Every week notable happenings occur in the social media environment that are instructive and that merit attention. There are numerous resources to follow to keep informed about social media. We find that we can stay on top of most of it by following five of the most recognized social media and technology publications online, including:

▶ TechCrunch (http://techcrunch.com/)

▶ Mashable (www.mashable.com)

▶ ReadWriteWeb (www.readwriteweb.com)

▶ GigaOM (www.gigaom.com)

▶ TechMeme (www.techmeme.com)

Keeping abreast of social media industry news is as easy as spending 10 to 15 minutes a day browsing through the new headlines and articles of social media blogs. Very quickly you will be considered your company's foremost resource on social media, an enviable and valuable position!

Wrap Up

To effectively manage operational monitoring and reporting, you need to implement and use various tools to prevent data loss before information is leaked and track relevant mentions that have already been published online. Most companies face the challenge of employees not using the Internet appropriately, and monitoring compliance with internal policies and with regulatory requirements is a daily tactical activity. Protecting data involves a combination of utilizing alerting systems, trend tracking, and archiving logs. Whereas data loss tools prevent possible information leaks by company employees, monitoring tools identify recently published information that may be of interest to the company.

Improvement Checklist

☐ Have you developed a detailed operations manual and disseminated it to employees and possibly the general public?

☐ Are you monitoring daily for keywords and phrases?

☐ Are you monitoring specific social media blogs and sites for updated news?

Reputation Management Monitoring & Reporting

Throughout this book, we have stressed the importance of monitoring your organization's social media presence through a process known as *reputation management.* How do you go about managing your reputation? First, you must first determine what you are going to monitor, whether it is employee activity, public communications, competitors, or your industry. Second, you determine the key search terms that will provide the information you need. And, finally, you have to implement the necessary tools and processes to provide an ongoing data stream to monitor and report accurately. When utilizing the available online reputation management systems for social media, you must take these issues into account:

▶ How diverse is your company and in what context do you build your reputation?

▶ Are you trying to anticipate customer needs and customer attacks?

▶ What's at stake if your reputation is damaged?

▶ How much control can you possibly have over Internet communication channels and online mentions?

▶ How can you track your reputation?

▶ Can you find accurate information about your reputation?

This chapter reviews the processes that are necessary for developing your reputation management capabilities, specifically

▶ Online reputation management

▶ Setting up a monitoring system

▶ Establishing a baseline and comparing historical periods

▶ Using what you learn

Case Study: Uncontrolled Reputation Damage

The issue of reputation management has now gone beyond mere brand stewardship and is at the very front lines of Internet privacy, litigation, and corporate security. A tragic but relevant example of privacy loss happened with the California Highway Patrol.[1] In October 2006, eighteen-year-old Nikki Catsouras died after losing control of her father's Porsche 911 and colliding with a toll booth. The California Highway

---

[1] Christopher Goffard, "Gruesome Death Photos Are at the Forefront of an Internet Privacy Battle," *Los Angeles Times* (May 15, 2010), http://articles.latimes.com/2010/may/15/local/la-me-death-photos-20100515/3.

Patrol (CHP) took photographs of the gruesome accident scene, a standard practice in fatal vehicle accident procedures. Unfortunately for the Catsouras family, two CHP employees forwarded the photos internally and to friends via e-mail. The leaked photos quickly spread and were eventually posted across the Internet. In addition, fake MySpace accounts were created by "Griefers" and e-mails of the photos sent to Nikki's parents, which caused further grief. The California Court of Appeal for the Fourth District on February 1, 2010, ruled that the Catsouras family has the right to sue the defendants (the CHP) for negligence and intentional infliction of emotional distress. The pending lawsuit and possible compensation for the family is expected to cost millions. The personal actions of two employees have cost the CHP its reputation and potentially millions of dollars. The question arises, could this have been avoided?

A number of things were wrong with this process. What should have happened with these pictures? The first question to be answered is did the CHP know that they were not supposed to share those pictures and did that break any specific laws? This is an obvious question, but many organizations do not provide any training about how to handle data, especially regarding social media usage. The Pew Center on the States says that according to the 2008 Grading the States Report training hours for state employees averaged 22.1 hours per year. Per-employee training expenditures averaged $417 per year, or 1.3 percent of payroll. There is no real breakout for social media or security training.

The next question to address is how the photos are stored and who has access to transmitting that information. If the CHP was monitoring all entry and exit points for data, they could potentially have blocked the files from leaving the organization if they were labeled confidential. Security technology such as McAfee's data loss prevention solution could have blocked outbound confidential data.

Other questions include should an organization monitor not only e-mail communication but also their employees' social media profiles as well? What was CHP doing to monitor activity on a daily basis? Could careful monitoring of personal activity shed light on the character of these two individuals and raised suspicion as to possible future actions? Could the monitoring of online bulletin boards and forums alerted the CHP to the leaked photo, allowing for a quicker response? A search today returns over 77,000 results, including many of the horrific images. Reputation.com, hired by the family, did attempt to remove the graphic photos of the crash, but those photos are still available. Once data gets on the Internet, even active management will find it hard to remove that data. Reputation.com claims to have persuaded websites to remove 2,500 of the photographs but understands that removing them from the Internet completely is an impossible task.

A policy built on the H.U.M.O.R. Matrix would have made employees of CHP aware that they are being monitored and possibly dissuaded potentially damaging actions. This tragic case can be translated to any organization dealing with sensitive information such as hospitals, lawyers, and financial institutions. Effective reputation management means investing in the resources to monitor and react to online reputation management (ORM) issues. Once the issue has been flagged, your social media policy should identity the steps and resources needed to deal with the situation.

Online Reputation Management

According to Wikipedia, "Reputation management is the process of tracking an entity's actions and other entities' opinions about those actions; reporting on those actions and opinions; and reacting to that report creating a feedback loop." They further define "Online reputation management (or monitoring) as the practice of monitoring the Internet reputation of a person, brand, or business, with the goal of suppressing negative mentions entirely, or pushing them lower on search engine results pages to decrease their visibility." A solid ORM solution needs to provide an organization with a combination of real-time and digest (daily preferably) reports. One or more relevant key terms should be identified and monitored across sites such as Google News, Google Blog Search, Technorati, Del.icio.us, Furl, Flickr, Yahoo!, MySpace, Twitter, Facebook, and as many other social media outlets as possible. A good ORM practice goes to the places frequented by your customers to monitor, report, and react to their sentiments about your brand.

Companies that listen and monitor the social space are in a better position to respond and defend their brand against potential attacks. Recently a number of services have become available to make this process easier and more effective. Companies such as Reputation.com, Radian6, Keotag, and Sprout Social all offer varying levels of online reputation management. Many of these tools are easy to use. Figure 16-1 shows results using Sprout Social after signing up in about ten seconds.

In the case of the Catsouras family and the CHP, both parties had an interest in monitoring and removing the leaked information as quickly as possible. Several of the tools listed could have helped provide real-time information on postings. The creation of a series of keywords would have alerted the CHP to the breach and swift legal action could potentially have stemmed the viral tidal wave. It is imperative that an organization has the information that it needs to act quickly to secure its reputation as time is of the essence. Within a few hours, the social web can damage or, in some cases, destroy a centuries-old brand. Understanding the reports generated by your reputation management solution and following an established action plan can greatly reduce the damage caused by possible ORM threats.

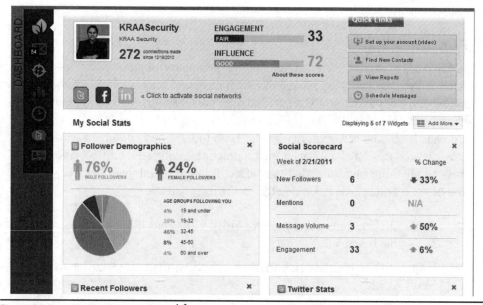

Figure 16-1   *Using Sprout Social for reputation management*

Brand Equity

We have already mentioned a number of social media monitoring tools, such as Reputation.com and Sprout Social. The data you monitor for will differ significantly across different industries. Various tools may have a slightly different impact by industry, but as a general rule, you should be able to utilize the same tools across industries.

The key areas we identified in Chapter 2 as being key targets for implementing new tools for brand and employee monitoring and reporting are

▶ **Brand equity**   Determine brand equity by tracking users of the company's social media profiles along with social media mentions about your company and sentiment about your company. Identify risks to brand equity by implementing tools to monitor all news about the brand name.

▶ **Brand attack**   Identify attacks against the brand by implementing tools to monitor all negative mentions about the brand.

▶ **Defense techniques**   Develop defensive capabilities against brand attacks.

▶ **Crisis management**   Develop crisis management capability.

▶ **Employee monitoring**   Should be coordinated between IT and Human Resources.

How JAG's Doing

In Chapter 11, we identified a number of measurements for reputation management. After having reviewed the processes and controls, we can use our test company JAG Electronics to determine what kind of positive changes can be implemented based on the H.U.MO.R. Matrix. After implementing various tools and techniques, JAG has reached a new maturity level. These tools, when combined with employee education about social media practices, will reduce JAG's risk of missing anything important that may affect it in the social media space. At the end of six months, JAG has made the following changes:

▶ **Capability to determine brand equity**   JAG has hired a company to determine brand value.

▶ **Capability to identify risk against brand equity**   JAG has set up Google News Alerts.

▶ **Capability to identify attacks against the brand**   JAG is using Social Mention.

▶ **Defense capabilities against brand attacks**   JAG has hired a company like Reputation.com to reduce the impact of any attacks and bad mentions.

▶ **Crisis management capability**   JAG has hired a public relations firm to manage communications.

▶ **Capability to coordinate between Marketing and IT**   JAG has implemented new monthly management meetings to coordinate all social media projects across departments.

▶ **Tools to manage reputation**   JAG has signed up for Radian6 and IceRocket to track and monitor their online presence.

Reputation Management and Employees

Employees will actually be more aware of how they are using social media once you have reports on their activity available. The challenge is the vagueness in the laws governing what you can do when you identify an employee talking about the company on social media platforms. The posting of confidential information is easy to identify and there are historical cases that equate posting to social media to sending out confidential material using other platforms.

Recently, in November 2010, the National Labor Relations Board filed a complaint against American Medical Response of Connecticut (AMRC), the reason being that AMRC fired an employee for negative comments posted about her supervisor on her personal Facebook page from her home computer.[2] The NRLB says the social media policy as well as the action is illegal under Section 7 of the National Labor Relations Act:

> An NLRB investigation found that the employee's Facebook postings constituted protected concerted activity, and that the company's blogging and internet posting policy contained unlawful provisions, including one that prohibited employees from making disparaging remarks when discussing the company or supervisors and another that prohibited employees from depicting the company in any way over the internet without company permission. Such provisions constitute interference with employees in the exercise of their right to engage in protected concerted activity.

You may capture information with your monitoring and reporting, but there is a difference between confidential data such as the photos of the Catsouras accident versus opinions and gossip, and your social media policies now have to straddle this fine line.

Setting Up a Monitoring System

Now that you have selected your ORM solutions, you need to track your mentions continuously; monitoring is not a onetime activity. Your monitoring should include any and all products, services, and industries in which the organization is active. Additionally, all key executives, partners, and suppliers should be added to the ORM watch list. These alerts will help identify possible HR or PR situations or possible disruptions in the supply chain. To set up a simple monitoring system, you will need to do the following:

1. *Create a database of keywords applicable to your organization.* Your keywords should include your products and services, key team members' names, company names, and any other key areas of industry involvement. In JAG's case, it will monitor its key employees. You can also create a keyword list of competitor names.

---

[2] National Labor Relations Board Steps in on Facebook Postings as Protected Employee Activity, Modern Media Institute (November 9, 2010), http://www.modernmediainstitute.com/2010/11/national-labor-relations-board-steps-in-on-facebook-postings-as-protected-employee-activity.html.

2. *Google vanity search.* Search for each of the keywords identified in Step 1. Google Search allows for special "operators" to be used in your searches to help improve your results. For example, you can search for a specific phrase or word order by adding quotation marks " " around your query. To search specifically for a person's full name, enter his or her whole name in quotation marks. Use the minus (–) operator in your query to make your search more specific by excluding certain terms. For example, to find Coca-Cola as a competitor and not as a product for purchase, exclude product sales from your results by searching for [**Coca-Cola-sale**]. The plus (+) operator is also helpful. When you add a plus (+) in front of a word, it tells the search engine that you want only that word and none of its synonyms, so you can get results for [**+happy**] without also getting results for "cheerful" and other similar words.

3. *Set up Google Alerts to be notified if and when you or your organization or service is mentioned.* Go to Google Alerts and create a series of alerts based on your keywords and select to be notified via e-mail when the alert is triggered. Figure 16-2 shows how you would set up the alert for "coca-cola."

4. *Integrate a paid ORM service into your H.U.M.O.R. Matrix.* As mentioned previously, a number of paid services, such as Radian6 and Compete.com, will monitor and provide reports in real-time or digest format.

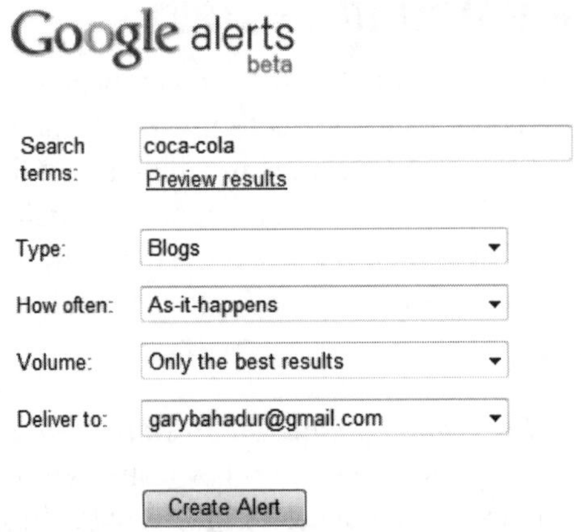

Figure 16-2 *Google Alerts setup for Coca-Cola*

5. *Now that you have set up the internal, company-centric alerts, you should create ORM alerts for your competitors, industry mentions, key customer centers, and/or geographic locations.* All of this data should be fed into a real-time monitoring system with triggers to alert defensive systems should a potential threat hit occur.

We mentioned using a number of the free tools here. By using some of the more robust commercial tools, you can automate this process and make it easier to handle. Any company with a small or large budget can implement enough tools to keep abreast of activity concerning its brand.

Establishing a Baseline and Comparing Historical Periods

Success, it is said, cannot truly be measured unless one knows where she or he has started from. This can also be applied to reputation management. If an initial search returns negative results, these results should be monitored alongside your efforts to mitigate these findings. Measuring the polarity of certain postings or search results will identify the sentiments expressed. By utilizing open source software tools like RapidSentilyzer BuzzBoard (www.rapid-i.com), which automatically collects the latest news about your company, your products, and/or your competitors, you can automate sentiment analysis on large collections of texts such as web pages, discussion groups, blogs, and real-time social media chatter on sites like Twitter for a very low cost.

Other sites like SocialMention.com assign a rating system to your query based on four key areas: strength, sentiment, passion, and reach (http://socialmention.com/faq):

▶ **Strength** Strength is the likelihood that your brand is being discussed in social media. A very simple calculation is used: phrase mentions within the last 24 hours divided by total possible mentions.

▶ **Sentiment** Sentiment is the ratio of mentions that are generally positive to those that are generally negative.

▶ **Passion** Passion is a measure of the likelihood that individuals talking about your brand will do so repeatedly.

▶ **Reach** Reach is a measure of the range of influence. It is the number of unique authors referencing your brand divided by the total number of mentions.

Using a tool like Social Mention on your name or a company name, you can track interesting results. A recent search for Jason Inasi and McGraw-Hill returned the data shown in Figures 16-3 and 16-4, respectively. You will notice that it is not complete or completely accurate. There is a lot of data to be pulled. This is why you need several additional tools, such as HowSociable and IceRocket, to get a complete picture. You will get different types of results on people versus companies versus key search terms. But if you are consistent over time and your Community Manager is actively engaged, you will be able to refine your results.

By measuring your combined Social Mention score over time, you can determine the effects of your social media actions. This real-time litmus test also provides insight into trending negative sentiment and can assist in identifying any potential threats.

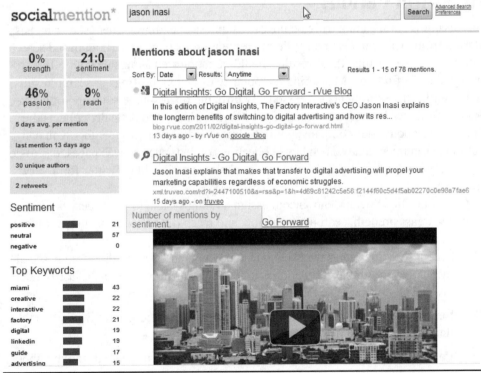

Figure 16-3   *SocialMention.com results for Jason Inasi*

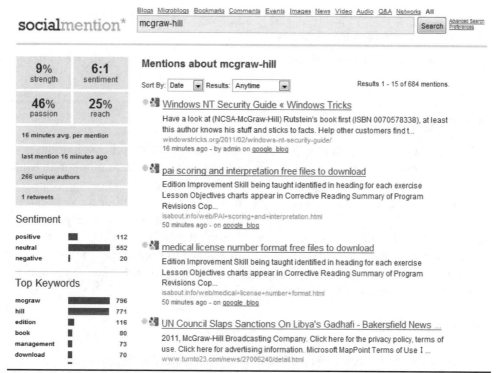

Figure 16-4   *SocialMention.com results for McGraw-Hill*

How to Make Good Use of Reputation Information

Whether it's accurate or not, complete or incomplete, balanced or skewed, the "information" that the public sees about your company defines their perception of who you are. One distorted blog post of your product could have a huge effect on your company, whether it's true or not. With a proactive approach to gathering information about who is attacking your reputation, you can defend against any brand attacks quickly and manage the story. By managing your reputation proactively, you can

▶ Efficiently collect, aggregate, and disseminate information about your brand

▶ Anticipate threats and react quickly

▶ Defend against geographically diverse sources

▶ Facilitate cooperation between business partners to defend a brand

▶ Communicate facts to customers

▶ Provide cost-effective feedback and perception management with free tools

Wrap Up

Online reputation management (ORM) is a critical and ongoing process in today's socially networked world. The first step is to decide what should be monitored. Most companies need to monitor employees, the public, competitors, and perhaps the overall industry. The second step is to determine how best to monitor for key search terms and important activities relevant to your company. How to accurately report this data is next. Finally, you have to keep updating the tools you use. As the social media landscape changes, new tools will be developed to keep abreast of the changing environment. To effectively complete your H.U.M.O.R. Matrix, you must implement some form of ORM solution.

Improvement Checklist

☐ Does your ORM solutions consist of a combination of real-time and digest reports?

☐ Have you created a database of keywords applicable to your organization?

☐ Are you monitoring keywords applicable to your competitors, industry, suppliers, and products?

☐ Are you keeping track of your measurement baseline strength, sentiment, passion, and reach against stated organization goals over time?

Social Media 3.0

Assessing Your Social Media Strategy

Y ou have come a long way since the first chapter where you learned to assess the online environment in preparation for securing your company's social media presence. Since then, we have covered a lot of ground, including:

▶ Creating a framework for your security policy through the H.U.M.O.R. Matrix

▶ Identifying threats

▶ Developing strategies and best practices

▶ Creating social media policies and procedures

▶ Implementing monitoring and reporting systems

In this chapter, we explore what you've learned and identify some of the challenges that remain.

How JAG's Doing

Our fictional company, JAG, has also come a long way since the beginning of the book. When JAG first evaluated itself on the H.U.M.O.R. Matrix, the company rightfully rated itself as performing poorly in all the areas. With regards to social media, the company had no policies, was not protecting their intellectual property, had not allocated budget or resources to social media, had no tools or systems in place, and were not monitoring relevant mentions online. Not only was JAG unprepared to deal with any situation that might arise, it was not even dedicating any time to understanding which opportunities social media could have afforded its business. Issues ranged from hiring people to understanding the company's competitiveness to creating positive word-of-mouth marketing.

Over time, JAG came to understand the importance of evaluating its social media risk exposure and, as a result, developed and implemented policies and procedures for the organization. JAG trained employees in the secure use of social media, on company expectations, and on ways to interact with JAG customers online. JAG also implemented monitoring tools to reduce the risk of reputation attacks and to measure the impact of public sentiment on its business model. In Table 17-1, you can see that JAG has gone through the exercise of updating the measurement of its security posture in the H.U.M.O.R. Matrix. Looking at the H.U.M.O.R. Matrix now, JAG has made headway in each area and can rate itself as "Average," or more mature, in all of them.

HUMAN RESOURCES 1-Poor 2-Average 3-Best Practice	Maturity Level Reached Within 6 Months	Maturity Level Desired Within 12 Months
Human Resource Policy		
Specific social media security policy	**3**—Implemented	3
Social media conduct defined by HR	**3**—Implemented	3
Capabilities of HR to manage social media	**2**—Tools implemented, manual review process	3
HR's dissemination capabilities	**2**—Working on interdepartmental coordination	3
Capability to engage employees through policies and processes	**2**—Policy issued and training to be done	3
Capability of HR to manage training	**2**—Implemented	3
Capability of HR to communicate policies	**2**—Implemented	3
Capability of HR to respond to social media breaches	**2**—Working with outside PR firm	3
IT Security Policy		
Applicability of social media policies	**2**—Implemented	3
Social media security technology defined in IT policies	**2**—Implemented	3
Capability to respond to social media breach	**2**—Working with HR and Marketing	3
Training Regimen		
Training for employees on social media usage	**2**—Manual process in place	3
Training for employees on social media security issues	**1**—Needs automated process	2

Table 17-1   *JAG's Changed Social Media Environment After Six Months*

UTILIZATION OF RESOURCES 1-Poor 2-Average 3-Best Practice	Maturity Level Reached Within 6 Months	Maturity Level Desired Within 12 Months
Technology		
Appropriate technology in place to track user access to social media	2—Implemented, URL filtering in place	3
Appropriate technology in place to track regulations in social media utilization	1—Need to track all regulations	2
Appropriate technology in place to track data storage in social media utilization	2—Implemented, each site documented based on data stored	3
Appropriate technology in place to track access to data to social media utilization	2—Implemented, all access documented	3
Appropriate technology in place to track shared services for resources in social media utilization	1—To be implemented	2
Appropriate technology in place to track business continuity to social media utilization	2—Implemented, BCP plan developed for each site	3
Appropriate technology in place to provide support services for social media utilization	1—To be done	2
Intellectual Property		
Ability to track inappropriate use of intellectual property	2—Implemented with tools such as Social Mention	3
Ability to track inappropriate use of third-party intellectual property by company	1—To be implemented	2
Copyright		
Ability to track copyright data of the company	2—Implemented with tools such as BlogSearch	3
Ability to tract inappropriate use of third-party copyrights by the company	1—To be implemented	2

Table 17-1   *JAG's Changed Social Media Environment After Six Months (continued)*

MONETARY CONSIDERATIONS 1-Poor 2-Average 3-Best Practice	Maturity Level Reached Within 6 Months	Maturity Level Desired Within 12 Months
Track budgetary spending for social media	2—Budget created by Marketing and IT	3
Cost of tools needed to track participation	2—Quarterly meeting scheduled to review budget spent on social media tools	3
Cost of tools needed to track social buzz, on a real-time basis	2—Software services purchased	3
Cost of tools needed to measure brand awareness	2—Tools like Radian6 in place	3
Cost of tools to track positive, negative, or neutral mentions	2—Tools like Social Mention setup	3
Cost of tools acquired for measuring monetary spending for social media security tactics, software, and person-hours	2—Manual tracking of budget items	3
Value of brand equity determined	2—Using an outside PR firm to measure	3

OPERATIONS MANAGEMENT 1-Poor 2-Average 3-Best Practice	Maturity Level Reached Within 6 Months	Maturity Level Desired Within 12 Months
Operations identified for social media	2—Daily operations identified	3
Operations responsibilities clearly defined by department	2—Implemented, guidelines by each department	3
Operations mapped to social media policies	2—Implemented	3
Active monitoring of social media threats	2—Using tools like Radian6	3

Table 17-1   *JAG's Changed Social Media Environment After Six Months (continued)*

OPERATIONS MANAGEMENT 1-Poor 2-Average 3-Best Practice	Maturity Level Reached Within 6 Months	Maturity Level Desired Within 12 Months
Asset management of social media sites being used in the company	2—All social media sites used have been identified	3
Tracking of employees allowed to use social media	2—Implemented with monitoring software	3
Education of operators who manage social media security tools	2—Done by HR	3
Process for determining data usage and storage in social media sites	1—Need more processes	2
Recovery process for restoring information from social media sites for business continuity plan	1—Need more processes	2
REPUTATION MANAGEMENT 1-Poor 2-Average 3-Best Practice	Maturity Level Reached Within 6 months	Maturity Level Desired Within 12 Months
Capability to determine brand equity	2—Working with outside PR firm	3
Capability to identify risk against brand equity	2—Using service like Radian6	3
Capability to identify attacks against the brand	2—Using service like Radian6	3
Defense capabilities against brand attacks	1—To be implemented	2
Crisis management capabilities	2—Using outside PR firm	3
Capability of Marketing and IT to coordinate	2—New weekly processes in place	3
Tools to manage reputation	2—Several tools like Social Mention and IceRocket in place	3

Table 17-1 *JAG's Changed Social Media Environment After Six Months (continued)*

The Challenges Ahead

A secure social media environment is one in which you are ready to respond to, report on, and remediate situations quickly and effectively. To do so, however, corresponding systems and policies must be implemented in advance. As your company's social media presences grows, you'll be faced with increasing security challenges. Your strategy and policies have to evolve over time as the tools and business processes change, and in social media these changes will be frequent.

Determine the Implementation Processes

When assessing your company's social media usage using the H.U.M.O.R. Matrix, some vulnerable areas will be immediately apparent and the priorities for implementation clear. For example, no policy allows employees to post whatever they want and open the company to attacks. If you have no policy and no monitoring tools in place, the risk is greater that employees can send out confidential information over social media channels and you would not know about it. As you identify the weaknesses in your environment, the steps you need to take to reduce your risk of confidential exposure and reputation damage will become clear.

Social media is evolving at a rapid pace with corresponding innovation in the tools available for participating online. This means that employees are most certainly using unauthorized social media tools during work hours, which can place the company at risk of data loss or reputation damage. Inventorying the universe of applications being used to understand the risk exposure in the work place and monitoring information being posted outside of the work place are key. In addition, you need to implement social media policies that outline not only expected behavior when representing the company, but also which applications are safe to use and how to use them. Employees also need to understand when it is appropriate to respond to queries about the company, and when such responses should be handled by spokespersons assigned to community management.

Make inventorying the company's intellectual property, trademarks, and copyrights a priority in order to prevent information leaks and wrongful use of logos and brands. Part of this process may actually entail creating digital versions of logos and brands for use by employees and the public.

Finally, it is important to implement monitoring tools to measure social media activity online—by employees, customers, and competitors. Listening and learning from online mentions both informs future implementations and provides a daily check on how well your company is performing.

Security Is a Moving Target

Any current implementation of social media security is a temporary panacea at best. This is because there are a plethora of social networks, each one with their own security holes and privacy risks. The social networks themselves are continuously changing and updating their privacy protections, often reducing privacy for commercial reasons, as is the case with Facebook. Nonvigilant users may wake up to find their once-protected information is no longer safe. You cannot rely solely on the social media networks to provide you with warning and security. Also, new types of social sharing websites are being invented that redefine how people interact with other. Currently, question and answer websites and mobile photo–sharing services are gaining quick adoption. Generally, new social media websites and mobile services are well integrated into existing social networks with millions of users. The ability to instantly geotag, share photos, and then distribute those photos through accounts on multiple websites poses new security challenges, such as the loss of confidential data through mobile phone uploads. These challenges are difficult to foresee, other than to know that the social web is akin to dunes in a desert with ever-shifting sands. The only way to protect yourself from future risk is to draw lessons from your current security implementation, keep up to date with new services and changes to existing services, and regularly reassess the environment.

Continuous Changes in Management and Policy

Considering how quickly social media changes, it is important to also note how quickly services are adopted and how quickly people learn to use those new services. There is a learning curve to using social media in general, and society as a whole seems to be progressing along this learning curve by participating more and sharing more openly. Furthermore, each new platform has its own quirks that users must learn and master.

This means that any company's customers will become more active online over time and will be present on more social networks. Employees will follow this trend, adopting new social networks and participating more openly.

Because of these dynamics, social media policies, procedures, controls, and monitoring must be updated regularly to keep up with changes in use and behavior. Outdated systems and policies pose the greatest threat by promoting a false sense of security.

Check Your Sources

As we get more and more information through social networks and blogs, we risk losing what institutional media provided in the 20th century: credibility through a recognized media brand name that anointed each article with the authority of the media outlet. When we read the *New York Times,* we know that certain standards are maintained with respect to professionalism, editorial process, quality of research, and ethics (and, even there, debates over accuracy of reporting arise occasionally). When we read any particular blog, however, how can we be sure it's trustworthy? How can we know that what is written has been researched and represents the truth? Does your policy require validation of sources of information before any story can be referenced or re-tweeted?

Digital literacy is a vital competence for dealing with the social web, a skill that must be mastered by companies participating online. Knowing what information to pay attention to and when and how to respond requires a fair amount of judgment, sophistication, and research. Before acting on social media mentions, it is important to know whether it comes from a familiar and trusted source and, if not, how to qualify the authority, credibility, and influence of the mention.

Multiple solutions to this problem can be combined. The first solution is to build a social layer into existing customer relationship management (CRM) systems to identify where your main customers participate online. Which blogs do they read and which social media platforms are they participating in? Knowing this both allows for more precise monitoring of mentions, as well as informs marketing about where promotional initiatives should be conducted and targeted.

The second solution is to cross-check the author of any social media mentions with the other social networks he or she may participate in. For example, does the author have a LinkedIn profile, and if so, does the author include third-party testimonials? While there is no centrally trusted identification mechanism on the Internet, some social networks like LinkedIn and Facebook can serve as proxies precisely because people "vouch" for each other through connections and testimonials. Mentions by anonymous people should be researched more thoroughly, as anonymity by definition destroys credibility, however.

The third and most important solution is to research mentions by verifying the facts. This may include contacting the employee at the point of customer interaction, if a service problem occurred, or contacting the customer directly, if he or she is complaining about a product defect.

Authentication Systems Are Changing

There has been a sea change online in the way that users register as website members. People used to fill out forms with their name, e-mail, password, and other details, depending on the website. More and more, however, we are seeing third-party authentication systems and, in particular, Facebook Connect. People who are members of Facebook can join a new website just by using the Facebook Connect button, which loads the users' details from their Facebook account. Other websites may use competing authentication mechanisms, generally provided by Twitter, Google, or some other services.

As these systems become more widely adopted, people come to expect them more on websites. This also means that information is being shared more quickly and more easily, sometimes automatically, between websites and social networks. By making it simple for people to share across networks, the speed of information sharing has increased, as has the need to monitor social media activity around brand mentions on multiple sites.

Whether people authenticate through a social network or by using e-mail, identifying individuals using fake social network profiles that nevertheless look real, or using webmail addresses under new pseudonyms, can be difficult. To a certain extent, it's relatively easy to remain anonymous on the Internet, and authenticating individuals and verifying their identity can sometimes be a challenging. Competitors may pose as customers, and employees may pose as anonymous individuals. Such activity may be problematic in that identities may eventually be discussed by tracking IP addresses, with sometimes embarrassing and expensive consequences for companies or individuals. In a landmark case in 2009, New York State Attorney General Andrew M. Cuomo secured a $300,000 settlement from cosmetic surgery firm Lifestyle Lift, over the publishing of false positive consumer reviews on Internet message boards and websites.[1]

Brand Attacks Are Hard to Track

Anonymizing technologies are prevalent and anonymous attackers can go to great lengths to hide their tracks. With potential attacks emanating from foreign countries and being organized in foreign languages, it can be hard to foresee and track attacks against your brand.

---

[1] Attorney General Cuomo Secures Settlement with Plastic Surgery Franchise That Flooded Internet with False Positive Reviews, Office of the Attorney General (July 14 2009), http://www.ag.ny.gov/media_center/2009/july/july14b_09.html.

The online forum, 4chan, and members who use the moniker "Anonymous," have become famous for their ability to generate popular Internet *memes* (a concept that spreads via the Internet) as well as for carrying out coordinated denial of service and other types of attacks against companies, government agencies, and other websites. 4chan's users have carried out some of the highest-profile collective actions online, particularly against the Motion Picture Association of America (MPAA), the Recording Industry Association of America (RIAA), and MasterCard. Anonymous members, recruited through posts on 4chan boards, subsequently initiated their own attacks in defense of WikiLeaks, as we covered in Chapter 3. Tracking the sentiment of hacktivist (hacker activist) groups such as those present on 4chan can go a long way toward preparing your brand for attacks, as well as helping you understand the likely timing of such attacks.

Active Reputation Management

Coordinated collective attacks can seriously damage brand assets and websites. To guard against these attacks is the key to your security program. Equally important, however, is maintaining continued vigilance about mentions of your brand. The end result of a social media attack is brand damage, in most cases, versus damage to computer assets. An accumulation of negative brand mentions around service or product features can do lasting damage to a company by destroying brand value that has taken years to build. The principal competence in reputation management is the ability to respond, report, and remediate situations affecting a brand's reputation. When this is not handled properly, the brand can suffer or even be destroyed. When the group Anonymous hacked into the e-mail of the Internet security company HBGary Federal in February 2011, the brand suffered a major hit.[2] HBGary was presenting at the RSA Security conference and was forced to pull out of the conference. HBGary did not come out with a strong response quickly. There were a number of negative stories about the company and the leaked e-mails that revealed the private communications within the company. Once a security company has been penetrated, how can that company possibly recover from the lack of trust around the company's ability to deliver quality service? Could HBGary have responded in a more coordinated manner to defend its reputation? We will never know; the company response processes were definitely not exceptional. But considering that HBGary is still in business does show that the company is repairing its reputation and customers are still relying on its services.

---

[2] Josh Halliday "Anonymous: US Security firms 'Planned to Attack WikiLeaks,'" *The Guardian* (February 15, 2011), http://www.guardian.co.uk/media/2011/feb/15/anonymous-us-security-firms-wikileaks.

Respond

The ability to respond depends on

▶ Having systems in place that monitor mentions

▶ Understanding the authority and influence of people posting the mentions

▶ Having trained Community Managers in place

▶ Leveraging existing relationships with the community

▶ Maintaining an active presence on social networks

These capabilities and competencies benefit from the learning associated by building them up over time. In other words, a company is severely curtailed in its ability to communicate effectively without these capabilities in place.

The ability to respond effectively also depends very much on being able to respond quickly. A quick response is monitored in minutes and hours—not days. When rumors and innuendos start, it is best to address them as soon as possible by establishing the facts and by opening up lines of communication with the community.

Report

Reporting on social media mentions instills a discipline and gives valuable experience in analyzing the results. Over time, the company learns what are the most important terms and related terms to track, where the mentions are occurring, who is doing the mentioning, and when those mentions are likely to occur. Reporting also acts as an early warning signal by highlighting changes in consumer sentiment when they occur. Reporting helps link marketing and promotional activity with consumer perceptions and identify possible backlash or attack. Finally, reports can form a part of a chain of custody documentation and records and can provide important context around situations that do develop. For reports to be effective, they have to be operationally useful by providing data that supports the decision-making process.

Remediate

Successful reputation management depends on the ability to remedy troublesome situations. Beyond responding, remediating involves business processes and key stakeholders within the company. When a company's community of customers discusses problems in service delivery, product features, customer service, or other aspects of a company, action must be taken to meet customers' expectations. If they are misinformed, then it is a matter of communicating the facts in a forum and a tone that is meaningful for customers. For example, as we discussed in Chapter 3, when Taco Bell was faced with social media attacks against the quality of its meat, Taco Bell successfully addressed the community's concerns about its ingredients through an extensive social media response. On the other hand, when customers have legitimate concerns, then Community Managers must be able to take the message back to senior management and steps must be taken to address the problems. Thus, when Domino's Pizza suffered the ignominy of prank videos posted by two of its employees, the brand took actions to review its processes and to improve the quality of the food it serves. These internal changes were supplemented by wide-reaching advertising campaigns highlighting the company's efforts in shoring up its reputation.

Wrap Up

The new social media tools that are being released almost daily create a unique challenge for companies trying to reduce risk. Employees, customers, and competitors have the capability to damage your company. A framework such as the H.U.M.O.R. Matrix is necessary to assess threats, implement controls, and provide continuous monitoring and reporting.

Some challenges remain in setting up a secure environment for social media. Security is a movable target and any implementation of social media security is a temporary remedy at best. Coordinated collective attacks can seriously damage brand assets and websites, and a key to security is to guard against these. Equally important is maintaining continued vigilance around mentions of your brand. The principal competency in reputation management is the ability to respond to, report on, and remediate situations affecting your brand's reputation. Effectively managing the brand's reputation involves a series of skills that take time to implement, involve technical tools and systems, require human resources to evaluate, and rely on business processes and effective digital literacy training. Successful reputation management depends on the ability to remedy situations by opening up lines of communication with the community and by being able to effect change within an organization to address the community's concerns.

The Future of
Social Media Security

Facebook surpassed Google, Yahoo!, and Microsoft in user engagement in 2010 with users spending 12.7 percent of their time on Facebook. Facebook also accounted for 10 percent of all U.S. page views in 2010 according to comScore's "2010 U.S. Digital Year in Review" study.[1] This explosive growth in social media usage illustrates the tangible shift into the social engagement era.

Today, the mobile device that you use to update your social platforms can also communicate with your car, home, vending machines, and a host of other connected devices. The number of Internet-connected devices passed 5 billion in 2010 and are forecast to reach 22 billion by 2020, according to IMS Research.

Social media is integrated into our personal and business lives. These two lives are converging, which will continue to offer opportunities and cause problems. The offline world becomes smaller as the online world becomes more integrated with all aspects of business. Social networking sites have evolved beyond just connecting people: they are global business platforms, now connecting just about all businesses and services. As more information becomes part of this new platform, every bit of user and company information will be made available. This poses a problem that we are already experiencing regarding the privacy of information—or the severe lack of it.

This lack of privacy will keep some people from joining the evolving social platforms, possibly impacting growth and adoption in communities or even cultures. How can privacy and security risks and concerns be overcome? Is there—or will there be—a data protection model that can be put into place to convince the late adopters to move into social networks?

In this chapter, we will identify the major upcoming concerns in social media and what can be anticipated to address the new challenges. We will face issues with the way everything will be interconnected; the erosion of privacy will be an ongoing phenomenon; and the regulatory environment may catch up to help or hinder consumer and corporate protections.

The Internet of Things

If everything is connected, the playing field between large and small companies should level out. All companies now have the opportunity to conduct product development with direct feedback and communications with their potential customers during the product development lifecycle. Social media has made this a much simpler task. More reliable data is now available in real time. The result of the interconnected

---

[1] The 2010 U.S. Digital Year in Review, comScore (February 7, 2010), http://www.comscore.com/Press_Events/Presentations_Whitepapers/2011/2010_US_Digital_Year_in_Review.

platforms is a product development process customized as per the changing tastes of the people and, presumably, this process can provide a better product. With social media, you can easily post surveys and research and development information on social networking sites and launch prototypes to gauge feedback.

This changes how companies launch products and even speeds up the process. But speed can sacrifice security in the race to get a product to market. This may produce more security holes if web applications no longer go through long testing phases. With social network vulnerabilities, customer confidential data stored in these cloud services can be at greater risk, which we discuss in more depth in the next section of the chapter.

Social media also makes doing a lot of things less expensive. If your product does not need huge advertising dollars for magazine ads or television ads, your budgets change, and presumably your marketing budget decreases. A small company can compete with large company in marketing a new product using social networks. The expense changes so significantly that more products from smaller companies can make it to market. Many companies formally appoint social media managers (Community Managers) to handle social marketing through social media sites, gaining insights from users. This new role may add a new headcount to the budget but there are numerous areas for cost savings using social media platforms. Twitter and Facebook Fanpages are free! The winners will be those who can engage with their communities, not those who can spend more on marketing.

The next generation of Internet applications using Internet Protocol version 6 (IPv6) will be able to communicate with devices attached to virtually all electronic objects. This system should, therefore, be able to identify any kind of object and could potentially encode 50 to 100 trillion objects, as well as follow the movement of those objects. Cellular and emerging technologies such as Internet television, tablets, networked appliances, and ebook readers are major contributors to this growth.

Collaborative communities are developing around this interconnected world with social media acting as the catalyst in the activation, development, and deployment of individual community initiatives. These communities, though in their infancy, are driving the development of hundreds of products, services, policies, and even governments. A good example of this use of social media is the revolution in Egypt. Twitter and Facebook were two main sources of communication. The government even attempted to shut down Internet access to block communications. The use of social media tools in the Arab Spring revolutions in the Middle East inspired Salesforce.com's CEO, Marc Benioff, to unveil new social networking tools (http://www.reuters.com/article/2011/08/31/us-salesforce-idUSTRE77U5PC20110831).

With this much growing influence, it is essential that we understand the role security will play in this rapidly evolving Global Brain.

Evolving Threats to the "Global Brain"

The "Global Brain," a term coined by Peter Russell in his 1982 book *The Global Brain*, is the concept of a worldwide intelligent network involving people, data, and communication with the technologies they use interconnected into a ubiquitous processing system for the planet. One can argue that social media has been the biggest paradigm shift of the Internet era to date. As Internet-connected devices become faster and more intelligent and take over more responsibilities for us, so too do the threats posed by advances in hacking, malware, and viruses. Instead of a single Internet-connected computer, we now have potentially dozens of devices all accessing and distributing personal data across multiple interconnected platforms that are much easier to attack.

Your car's GPS or mobile phone's location-based services can be used to track and monitor behavioral patterns. These patterns can then be used for corporate espionage, data theft, or even physical threats. For example, in a recent social media–related attack, a 19-year-old man from Mexico, Pedro Lopez Biffano, is accused of kidnapping more than a dozen people after befriending his victims on social networking sites.[2] He would "friend" them and then trick them into meeting him, at which point he kidnapped and held them for ransom. If a person is active on social networks, "friends" can build complete profiles of everything that person does—finding out where he or she lives, hangs out, travels, all in real-time.

The ability to poach information from multiple social media accounts and across multiple devices, while convenient, has proven to be disastrous when breached. Because it costs almost nothing to capture this information, attackers have lower monetary barriers to setting up new scams and launching attacks. In the case of Pedro Lopez Biffano, no significant amount of money was needed to use Facebook and then trick people he "friended" into meeting him. As everything becomes connected, privacy concerns are not yet been addressed by companies or regulations to protect the end user properly. And new technologies will move control from centralized servers to things like mobile devices and user-controlled environments that will become more difficult to restrict, with the user taking on even more responsibility for his or her own security.

---

[2] "Mexican Teenager Used Social Websites to Kidnap People," NDTV (January 17, 2011), http://www.ndtv.com/article/world/mexican-teenager-used-social-websites-to-kidnap-people-79781.

Loss of Control

The product marketing lifecycle changes when your users can take your content, modify it, and launch their own word of mouth marketing campaigns on your behalf if they really like your product. When this happens, it's great, but you can also lose more control of aspects of marketing as consumers have much more freedom on social networks and have the ability to even modify your content. Social networking sites pose a greater risk of IP theft, and the viral nature of these sites can lead to the easy dissemination of your data before you even know what's happening. Increasing challenges that companies face include:

▶ Losing control of the brand message

▶ Trying to control the end user

▶ Inability to measure what's impacting the brand

▶ Consumers changing the brand's message

▶ Losing money without a tangible ROI on social media

Product and Data Threats

The main risk a company faces is the threat to data security in product development efforts using social media sites. Crowd sourcing can open your company to competition. Great ideas are hard to come by, copying an idea is very easy, and if those doing the copying have the monetary backing, and the ability to execute quickly, they can perfect the product, launch it, and gain market share over your company.

Corporate espionage is much easier using social media sites, as is creating disinformation. Research on people and competing projects is simpler to gather. Employees post details about projects they are working on or locations where they are going such as customer or partner sites. Data theft becomes easier because attackers know more about their target. With the availability of so many data points about a person and company on the social web, social engineering attacks are more prevalent and will continue to increase.

Privacy issues and identify theft are skyrocketing. "Becoming" someone else is simpler because so many parts of that person's life are on social networks. This enables social engineering and authentication mechanism attacks, which can easily damage personal as well as company reputations.

Erosion of Privacy

Nothing a consumer or a company puts out into the social sphere is private. Once your employee sends some confidential information, whether by mistake or on purpose, it is just about impossible to pull it back in. If you want privacy, then opt for offline social exchange of information. But this is just not practical for business in today's world. Once a social networking site has your data in its applications, you lose control of how that data can be used. You no longer have a controlled environment for containing your corporate data anymore.

If you complain about your irritating boss, talk about the latest project you are working on, or post pictures about what you did on your sick day, it is out there for your "friends" to discuss. As applications connect to your profile and become, in essence, friends, they will be able to interact with your data automatically, target you based on what you are posting or tweeting, and make it easier to harvest every bit of information about you in a programmatic manner. As you discuss what you will be doing and where you are going, you are expanding the privacy threat into your physical location.

Geolocation Targeting

Applications are moving toward geolocation functions. "Apps" being developed for smartphones are adding geolocation functions to target your current location. An app such as Facebook Places can geolocate where you are so your friends can find you. Foursquare allows your friends to join you at a venue. You may use the app AroundMe to find the nearest restaurant, hotel, or even hospital. There are tremendous benefits to geolocation services. But with great power, comes great responsibility. Are these apps protecting you from potential attackers? Or do they even give you the ability to restrict and block your geolocation?

For instance, let's say you are about to meet a new prospective client at his office for lunch. You "check-in" with Foursquare to the customer office location. You are giving a lot of information to a potential attacker in the physical world about where you are and who are meeting with. If you take a picture of the venue and upload it with your iPhone to TwitPic with the geotag feature turned on, someone viewing the picture can get the longitude and latitude of the where you took the picture. Predators can discover your physical location by tracking you on the social networks you use such as Gowalla, Facebook Places, or Foursquare and target you for personal reasons or perhaps to conduct corporate espionage. Many mobile applications being sold now have some location-based service functions, making it easier to share data with other sites—and making it easier to track your movements.

Attack of the Appliances

Privacy infringement and identity theft have so far come from traditional places such as web applications, stolen databases, and now social media scraping of information. Compiling a list of data points about a person or company from all the social media platforms they use is easy. With the growth of networked devices, connected devices have moved from your mobile phone and TV to your home security system and even your central air conditioning; now and in the future even more information is being ported to the Internet and used by social media sites. Your interests, the things you buy and use daily, are part of these connected devices. This valuable information can be used for good and evil. When each device is networked, and potentially connected to the Internet, that usage data could be valuable. Consider the real danger of a virus or malware being able to disable your Internet-connected home security system and the real impact that could have on your security.

Attack of the Brands

Everything your company puts out on the Internet, either through corporate marketing or through employees posting on their personal time, contributes to the big database in the sky that is your brand. All of your customers and potential customers and competitors have access to the same information about your brand and can contact you or contact the world and say whatever they want about your brand. Many companies track messages about their brand. When companies gain an insight into consumer behavior, they work their advertising strategies around that.

These same information-gathering techniques can be used by your competitors to understand everything about your company and find weak points in your brand to attack. If the competitor sees consumers like your product, they might easily copy the concept and launch a competing line. If they see consumers are unhappy about your product, they can use that to steal customers and damage your reputation. Your competitors can be even more vicious and unethical by creating fake profiles and posting embarrassing messages, lies, or misleading statements using your name. We foresee corporate espionage escalating to brand attacks more often as hiding behind fake profiles becomes easier. Competitor attacks will only escalate as this becomes more readily understood.

"You R Owned!"

The evolution of all this information on the Internet has become a question of ownership. Who actually owns their personal information and the database of the messages you sent that are stored on a server owned by Facebook or Twitter? If the Library of Congress is already cataloging Twitter messages, does that mean the Government owns your tweets? More and more people are raising the question of privacy after Facebook revealed that it stores and owns the database of the wall posts sent by its users. With its ambiguous privacy policy, Facebook has the right to use and keep the information, even if the users have deleted their profiles. Facebook has since changed its privacy policy, but what happens a year from now— can they change it back? How about the 20 other social media sites you or your company use? What is their policy on information ownership? Once you send your information out and it is stored on a server you do not control, it is effectively lost to you.

Inconsistent Regulations

As more and more companies lose consumer data through hacker attacks, misconfigurations, and uneducated user activity, government officials have begun to take notice. Many countries are enhancing their consumer privacy protection laws. Many industries have regulations about how consumer data is managed. As attacks become easier and the voting public is impacted, they will force the government's hand in adding some regulations to social media. And as you do business in different countries, you will have to contend with multiple laws. Contending with varying laws and regulations will increase the cost of doing business.

At this point, the regulation of social media across countries is inconsistent and can affect your security. In November 2010, the EU Commission announced a strategy to "protect individuals' data in all policy areas, including law enforcement, while reducing red tape for business and guaranteeing the free circulation of data within the EU."[3] The EU Commission's strategy sets out proposals on how to modernize the EU framework for data protection rules through a series of key goals:

> Strengthening the Rights of Individuals so that the collection and use of personal data is limited to the minimum necessary. Individuals should also be clearly informed in a transparent way on how, why, by whom, and for how long their data is collected and used. The question of who owns your private data has become a major issue for both corporations and governments and will continue to provide challenges in the years to come.

---

[3] European Commission Announces Intention to Strengthen EU Data Protection Rules, K&L Gates (November 19, 2010), http://www.ediscoverylaw.com/2010/11/articles/news-updates/european-commission-announces-intention-to-strengthen-eu-data-protection-rules/.

According to the Pew Internet & American Life Project,[4] 24 percent of Internet users who sought online support for health issues in forums have signed in with their real name and e-mail address. Every statement, question, and response they posted is now stored in the cloud or on a hard drive somewhere. But different countries will handle this real data in various ways. If you are from the U.S., you have fewer privacy restrictions placed on your data than if you signed into this health portal from Germany where the EU data privacy laws are stronger.

The Best Defense Is a Good Offense

The first step in overcoming your concerns about privacy and security risks is to take charge of the education requirements necessary to use social media responsibly. We obviously advocate implementing a process to handle any type of social media platform you use now or in the future. With a consistent process, a company will not be taken unawares as new social media tools become popular and consumers and employees migrate to different sites. Online and in-person training programs are available to corporations. These programs cover how to use social media wisely and how employees can learn all the basic security requirements they need to be part of any technology being used today and in the future.

Second, with the right tools in place, you can defend your company, your brand, and your privacy. We have discussed a number of tools to aid this process, and each month new tools to address social media are being released. Like any job, without the right tools, you will be unable to meet your goal. Whether you use free or paid tools, they are available, just keep up to date with what can actually help you manage your social media landscape.

Third and finally, be proactive in managing your social media reputation. If a story comes out, whether positive or negative about your company, you can instantly act and manage the story to a certain extent. Your company can put out true responses to a lie; your company can effectively communicate about things your company may have done wrong; and your company can build upon positive mentions quickly to expand the story and increase your brand value. The real-time capabilities you have should be used aggressively and proactively rather than slowly and reactively.

---

[4] 86% of Internet Users Want to Prohibit Online Companies From Disclosing Their Personal Information Without Permission, Pew Internet & American Life Project, http://www.pewinternet.org/.

Jumping into the Deep End

Believe it or not, there are many companies that have little or no knowledge of social media, much less social media security. They are hesitant to join in for many reasons but that doesn't stop third parties from affecting a brand in the social media sphere. How to address these challenges is part of the process we have put together in this book. By laying out a model for addressing the key concerns around social media security, a company can develop a plan that allows it to jump into social media usage.

Traditional security models, such as ISO standards and NIST standards, provide an understandable step-by-step guide to implementing a secure process for achieving security goals. This same process can be put in place for social media security, using the H.U.M.O.R. Matrix or some other model. This way, companies can gain a level of comfort in knowing they have a roadmap to follow.

Wrap Up

We have put together a step-by-step framework with our H.U.M.O.R. Matrix for you to track your social media security strategy. As social media technologies change, you must have a process in place that is flexible enough to provide the necessary tools to reduce risk, no matter the form of the technology being used. Threats will expand rapidly with the social web, but using the tools outlined in this book you can anticipate the changes and implement the right controls to mitigate potential disasters. Use social media securely and responsibly.

Please share your social media experiences with us at www.securingsocialmedia.com!

APPENDIX

Resource Guide

Your social media toolkit has to be complete to cover all the bases for monitoring and reporting on activity. We have utilized a number of different tools throughout the book. Some are multifunctional and some are very specific. The tools listed here are by no means the complete set of what is available, and with the quickly changing landscape of social media, some of these will be gone in a year or expand their capabilities. New tools will be coming on the market rapidly as well, so you have to keep up with your research for the types of tools you need.

Resource	URL	Description	Chapter	Paid/ Free
Addict-o-matic	www.addictomatic .com	Activity tracking tool	4, 13, 15	Free
Meltwater (formerly BuzzGain	http://buzz.meltwater .com/	Activity tracking tool	15	Paid
BuzzLogic	www.buzzlogic .com	Activity tracking tool	15	Paid
BuzzStream	www.buzzstream.com	Activity tracking tool	15	Free
Google Alerts	www.google.com/ alerts	Activity tracking tool	1, 3, 4, 13, 14, 15, 16	Free
Google Blogsearch	www.blogsearch .google.com	Activity tracking tool	12, 14, 16	Free
Google Insights for Search	www.google.com/ insights/search	Activity tracking tool	14	Free
HootSuite	www.hootsuite.com	Activity tracking tool	8	Paid
HowSociable	www.howsociable .com	Activity tracking tool	15	Free
IceRocket	www.icerocket.com	Activity tracking tool	2,12,13	Paid
Keotag	www.keotag.com	Activity tracking tool	16	Free
KnowEm	www.knowem.com	Activity tracking tool	10	Free
Lithium	www.lithium.com	Activity tracking tool	14	Paid
livedash	www.livedash.com	Activity tracking tool	15	Free
MyBuzzMetrics	http://www.nielsen-online.com/	Activity tracking tool	15	Paid
Samepoint	www.samepoint.com	Activity tracking tool	15	Free

Resource	URL	Description	Chapter	Paid/ Free
ScoutLabs	www.scoutlabs.com	Activity tracking tool	15	Paid
Seesmic	www.seesmic.com	Activity tracking tool	8	Free
Social Cast	www.socialcast.com	Activity tracking tool	12	Paid
Social Mention	www.socialmention	Activity tracking tool	1, 2, 13, 15, 16	Free
Socialmetrix	www.socialmetrix.com	Activity tracking tool	15	Paid
Sprout Social	www.sproutsocial.com	Activity tracking tool	15, 16	Paid
StatsMix	www.statsmix.com	Activity tracking tool	15	Free
Topsy	www.topsy.com	Activity tracking tool	13	Free
Trackur	www.trackur.com	Activity tracking tool	16	Free
Trendrr	www.trendrr.com	Activity tracking tool	15	Free
Yahoo! Pipes	www.yahoo .com/pipes	Activity tracking tool	3, 13	Free
Biz360	www.attensity .com/home/	Analytics	15	Paid
Compete.com	www.compete.com	Analytics	13	Paid
Dow Jones Insight	www.dowjones.com/ product-djinsight.asp	Analytics	15	Paid
Google Trends	www.google.com/ trends	Analytics	14	Free
Heartbeat	http://www.sysomos .com/products/overview/ heartbeat/	Analytics	15	Paid
RapidMiner	www.rapid-i.com	Analytics	16	Paid
SM2	sm2.techrigy.com	Analytics	15	Paid
SocialSafe	www.socialsafe.net	Backup and recovery	10	Paid
Blogger.com	www.blogger.com	Blogging	2	Free
WordPress	www.wordpress.com	Blogging	2, 6, 13	Free
Symantec Vontu	www.vontu.com	Data loss prevention	2	Paid
Trustwave Vericept	www.vericept.com	Data loss prevention	2	Paid
Facebook Places	www.facebook.com/ places	Geolocation tool for social networking	3, 12, 13	Free
Foursquare	www.foursquare.com	Geolocation tool for social networking	2, 3, 8, 10, 13	Free

Resource	URL	Description	Chapter	Paid/ Free
Slideshare	www.slideshare.com	Information sharing portal	10	Free
Wikipedia	www.wikipedia.com	Information sharing portal	6, 13	Free
Gowalla	www.gowalla.com	Location-based tool	3, 8	Free
Scvngr	www.scvngr.com	Location-based tool	3	Free
Tagged	www.tagged.com	Location-based tool	10	Free
TwitHire	www.twithire.com	Micro-blogging job search	12	Free
TwitJobSearch	www.twitjobsearch.com	Micro-blogging job search	12	Free
TweetDeck	www.tweetdeck.com	Micro-blogging tool	3, 8, 13	Free
Twitter	www.twitter.com	Micro-blogging tool	2, 4, 6, 10, 13, 16	Free
FireEye	www.fireeye.com	Monitoring tool	13	Paid
Specter 360	www.specter360.com	Monitoring tool	13	Paid
Digg	www.digg.com	News aggregator	10	Free
Google News	news.google.com	News aggregator	16	Free
Meltwater	www.meltwater.com	News aggregator	13	Paid
Reddit	www.reddit.com	News aggregator	2	Free
StumbleUpon	www.stumbleupon.com	News aggregator	2	Free
Technorati	www.technorati.com	News aggregator	3, 16	Free
Yahoo!	www.yahoo.com	News aggregator	16	Free
Basecamp	www.basecamphq.com	Online project management	2	Paid
Flickr	www.flickr.com	Photo-sharing website, social networking	2, 10, 16	Free
Dupli Checker	www.duplichecker.com	Plagiarism checker	13	Free
The Plagiarism Checker	www.dustball.com/cs/ plagiarism.checker	Plagiarism checker	8	Free
PlagiarismDetect	www.plagiarismdetect .com	Plagiarism checker	13	Free

Resource	URL	Description	Chapter	Paid/ Free
Brandwatch	www.brandwatch.com	Reputation management	15	Paid
Naymz	www.naymz.com (now visible.me)	Reputation management	16	Free
Radian6 Salesforce	www.radian6.com	Reputation management	1, 3, 12, 13, 15	Paid
Reputation.com	www.reputation.com	Reputation management	1, 3, 8, 13, 14, 15, 16	Paid
VocusPR	www.vocus.com	Reputation management	15	Paid
WhosTalkin.com	www.whostalkin.com	Reputation management	15	Paid
Del.icio.us	www.delicious.com	Social bookmarking	16	Free
Furl	www.diigo.com/	Social bookmarking	16	Free
Bebo	www.bebo.com	Social network	10	Free
Facebook	www.facebook.com	Social network	2, 4, 6, 8, 10, 13	Free
Google+	plus.google.com	Social network	2	Free
Google Buzz,	www.google.com/buzz	Social network	2	Free
hi5	www.hi5.com	Social network	10	Free
LinkedIn	www.linkedin.com	Social network	8, 10, 13	Free
MySpace	www.myspace.com	Social network	2, 10, 16	Free
Tumblr	www.tumblr.com	Social network	10	Free
Squid Proxy	www.squid-cache.org	URL filtering	13	Free
Bitly	www.bitly.com	URL shortening	3	Free
Kiss.ly	Now bitly.com	URL shortening	4	Free
TinyUrl	www.tinyurl.com	URL shortening	4	Free
YouTube	ww.youtube.com	Video sharing	10	Free
McAfee Web Gateway formerly Webwasher)	www.mcafee.com	Web URL filtering	13,16	Paid
Websense	www.websense.com	Web URL filtering	2	Paid

Index

B

backup and recovery strategies, 38
banning social media at work, 227–228
baseline reputation data, 291–293
best practices. *See also* social media
    security policy
        evolution of security, 106
        sample security policy for, 127–134
Biffano, Pedro Lopez, 314
Bit.ly, 59
BlackSheep, 93–94, 115
blocking intellectual property use, 170
Blogger.com, 209
blogs
        copyright infringement on, 199
        FTC regulations for, 143–144
        military use of, 188–189
        searching with Google Blog, 258–259
        security policies regarding, 109, 111–112
        threats via, 71
        unauthorized reprinting of, 238–239
botnets, 74
brand attacks
        assessing potential damage of, 86
        attempts to ruin brand, 207
        by competitors, 317
        Domino's, 204–206, 207
        hacking as, 68–69
        responding to, 156–159
        tracking anonymous, 306–307
        types of attackers, 72
brands. *See also* brand attacks
        attempts to ruin, 207
        creating management plan for, 191–192
        defined, 206
        management control rooms for, 150–151,
            266–267, 276
        monitoring data for, 287
        potential loss of control, 315
        role of brand evangelists, 152
        training employees to advocate, 54
British Petroleum (BP), 4–6
*Buckly H. Crispin v. Christian Audigier, Inc. et
    al,* 62
budgets. *See also* monetary considerations
        determining social media, 34–36,
            254–255

implementing security with limited,
    256–260
improvement checklist for, 264
including social media tools in, 186
security, 34–35
solving security with big, 260–262
Burger King, 223–224
business continuity plans, 38
businesses. *See* organizations

C

California Highway Patrol (CHP), 284–286
capabilities
        assess technical, 28
        mapping, 166–167
Catsouras, Nikki, 284–285, 286
CBT training, 263
cease and desist letters, 210–211
Chilling Effects Clearinghouse, 210–211
clickjacking, 68
cloud computing
        cloud-based applications, 29, 30
        risks in, 38–39
Comcast, 207
communications. *See also* blogs; content;
    intellectual property
        disseminating policy changes, 280
        laws regulating financial, 225–226
        safeguarding, 12
        telling employees about operating
            strategies, 193–194
community management
        functions across departments, 152–153
        resources and tasks in, 150–152
Community Manager
        coordinating with other departments,
            120–121
        directing cross-functional teams, 154
        disseminating social media policy,
            158–159
        hiring and training, 138
        interfacing with other departments,
            119–120
        managing medium company challenges,
            148–149
        modifying Facebook privacy settings,
            147–148